MARX

'Vincent Barnett's *Marx* is a refreshing and original interpretation of Karl Marx's work and life. It is clearly written and well educated, and will be sure to become a standard text for any serious student of history and politics.'

Matthew Worley, *University of Reading*

Karl Marx has been portrayed in equal measure both as a political prophet who foresaw the end of capitalist exploitation, and as a populist Antichrist whose totalitarian legacy has cost millions of lives worldwide. This new biography looks beyond these caricatures in order to understand more about the real Karl Marx: about his everyday life and personal circumstances, as well as his political ideology.

The book tells the life story of a man of ideas, showing how his political and economic thought developed alongside his life and practical work. Vincent Barnett seeks to paint Karl Marx not as a static, unwavering character, but as a man whose beliefs developed dynamically over time. The book explores his personal background, and problems of personal income and family health. It also examines the influence of Hegel's method on Marx's work, and Marx's relationship with Engels.

This lively, up-to-date guide to the life of Karl Marx provides an excellent starting point for students in history, politics and philosophy, and for all those with an interest in Marxism and political ideas.

Vincent Barnett has been a research fellow on a wide variety of History, Russian Studies and Economics projects at various UK universities. His publications include *A History of Russian Economic Thought* (2005), *The Revolutionary Russian Economy, 1890-1940* (2004) and *Kondratiev and the Dynamics of Economic Development* (1998).

ROUTLEDGE HISTORICAL BIOGRAPHIES

SERIES EDITOR: ROBERT PEARCE

Routledge Historical Biographies provide engaging, readable and academically credible biographies written from an explicitly historical perspective. These concise and accessible accounts will bring important historical figures to life for students and general readers alike.

In the same series:

Bismarck by Edgar Feuchtwanger
Edward IV by Hannes Kleineke
Emmeline Pankhurst by Paula Bartley
Gladstone by Michael Partridge
Henry VII by Sean Cunningham
Henry VIII by Lucy Wooding
Hitler by Martyn Housden
Lenin by Christopher Read
Louis XIV by Richard Wilkinson
Mao by Michael Lynch
Martin Luther by Michael Mullet
Martin Luther King Jr by Peter J. Ling
Mary Queen of Scots by Retha M. Warnicke
Mussolini by Peter Neville
Nehru by Ben Zachariah
Oliver Cromwell by Martyn Bennett
Trotsky by Ian Thatcher

Forthcoming:

Neville Chamberlain by Nick Smart

MARX

Vincent Barnett

LONDON AND NEW YORK

First published 2009 by Routledge
2 Park Square, Milton Park, Abingdon, Oxon OX14 4RN

Simultaneously published in the USA and Canada
by Routledge
270 Madison Ave, New York, NY 10016

Routledge is an imprint of the Taylor & Francis Group, an informa business

© 2009 Vincent Barnett

Typeset in Garamond by Saxon Graphics Ltd, Derby
Printed and bound in Great Britain by TJ International, Padstow, Cornwall

British Library Cataloguing in Publication Data
A catalogue record for this book is available from the British Library

Library of Congress Cataloging in Publication Data
Barnett, Vincent, 1967-
Marx / Vincent Barnett.
p. cm. -- (Routledge historical biographies)
ISBN 978-0-415-43591-8 (hardback) -- ISBN 978-0-415-43592-5 (pbk.) 1.
Marx, Karl, 1818-1883. 2. Communists--Biography. 3. Communism--History.
4. Philosophy, Marxist. I. Title.
HX39.5.A53B37 2009
335.4092--dc22
[B]
2008041118

ISBN10: 0-415-43591-9 (hbk)
ISBN10: 0-415-43592-7 (pbk)

ISBN13: 978-0-415-43591 -8 (hbk)
ISBN13: 978-0-415-43592 -5 (pbk)

Contents

LIST OF PLATES

PREFACE

The inspiring yet daunting task of writing a historical biography of Karl Marx for the early twenty-first century has fallen to someone who has been engaging with Marx's writings and legacy since the mid-1980s. Two particularly important intellectual debts that have been accumulated since this time require explicit acknowledgement. My initial study of Marx was facilitated by valuable time spent as an MA student with Professor David McLellan at the University of Kent at Canterbury. Immediately after this I was privileged enough to become a PhD student of Professor James White at the University of Glasgow. Aspects of both of their original and pioneering interpretations of Marx can be found employed in this book, as the references clearly attest. I have, however, added various new elements and some conceptual twists, which mean that neither of the above-mentioned authorities should be held in any way responsible for the account of the subject that is presented here.

It also requires acknowledgement that my previously published work in Russian and Soviet history has been particularly concerned to highlight neglected historical alternatives, and that this has proved (surprisingly) to be a rather controversial approach. Even after the collapse of the USSR at the end of the 1980s, the pernicious but decaying influence of Stalinism was found to be alive and well in certain areas of academia. The Cambridge economist J. M. Keynes famously remarked that political leaders were often only regurgitating the ideas of obscure academic scribblers of the past, but to find that academic scribblers were regurgitating the ideas of past political tyrants has been a chastening experience. I therefore welcomed the opportunity of return to the original source that was employed in Stalin's political distortions, and thanks are due to Professor Robert Pearce for his encouragement in this regard. He also provided very relevant comments on the chapters as they were being composed.

CHRONOLOGY[1]

Year	Life	Writings
1818	Birth	
1835	University of Bonn	
1836	University of Berlin; Engagement to Jenny von Westphalen	
1837	Studies Hegel's philosophy	
1838	Death of Heinrich Marx	
1839	Begins Doctorate	
1841	Achieves Doctorate	'Doctoral Thesis'
1842	Moves to Cologne; Becomes editor of the *Rheinische Zeitung*; First meets Friedrich Engels	
1843	Marries Jenny von Westphalen	'Critique of Hegel's Philosophy of Right'
1844	Birth of daughter Jenny; Becomes close to Engels	'Economic and Philosophical Manuscripts'
1845	Moves to Brussels; Birth of daughter Laura; *Condition of the Working Class in England* by Engels; Marx and Engels visit the UK; Marx relinquishes Prussian citizenship	'Theses on Feuerbach'; *The Holy Family* (with Engels)
1846	Birth of son Edgar	'The German Ideology' (with Engels)
1847	Joins the Communist League	*The Poverty of Philosophy*

Year	Life	Writings
1848	Moves to Paris and then Cologne; Follows revolutionary outbreaks across Europe closely; Becomes editor of the *Neue Rheinische Zeitung*	*The Manifesto of the Communist Party* (with Engels)
1849	Trial for incitement; Moves to London; Birth of son Guido	*Wage Labour and Capital*
1850	Death of Guido; Works on a proposed 'Critique of Political Economy' sporadically throughout the 1850s	*The Class Struggles in France*
1851	Birth of daughter Franziska; Birth of illegitimate son Frederick Demuth	
1852	Death of Franziska; Dissolves the Communist League	*The Eighteenth Brumaire of Louis Bonaparte*
1853		*Story of the Life of Lord Palmerston*
1855	Birth of daughter Eleanor; Death of Edgar	
1856	Moves to a superior house	*Revelations of the Diplomatic History of the Eighteenth Century*
1857–8		'Outlines of a Critique of Political Economy'
1859	First published results of his prolonged study of economics	*A Contribution to a Critique of Political Economy*
1860	Continues work on the 'Critique of Political Economy' in the 1860s; Falsely accused of forgery	*Herr Vogt*
1861	Analyses the American Civil War	

Year	Life	Writings
1862	Application to become a clerk is rejected	
1863	Death of Henrietta Marx; Skin condition worsens	'Theories of Surplus Value'
1864	Founding of the First International; Death of Wilhelm Wolff	
1867	The first volume of the 'Critique of Political Economy' is finished; Travels to Germany to deliver the manuscript to the publisher	*Capital* (vol.1)
1868	Marriage of Laura	
1869	Starts to learn Russian	
1870	Engels moves from Manchester to London	
1871	Hails the Paris Commune	*The Civil War in France*
1872	Marriage of Jenny; Russian translation of *Capital* (vol.1); Second German edition of *Capital* (vol.1)	
1874	Criticises M. Bakunin's anarchism; Failed attempt at British citizenship	
1875	French translation of *Capital* (vol.1) is completed	*Critique of the Gotha Programme*
1877–8	*Anti-Duhring* by Engels	
1881	Death of Jenny Marx; Various illnesses worsen	'Letter to Vera Zasulich'
1882	Travels across Europe as convalescence	
1883	Death of daughter Jenny; Death of Marx	
1885		*Capital* (vol.2)

Year	Life	Writings
1887	English translation of *Capital* (vol.1)	
1894		*Capital* (vol.3)
1895	Death of Engels	
1905–10		*Theories of Surplus Value*

Notes

1   Writings given in italics were published in the years that are indicated, but other writings were not issued in print until a later time.

INTRODUCTION

The philosophers have only interpreted the world in different ways; the point is to change it.[1]

Karl Marx is probably the most influential philosopher, historian and social theorist of modern times. Within forty years of his death, a small but significant minority of the world's population were living within a socio-economic system that claimed to be constructed using his ideas as their main inspiration. Within seventy years of his death, very important and sizeable parts of the world's population were living under such systems. No writer before or after Marx can claim anything like as much impact upon world affairs. The content of Western philosophy has been conceived as extended footnotes to Plato, but Plato never exerted as much influence on the ordinary lives of as many citizens on planet Earth as Marx so rapidly achieved. Comparison to figures such as Jesus Christ would be most appropriate in order to indicate the sheer scale of Marx's influence on human life. Indeed some have even analysed Marxist doctrine as a secular form of religion.

And yet, one hundred and thirty years after his death in 1883, the societies that claimed to be based on his ideas have collapsed in spectacular fashion, and Marx's sworn enemy – private capital – has trampled over his crumbling legacy with almost unbelievable ease and audacity. If the twentieth century was defined as the century of Marx's phenomenal success, the twenty-first century has begun with Marx's abject failure. Nothing less than the total rout of revolutionary socialism on an international scale was observed in the 1990s, at a pace that most commentators had previously thought was impossible. To paraphrase the eleventh thesis on Feuerbach – Marxists had only changed the world in transient ways. The point was to change it permanently.

In fact it could be argued that the longer-term impact of Marx's ideas was to make capitalism more durable than it was before his influence, rather than to facilitate its imminent demise. Not long after the alternative of Soviet-style communism had been attempted and almost universally discredited, capitalism was invariably seen as the only economic game in town. Marx's firebrand critique of capitalist production had lost some of its potency, largely because the alternative turned out in some ways to be much worse. Marxism as a campaigning social movement in the West seemed to have met with something that a political tragedy was not supposed to meet – namely, a dull ending.

However, as Marx himself observed, science would be superfluous if the appearance and essence of things always coincided. One area in which his legacy still remains intermittently respectable is his influence upon the intellectual development of a number of related academic disciplines, mainly (but not exclusively) sociology, political science, philosophy and economics. Marx might be revolving in his grave if he realised that he had not changed the world in the practical manner that he had desired, but rather had only interpreted the world in various original and insightful ways. Or he might (more wisely) recognise that this was not an either/or situation – that it was possible to change the world simply by reinterpreting it. If this latter point is conceded, then his legacy remains a lasting and a genuine one, as this biography will attempt to demonstrate.

THE APPROACH ADOPTED

Marx has often been interpreted as all things to all people. To his devout followers, he was revered as a political prophet who foresaw and (for a while at least) helped to bring about the end of capitalist exploitation, and who laid the foundations for the creation of a future socialist utopia. To his sworn enemies, he was reviled as the political anti-Christ, a stateless Jew who sought to socialise everything (including women) and whose totalitarian legacy has cost millions of lives across the globe. Both of these partial caricatures still retain some of their potency today, but they are a long way from the truth of the historical person 'Karl Marx' as he went about his everyday activities. In the bulk of this book such sweeping judgements will be shelved in favour of an attempt to reconstruct something of the real Marx as he lived his life and developed his thoughts.

Marx's significance is inextricably bound up with his political legacy and with the political attitudes of those who have studied him. As the eminent historian E. H. Carr correctly prescribed, in order to fully understand historical analysis you must first understand the historian who wrote it. It will be maintained here that in order to be comprehensive when studying socio-political matters, equal sympathy must be given to all the major mainstream currents in political thought. Put another way, the element of truth that is contained within all major political philosophies that is objectively held as being the case must be equal. Hence, the author of this book will maintain an equal sympathy for conservatism, liberalism and socialism, and can readily comprehend how each of these currents adds something important to an overall understanding of political life. Each stream of political philosophy by itself, however, is one-sided and incomplete. Marx of course never claimed to be politically neutral – quite the opposite in fact – but this biography will aim to be both sympathetic and critical towards his ideas in equal measure.

A significant feature of the structure of the book that needs to be explained is that it is divided into parallel chapters. The first chapter of each pair focuses mainly on Marx's life and practical work in a given period of time, while the second chapter of each pair focuses mainly on his ideas in the same period. The reason for this division is so that readers can navigate their way through the book by following only the first or only the second of each pair of chapters if they so desire. Alternatively, they may read through all the chapters in sequential order. The first chapter of each pair contains only a limited and basic presentation of Marx's ideas, so that readers who find the theoretical aspects of his work difficult to follow can still find much of interest to engage with. In the second chapter of each pair, full compass to a presentation of Marx's wide range of conceptual innovations is allowed ('the gloves are off'), which means that the level of discussion will inevitably be higher. A great effort is made to explain his ideas in as clear and as straightforward a manner as is possible, but the subject itself necessitates that complex notions and special terms are deployed with some regularity in the second chapter of each pair.

Another significant feature of the book is that it focuses most consistently on what Marx himself undoubtedly believed was his most important intellectual project – his economic studies – rather than on his day-to-day political struggles or his non-economic work. This is for three reasons. First, Marxist political movements are today only a pale reflection of what they once were, whereas Marxist economic theory still has some resonance as an intellectual current. Second, many existing accounts of Marx focus in detail on his political struggles and daily life, and interested readers can readily consult these works. Third, understanding Marx's economics is essential to understanding his real legacy, yet the intellectual genesis of his approach is often misconstrued and poorly explained. All these reasons indicate that an account of Marx's economic studies should be the centrepiece of any analysis of his life and work that is written today. This is not to say that no account of his political views or his personal life will be presented – in fact, far from it – only that these elements must help to illuminate the guiding light of his professional life, the 'Critique of Political Economy'.

THE AIMS OF THE BIOGRAPHY

Given that the collapse of Soviet-style communism was the defining political event of the end of the twentieth century, an effort will be made in this biography to answer the question: can the seeds of this failure be identified in the thoughts, theories and attitudes of the founder himself? That is, how far are Marx's own ideas to blame for the inadequacies of Soviet-style communism, in terms of his lack of foresight regarding the requirements of constructing an alternative socio-economic system to that of capitalism? This question is certainly appropriate, as Marx wanted to be judged as the progenitor of a new mode of production, not simply as an academic writer or an economic historian.

Another point to emphasise is that this will be unashamedly a historical biography of ideas: that is, it is the life story of a man whose most lasting contribution to human endeavour was in the realm of the intellect and in understanding social and economic development. It is not the biography of a man of action or a man of affairs, even though Marx made many contributions to matters of practical political organisation that certainly deserve some coverage. This perspective is made clear when it is recognised that he changed the world in a dramatic way by simply thinking about the development of capitalist production while sitting in a chair in the British Museum, and then writing about it. The most significant novelty for the biographer thus resides in understanding the processes that were developing in Marx's brain, not in his 'outer' world or his daily life. The latter certainly impacted upon the former in various important ways, but it is the former that gives him a strong claim to a continued and lasting interest as an individual of world-historical importance. Thus this book is first and foremost a biography of Marx's mind – of how it began, how it developed, how it reached its pinnacle and then how it fell into decline.

One final aim of this biography is to shift attention away from his most obvious and immediate legacy as a political agitator, towards evaluating his longer-term and more permanent contributions as an intellectual. To an old-style Marxist this aim would probably be characterised as reactionary, as aiming to construct 'the academic's Marx' as against 'the revolutionary Marx'. This is really a false dichotomy, as Marx took his theoretical studies extremely seriously. But to the loyal conservative, this aim might also be seen as misguided, as Marx's ideas have (for them) been conclusively falsified in practice, and hence they deserve no further attention. The attitude of the convinced Marxist on this issue mirrors that of the loyal conservative in terms of the absolute certainty and finality of their beliefs. Each biographer has his or her own particular approach, and the one selected here (political neutrality, or, more accurately, full political complexity) has at least been clearly outlined and supported with some argument.

INTERPRETING MARX

Part of the controversial legacy that Marx left behind is the considerable disagreement, even today, about what he actually was. Of course he was a human being, but, beyond this, was he ultimately a philosopher, an economist, a political agitator, a populist demagogue, or even (as the title of one ridiculous book maintained) a Satanist? It will be the contention of this biography that Marx is best and most comprehensively conceived as a theorist of social economy, or – as the well-known anti-communist W. W. Rostow judged – as a general theorist of society in all its forms. Marx devoted the best years of his life to the study of economics, but he always stressed that economic forces were inevitably linked to social relations. He certainly accumulated a great deal of knowledge of subjects such as philosophy, economics and revolutionary politics, but as a theorist he brought this knowledge to bear most originally on documenting socio-economic structures in all their complexity. In this he was a pioneer explorer in fields of social science that had only previously been glimpsed by past theorists. The field today that this comes closest to is probably economic sociology, but even this term does not fully encompass all the subject areas that Marx had attempted to navigate.

There is no doubt that Marx remains today a hugely controversial figure, both for the left and the right. For the left, the question now is: to what extent were his ideas realised in the USSR and in other communist countries, and, given their collapse, are his ideas still relevant to today's multi-polar world of climate change, gender politics and religious fundamentalism? One of the basic political controversies of the twentieth century related to how far Marx was responsible for the horrific crimes of Stalinism, and hence to what extent Joseph Stalin was a faithful follower of Marx's socialist blueprint. One of Stalin's most vociferous political opponents, Leon Trotsky, was assassinated on Stalin's orders, in part for suggesting that Stalin had betrayed Marx's outline of communism, and hence this question once held great doctrinal significance. In more recent times, with the rise of other left-orientated oppositional movements such as feminism and green politics, the question became one of how far the traditional Marxian politics of class conflict were relevant to a more diversified post-modern world.

On the right, Marx was (and still is) vilified as the originator of communist autocracy, as an enemy of individual choice and as a contributor to the ongoing decline of moral standards. But do his ideas still present a real danger to democracy and to free enterprise today? A basic difference between Marxism and other left-wing political currents was that Marx claimed to provide an outline of an alternative economic system to capitalism – socialist planning. But the rise of New Right ideology in the 1980s secured a major victory against the rationality of central planning compared to that of the market. Mrs Thatcher's privatisation programme looks today to have been a practice run for the dismantling of socialist economies across the globe. Partly as a consequence of this defeat, most major democratic centre-left parties now accept market economics as a necessary compromise, and some are even messianic converts to neoclassicism. Given the decline of socialist economic institutions across the globe, the question for the right became one of securing the defeat of Marxian ideas in the wider sphere of social and political life, but this has proved a rather more intractable task.

The libertarian philosopher F. A. Hayek could not be clearer on Marx's responsibility for the political tragedies of the twentieth century. Hayek wrote: 'while the ideas of Hume and Voltaire, of Adam Smith and Kant, produced the liberalism of the nineteenth century, those of Hegel and Comte, of Feuerbach and Marx, have produced the totalitarianism of the twentieth'.[2]

Hayek was referring here to Marx's penchant for constructing a teleological (or end-state governed) conception of historical progress in which scientific 'laws' predicted the coming of the communist nirvana in a deterministic manner, a feature that Hayek also saw in the work of sociologists such as Auguste Comte and philosophers such as G. W. F. Hegel. However, this type of 'grand sweep' interpretation of Marx's legacy often loses its force when a more careful historical reconstruction of his work is attempted. Hayek might also be queried for employing a simplistic type of determinism of his own – that Smith's ideas produced liberal democracy, whereas Marx's ideas produced totalitarian corporatism.

In this regard it is absolutely essential to realise that the individual person 'Karl Marx' was not static or fixed in any way, but rather he developed his beliefs and attitudes dynamically over time. To isolate out any one element of this dynamic process leads to an overly simplistic understanding of his multifaceted significance. The sort of one-dimensional interpretive abstractions given by Hayek serve political purposes very well, and may even contain a germ of truth, but do not always aid scholarly understanding if they are presented in isolation. Hence one aim of this biography is to present a multifaceted portrait of Marx that does not conform to any of the pre-established political stereotypes of either the left or the right.

ECONOMIC AND POLITICAL THOUGHT BEFORE MARX

As this biography will give major prominence to the analysis of Marx's ideas, a brief sketch of the state of European thinking on political and economic matters before Marx is required, in order to set the scene for his own specific contributions. The two major political philosophies that had reached states of relative maturity in mid-nineteenth century Europe were liberalism and conservatism. Edmund Burke was a major representative of the latter; John Locke of the former. Locke's *Two Treatises of Government* of 1690 contained a classic statement of the theory of constitutional government and (limited) representative democracy, which were presented in opposition to ideas of a divine or absolute monarchy that had been disseminated in England before 1640. Burke's major work *Reflections on the Revolution in France* of 1790 was a critique of rationalist attempts at political change as exemplified by the 1789 revolution, favouring instead an evolutionary conception of the development of political institutions in which much weight was given to preserving existing customs and valuing social continuity. Both liberalism and conservatism were predominantly political programmes, although they both included support for the market economy as the necessary corollary to their favoured institutions of government.

Against these two mainstream currents, socialist political ideas were less developed in both conceptual and also practical form at the time of Marx's birth in 1818. William Godwin's *Enquiry Concerning Political Justice* of 1793 was part anarchistic and part socialistic in approach, extolling the virtues of reason and the perfectibility of human life. The first fully socialist classic of political thought was arguably Robert Owen's *A New View of Society* of 1813, in which the importance of circumstances in determining individual character was highlighted. Owen was part of a group of utopian socialist writers active at the beginning of the nineteenth century whose vision of an alternative society was powerful and inspiring, but whose account of the practical and organisational means to achieve their political aims on a mass scale was relatively underdeveloped. It was Marx's own claim, subsequently repeated by many of his followers and also by some commentators, that he was the first to provide a much more rigorous and sophisticated account of socialist political strategy, to focus this strategy on more realistic ends, and to connect this strategy with broader social movements. How accurate this evaluation really was will be reviewed in the conclusion to this book.

In the realm of economic ideas, the dominant current in the UK at the beginning of the nineteenth century was classical economics. This tradition associated free trade and private enterprise with material prosperity, and was heavily analytical in approach. It located the wellsprings of economic development in three factors of production – land, labour and capital – which were brought together most efficiently in the capitalist manufacturing process. One branch of classical economics – the theory of value – attempted to explain the origin of the numerical evaluation of commodities through price, for example by means of embodied labour. Another branch – foreign trade – analysed the international distribution of production and consumption. The virtues of free enterprise and the private ownership of land and factories were invariably extolled, as were the benefits of minimum government intervention in economic affairs.

It can be seen from this very brief outline that classical economics as a system of ideas painted a generally favourable picture of the market economy, and hence was compatible with both conservative and liberal political ideas. But the intellectual effort that had been expended on developing these various intellectual currents was huge, involving the work of many (usually quite wealthy) individuals over hundreds of years. What Marx would attempt in the main part of his own life can now be seen in its true context. He would try to replicate for socialist political ideas what classical economics was to conservative and liberal philosophy – that is, to provide a framework and a set of concepts of economic analysis that were compatible with socialist political ideas, while also making this philosophy more rigorous in itself. He set out to do this while living in quite difficult circumstances in terms of his personal income and family health.

It is true that Marx was not starting this major project in economic ideas totally from scratch, as a few socialist economic principles had previously been outlined. But his self-imposed task was still a mammoth one, as this area of the subject was underdeveloped in comparison with the existing principles of classical economics. The fact that he ultimately failed to complete this task, and also that what he did produce contained some significant errors and a lack of a satisfactory consideration of every issue, might now be a little more understandable. What is less understandable is that, after Marx's death, what he did produce was frequently treated as a fully complete bible of socialist economics by many of his followers. In fact it was far from complete, and it was certainly not intended by him to be revered as a quasi-religious text, as some of his disciples would treat it. But before Marx could begin on his life's work in the economic sphere, he had to come to terms with an early association with the German idealist philosophy of his youth and his country of birth.

HEGELIAN LOGIC

It will be argued throughout this book that the method of the German idealist philosopher G. W. F. Hegel (1770–1831) was of great importance to Marx both before and also during his protracted work on the 'Critique of Political Economy', his projected life's work in economic analysis. Because of this fact, an introductory account of the Hegelian approach to philosophical understanding is required in order to set the scene for what will follow. The reader should be forewarned: one reviewer of a book enticingly titled *The Secret of Hegel's Logic* concluded that the author had kept the secret very well. Certainly it is true that Hegelian or dialectical logic has a very different 'feel' from what most people today understand as the clarity of conventional or formal logic, but this does not mean that it cannot be explained in a relatively straightforward manner.

The general structure of Hegel's entire system of dialectical logic was composed of triadic progressions within triadic progressions, and this structure was also its basic defining characteristic. A triadic progression was composed of a conceptual term, then its direct opposite, and then a blended combination of the two terms viewed on a higher plane. The progression 'Being – Nothing – Becoming' was a basic example. Hegel's famous (yet frequently misrepresented) dialectical method thus involved three continuous steps. First, the stage of understanding, when the category in question was taken as fixed and given: for example 'Being'. Second, the stage of negative reason, when on further reflection, contradictions and opposites emerged from within the category: for example 'Nothing'. Third, the stage of speculation, when the identified contradictions were resolved within a new, higher category that contained within itself the previous two: for example 'Becoming'.[3] This method is frequently presented in over-simplified form as: thesis, antithesis, synthesis.

In another example, the first three chapters of 'the doctrine of being' from Hegel's *Science of Logic* (1816) – his most important exposition of the principles of dialectical understanding – were structured as follows:

a) Being (Being – Nothing – Becoming)
    |

b) Determinate Being (Determinate Being – Finitude – Infinity)
    |

c) Being-for-Self (Being-for-Self – the One and the Many – Repulsion and Attraction)

Here, various triadic progressions occurred within each term of a larger triadic progression. Hegel designed this dialectical method as a way of understanding movement across conceptual boundaries. This was not movement in a straightforward spatial or temporal sense, but movement between and within concepts or categories. It was thus the human mind that was generating this movement through its own thought processes. Hegel's method was not a description of change occurring in a conventional materialistic sense, but of the most basic movement that underlay all speculative understanding.

What was the basic difference between conventional or formal logic and Hegelian logic? Quite simply, in conventional logic 'A' and 'not A' were always opposites, whereas in Hegelian logic 'A' and 'not A' were also identical. Thus, in conventional logic the first two terms of a triadic progression (for example, 'Being' and 'Nothing') were permanently fixed as opposites, whereas in Hegelian logic 'Being' and 'Nothing' underwent a metamorphosis through an identity. They were posited as identical by means of the movement between the two opposing poles; this movement being the third term of the triadic progression, 'Becoming'. Conventional logic was static in this regard, and had no third term by means of which any two apparently opposite categories could be temporarily unified.

In presenting the logic of the unity of opposites in triadic progression, Hegel sometimes used a formulaic representation of the three terms involved. For example, 'Universality – Particularity – Individuality' was shown as U – P – I. Indeed, the entire structure of Hegel's *Science of Logic* followed this type of triadic progression, as a way of demonstrating

Hegel's belief that everything led up to the Absolute Idea (universal Mind fully conscious of itself): the final result of all philosophical development. Hence the structural progression of something was of special significance in Hegelian logic, in addition to the specific content that was under review.

Much confusion has arisen about the use of dialectical logic. The point of it was to elicit *understanding of concepts and their inherent development across meaning*. The statement that 'the unity of Being and Nothing was Becoming' was supposed to elicit an improvement in understanding in the conscious mind of how the motion of change permeated all things at a very fundamental level. The reader might either respond 'yes, I understand it' or 'no, it makes little sense to me'. In the latter case, the reader is unlikely to be a Hegelian. Marx certainly was a Hegelian in the early part of his life, and (perhaps) also to the very end, although such rarefied philosophy was a world away from many of the real-life issues that he would tackle in the main part of his life.

CONCLUSION

Some of the most important issues in interpreting Marx for the early twenty-first century have now been introduced, but this process of elucidation has a very long history. In Friedrich Engels' speech at Marx's graveside in Highgate cemetery on 17 March 1883, the process began of interpreting Marx's legacy for the generation that was immediately to follow. According to Engels, Marx's greatest contribution to human understanding was the discovery of two fundamental laws that operated in the socio-economic arena. The law of development of human history revealed how the production of the material means of subsistence formed the foundation on which the state and all ideology were constructed. The law of motion of capitalist production revealed exactly how the exploitation of the worker by the capitalist occurred though the extraction of surplus value. Engels' glowing evaluation was that Marx had been the world's greatest living thinker, comparable in importance to Charles Darwin, the discoverer of evolution by natural selection.

But Marx was, Engels continued, more than just a man of science. He was also a revolutionary fighter for proletarian liberation. Engels bragged that, as a consequence of this ongoing struggle, Marx was the most hated, slandered and calumniated man of his time. It might be a little surprising then, given the heated passions that Marx had apparently generated while he was alive, that he had died peacefully through natural causes in his armchair at 2.45 in the afternoon. In truth, Engels' evaluation of Marx's importance at the time of his death was unquestionably an exaggeration. It was true that Marx had generated much conflict within certain political circles during his lifetime, but his reputation as a social scientist was nowhere near as illustrious as Engels made it out to be in 1883. It grew substantially over time, arguably reaching a peak in the 1970s, but even then it did not match that of Darwin across the board. An attempt to delineate Marx's most significant contributions to social science will be made in this biography.

1

RULED BY A DEMON

Marx was undoubtedly a prodigious child of his European country of birth, even though he would later develop an internationalist perspective that sought to downplay the importance of national loyalties in determining mental attitudes. In terms of prevalent intellectual currents, in the first half of the nineteenth century Germany possessed some unique schools of thought that would affect Marx's progress significantly. For example, the analytical approach of the British classical economists (as exemplified by the work of Adam Smith and David Ricardo) was not in any way dominant. Instead Germany had its own indigenous tradition in political economy – the historical school – which championed protectionism as opposed to free trade, and developed contextually specific as opposed to universal principles of understanding. Key members of the older German historical school included Gustav Schmoller and Wilhelm Roscher, and Marx certainly knew of some representatives of this approach from an early stage in his life.

More immediately influential on the young Marx was an unbroken line of idealist philosophy that was dominant in Germany from the end of the eighteenth century to the middle of the nineteenth. This line began with Immanuel Kant's transcendental idealism and then passed through G. W. F. Hegel's absolute idealism. It was subsequently refracted across Hegel's German followers, such as Ludwig Feuerbach, before reaching Marx in modified form. Idealism promoted the notion that the ultimate reality was mind or mental processes. This was in contrast to materialism, which stated that the ultimate foundation of the universe was corporeal matter. One of the most significant threads that will run through this book is that Marx himself went on a long intellectual journey that can be characterised as travelling from the idealism of the Young Hegelians to the concrete specificity of the German historical school, on the way passing through the analytical approach of classical political economy and the humanism of French socialism. But how exactly did Marx begin on this fateful path, and what were the very early influences on his upbringing and schooling?

MARX'S CHILDHOOD

Marx was born in Trier (Treves), in the southern part of the Rhineland region of Germany, on 5 May 1818. At this time the Rhineland was one of the most advanced parts of Germany, although it was a long way behind the UK in purely economic terms. Located on the western edge of Germany, the Rhineland had acquired a reputation as being relatively forward-looking and tolerant. Marx later referred to instinctive feelings for right and law as the most important provincial characteristics of the Rhinelander.

In both politics and social development, the country of Marx's youth was noticeably different from the Germany of today. Trier's proximity to various border territories, such as France and the Netherlands, meant that its national allegiance had changed direction more than once over a significant period of time. Being close to the Belgian frontier, the Rhineland had been annexed by France during the Napoleonic wars, and in 1814 it was incorporated into Prussia. A flow of political émigrés had passed through Trier as a border city on a number of occasions. Viticulture dominated the rural economy of the region, and it was a protective tariff (as advocated by some representatives of the German historical school) that had helped to establish the vineyards of the river Mosel.

Marx's father, Heinrich Marx, was born in 1782, and he went on to practise law successfully in various courts in Trier. Heinrich was descended from a long line of rabbis, and Marx's mother, Henrietta Pressburg, was also of Jewish descent. Difficulties in Heinrich's legal career had necessitated his conversion to Christianity, as Jewish people were subject to various forms of discrimination in Germany at this time, some of them officially backed by law. However, as converted Protestants within a Catholic majority, the Marx family were still seen as outsiders. Not in any way extreme in support of his religious beliefs, Marx's father was much closer in spirit to the ideas of Enlightenment liberalism than those of religious dogmatism, and he became a town leader of the moderate constitutional party. Heinrich and Henrietta had nine children in total, five of whom died early in their lives (four from tuberculosis), leaving Karl as the eldest and initially most favoured son.

The Marx family certainly did not experience grinding poverty firsthand in their daily lives, although neither were they especially rich. Soon after Karl's birth they had moved into a ten-room house with an associated cottage and a vineyard, and had also employed two maids in family service. Heinrich and Henrietta were perhaps best characterised as middle class, which was somewhat ironic given Karl Marx's later insistence that only two classes had any real historical significance within capitalism – the ruling class and the working class. The Marx family was neither.

As a boy Marx was lively and animated, being known for the writing of satirical poems and for his sometimes over-enthusiastic playfulness. As a high school student between 1830 and 1835 he achieved a good academic record. An early friendship with the older (and wealthier) Baron Ludwig von Westphalen led Marx to an interest in romantic poetry, and idyllic walks with the Baron first sparked his life-long love of the plays of William Shakespeare. The Westphalen family lived in one of the most prestigious areas of Trier, and it was Ludwig Westphalen who first introduced Marx to French socialist writers such as Henri Saint-Simon. Marx was an avid learner, and one of his high-school essays, entitled 'Reflections of a Young Man on the Choice of a Profession', composed in August 1835, demonstrated some considerable depth of thinking for such a young potential poet. Marx mused revealingly:

> Those professions which are not so much involved in life itself as concerned with abstract truths are the most dangerous for the young man whose principles are not yet firm and whose convictions are not yet strong and unshakeable ... But the chief guide which must direct us in the choice of a profession is the welfare of mankind and our own perfection.[1]

Marx suggested in his essay that promoting individual perfection and the general welfare of all were not in fact contradictory goals; instead they complemented each other. Great men achieved personal nobility as perfected individuals through working for the common good. However, Marx had not yet found his own life's calling, and following in his father's footsteps he was sent to Bonn (as the nearest university town) in the autumn of 1835 to study law. He was seventeen years old.

During his first year at Bonn University Marx attended six courses, including lectures on philosophy, literature, and Greek and Roman mythology. The most frequent comment on his class attendance record was that he applied himself 'very industriously and attentively'.[2] He also joined the Trier Tavern Club in this period, eventually becoming a president. As a result of his sometimes over-enthusiastic drinking he was imprisoned by the university on one occasion, and in the summer of 1836 he was wounded in a duel, although not seriously. Duelling still existed in Germany at this time as a way of solving personal disputes. In Bonn Marx also started a lifelong habit of getting himself into financial debt (or finding himself in debt, depending on interpretation). Heinrich Marx decided that one year in Bonn was sufficient for his son's education, and he made plans to transfer Karl to Berlin.

BERLIN

Between leaving Bonn and transferring to Berlin, Marx became engaged to Jenny von Westphalen, his future wife and lifelong female companion. In personal terms, Marx's wife stands alongside Friedrich Engels as his closest and most long-lived confidant. Without the prolonged support of both of these two people it is unlikely that Marx would have achieved all that he did.

At the time of their engagement Marx was eighteen years old and Jenny was twenty-two. They had been friends for a considerable period of time before the formal engagement, which was unusual given a divergence in social standing. Jenny was the daughter of Ludwig von Westphalen, Marx's paternal friend. The Westphalen family was more prosperous than Marx's, and Jenny had a reputation as being a very desirable woman, possessing both beauty and an education. The engagement was initially secret and caused Marx's father some concern, as Karl was merely a student with an undecided future. But Marx made up for this uncertainty with genuine enthusiasm and by writing quantities of gushing love poetry. As an example:

> See! I could a thousand volumes fill,
> Writing only 'Jenny' in each line ...
> From the being of the wild waves' thunder.
> Truly, I would write it down as a refrain,
> For the coming centuries to see —
> LOVE IS JENNY, JENNY IS LOVE'S NAME.[3]

The object of this laboured incantation quickly became inseparable from her admiring suitor, and most commentators agree that they both genuinely loved each other from very early on in their relationship.

Marx arrived in Berlin in the autumn of 1836 and remained there for four and a half years. At Berlin University he continued his study of law and philosophy, and he attended the lectures of a progressive disciple of Hegel. He also attended the lectures of a disciple of the historical school as applied to law. These two viewpoints on jurisprudence were highly contradictory. The Hegelian approach emphasised that historical development was an immanently determined process, the expression of the unfolding of the Absolute Idea (or ultimate spiritual perfection) through historical time. The historical school, by contrast, emphasised the contingent nature of law – how it had evolved in piecemeal fashion through various social and economic conventions. Marx was to become a follower of the Hegelian approach to philosophy in his youthful writings, but the later Marx would react against elements of the Hegelian system to a significant extent. Hegel himself had held a chair in philosophy at Berlin University from 1818 to 1831, and Hegelianism was still a very strong tradition when Marx arrived in Berlin in 1836.

After realising that he could not reasonably study law without a detailed understanding of philosophy, Marx read a great deal of Hegel's works and also those of Hegel's followers throughout 1837, and he soon became a convert to the Hegelian system of understanding. Marx recorded this conversion in a letter to his father from November 1837. Marx explained how the composition of a (now lost) philosophical dialogue attempting to unite art and science had led him to a dialectical account of religion, nature and history, and thus to a full appreciation of the Hegelian system in its entirety. As a result of this complete doctrinal conversion, Marx reported that he subsequently experienced a period of vexed disturbance, sporadic elations and an ongoing feeling of sickness, indicating the cerebral depth at which he held his philosophical beliefs. What exactly this conversion meant in substantive terms, and also its meaning in terms of its influence on Marx's intellectual progress in later life, would become a very controversial topic for both the followers and the interpreters of Marx's ideas.

At this time Marx also became a frequent visitor to an informal club in Berlin that promoted the study of literature, philosophy and the liberal ideal. This club was a meeting point of the Young Hegelian movement, which was an unofficial association bound together by a left-leaning interpretation of Hegel's ideas. Hegel himself had become somewhat reactionary in his later political beliefs, and thus one of the main aims of the Young Hegelian movement was to rescue the 'true' radical Hegel from his older, more jaundiced self. Its key members were Bruno Bauer, who became a close friend of Marx, Adolph Rutenberg, Karl Koppen and Marx himself. Other Young Hegelian associates were Arnold Ruge, Bruno Bauer's brother Edgar Bauer, and Ludwig Feuerbach. Bauer was a lecturer in theology, and much of the focus of Young Hegelian writings at this time was directed towards criticising religious ideas.

During this period in his life, Marx still held to some small desire that he might become a successful writer of poetic verse in the unabashed romantic style of J. W. Goethe – although the previously quoted lines inspired by his love for Jenny indicated that such success was unlikely. In the early part of 1837, Marx dedicated a set of poems to his father that have survived for perusal today: 'Your awakening is an endless rising, Your rising an endless falling'. In truth the numerous 'serious' poems demonstrated only hack lyricism of the most unoriginal type, as Marx would later freely admit, but the few comic poems showed some genuine wit. One such poem, entitled 'Mathematical Wisdom', started as follows.

> We have boiled everything down to signs,
> And Reasoning's done on strict mathematical lines.
> If God's a point, as cylinder he just won't pass,
> You can't stand on your head while sitting on your —.[4]

However, Marx's poetic pretensions did not endure for very long at Berlin University, and the need to provide a more secure foundation for his future relationship with Jenny meant that he quickly gave up any lingering literary desires. Another factor was perhaps that whenever Marx's parents mentioned their son's (supposedly serious) poetry, it was reported that they would laugh to their hearts' content. Despite this unflattering family reception, a few of Marx's early poems were actually published in 1841.

In 1838 Marx's father Heinrich died while he was still in his mid-50s. A letter from Heinrich Marx to his son written the previous year (in March 1837) had read prophetically as follows:

> My heart often leaps at the thought of you and your future. Yet at times I cannot rid myself of sadder, more fearful ideas and intimations ... does your heart correspond to your head, to your talents? ... Your soul is obviously animated and ruled by a demon not given to all men; is this demon a heavenly or a Faustian one?[5]

Marx had been very close to his father, and Heinrich's death led to heightened financial difficulties for the Marx family. It also encouraged Marx to focus more directly on the choice of a career, and in response to this situation he decided to pursue a doctoral dissertation as the means to obtain a lecturing job at a university. During the next two years he worked diligently on his dissertation, which focused on aspects of ancient Greek philosophy, in particular the Epicurean current and its comparison with Democritus. It represented one of the most scholarly or non-polemical works that Marx would compose in his life, albeit only relatively so. In preparation for writing the dissertation Marx made substantial notes on a wide variety of topics within the general history of Greek philosophy, including the notion of the sage, and the writings of Plato and Socrates on religion.[6]

At the beginning of the dissertation itself, Marx outlined that he understood his chosen topic as an essential part of the larger birth, flowering and decline of Greek philosophy as a whole, with Aristotle conceived as its zenith. He categorised the Epicurean, Stoic and Sceptical philosophers as the philosophers of self-consciousness, a clear link to his own Hegelian background. Marx's approach was not purely historical, as he was concerned to apply his Young Hegelian beliefs to the subject at hand, and it is possible to see some similarities between the position of Greek philosophy after Aristotle and the fractured state of German philosophy after Hegel. Specifically, Marx favoured in the dissertation the Epicurean approach to conserving free will as human choice, as opposed to the mechanistic conception of nature as presented by Democritus. In the spring of 1841 Marx successfully received his doctoral degree from the University of Jena, which was held as an easier pass than Berlin. The title 'Dr Karl Marx' was the only scholarly appendage that was ever legitimately attached to his name; the epithet of 'Red Professor' being academically spurious.

However, it was not easy for Marx to obtain the university post that he had desired, and that had been the practical impetus for writing the doctoral dissertation in the first place. Bruno Bauer, one of Marx's closest colleagues within the Young Hegelian movement, was removed from a teaching job in 1842 owing to his controversial views. Bauer was the author of two works that were critical of respected versions of Christian evangelical history as being tendentious narratives. Religious ideas were taken very seriously in Germany at this time, and so Bauer's doctrinal transgressions were significant. This untimely lack of collegiate support was a serious hindrance to Marx's university aspirations, and instead he was forced to turn to journalism as a means of at least temporary support. In fact Marx's journalistic writings would turn out to be voluminous, as he was compelled to write for financial recompense throughout much of his adult life. Early in 1842 Marx sent an article on press censorship to Arnold Ruge, the editor of the *Deutsche Jahrbucher*. Ruge had previously published articles by Young Hegelians such as Bauer. This particular article by Marx was itself censored, as it highlighted contradictions within the censor's code, but this piece was the beginning of a long and successful association with polemical dialogue in journalistic form.

At the start of 1842, Marx began to plan the writing of a detailed analysis of Christian art, which was projected to include sections on religious art and the romantic school. He also wanted to compare Christian art with the pagan art of previous eras.[7] This approach linked both to the prevalent Young Hegelian concern with providing a critique of religious ideas as ideology, and also to Marx's own past interest in the history of art, as manifested in his attendance at lectures on art history given in Bonn University in 1836. However, Marx soon abandoned this idea in its comprehensive form, although his concern with aesthetics in the context of Hegel's conception of the place of art in the progressive development of the human spirit would re-emerge in philosophical form in the 'Economic and Philosophical Manuscripts' of 1844, which are also referred to as the 'Paris Manuscripts', after their city of birth.

PARIS

In April 1842 Marx moved for a short time to Cologne, where a new newspaper called the *Rheinische Zeitung* had recently been established. He became a member of the Cologne Circle, a group that was closely associated with this new newspaper, and he soon began to write for it. After contributing various articles, Marx wrote an informal outline for the newspaper's general orientation, and in October 1842 he was made the editor-in-chief. His editorship turned out to be very successful in terms of raising the paper's profile and circulation, and Marx began to acquire a formidable reputation as an outspoken polemicist on social and political topics. Indeed, the *Rheinische Zeitung* attracted so much attention that in March 1843 the government suppressed it, and Marx was thereby released from his editorial duties. Three months later he finally married Jenny von Westphalen.

Partly as a consequence ongoing censorship problem, Marx decided to emigrate from Germany, eventually arriving in Paris in October 1843. It was in Paris that Marx would compose the celebrated 'Economic and Philosophical Manuscripts', and where Jenny would give birth to their first child, a girl also called Jenny, both of these momentous events occurring in 1844. The 'Economic and Philosophical Manuscripts' came about partly because Marx wanted a more substantial grounding to his recently revealed philosophical supposition of human emancipation being achieved through the proletariat, and he thought that he could find this foundation in economic theory. They were also written (in part) as a consequence of Marx's realisation that material matters were more important than he had previously believed in determining mental attitudes, as he had come to understand through some of his journalistic writings on the practical problems of everyday life. Economic analysis promised a theoretical insight into such practical affairs.

Material matters continued to affect Marx's own family fortunes in a very immediate manner. In May 1842 one of Marx's brothers had died, and Marx returned to Trier in direct response to this tragedy. However, this visit led to the widening of a rift between Marx and his mother, Henrietta, who was not nearly as educated as her husband Heinrich or son Karl. Marx wrote a letter about this visit in July 1842 to Arnold Ruge, in which he explained that:

> I had to spend six weeks in Trier in connection with another death. The rest of the time was split up and poisoned by the most unpleasant family controversies. My family laid obstacles in my way, which, despite the prosperity of the family, put me for the moment in very serious straits.[8]

Marx's mother did not fully approve of Marx's choice of career, and had at one point cut off his allowance as a consequence. She had also acted to stop him from obtaining his share of his father's estate. The tone of the description of Marx's return to Trier was rather distant, suggesting that Marx had, psychologically, left his immediate family behind some time previously, possibly at the moment of his father's death in 1838. Marx's affection for his father had been perhaps greater than for any other family relative. His mother lived until 1863, but her later influence on her most famous offspring was slight.

In Paris some of Marx's closest colleagues were Arnold Ruge and Moses Hess, but he had known these fellow critics before reaching French shores: Hess, for example, being a member of the Cologne Circle. In August 1844 one Friedrich Engels (born in 1820) happened to be travelling across Paris and onwards to Germany. On 28 August Engels met Marx, by chance, in a well-known café in Paris, and an immediate intellectual affinity developed between the two men. A partnership was begun that would – literally – change the world, and would be severed 39 years later only on Marx's passing. Although both shared a strong penchant for radical politics, Engels' background was rather different from that of Marx. Being the child of a factory owner, Engels had already gained much practical experience of industrial life at the time of his fateful encounter with Marx. And although they were both middle class by education, Engels' family was much more financially stable than Marx's. Their characters and lifestyles were also quite different, and this issue deserves more detailed attention (see below).

This meeting was, however, not their very first encounter, as in November 1842 Engels had met Marx briefly and uneventfully while calling in on the editorial offices of the *Rheinische Zeitung*. From April 1842 until the end of the year, Engels had contributed regularly to this publication, writing articles on various topics such as Prussian newspaper laws, German liberalism and Rheinish music festivals. Engels was, like Marx, critical of liberal ideas in politics and philosophy, and instead leaned towards revolutionary socialism.

Excited by their obvious intellectual similarities, Marx and Engels decided to work together as writers and theorists of universal human liberation – a noble yet stormy pathway. Their first collaborative work was *The Holy Family* (subtitled characteristically 'A Critique of Critical Criticism'), which was written in the autumn of 1844 and published the following year in German. It was a detailed polemical consideration of the ideas of Bruno Bauer and his close circle. Bauer had been a close friend of Marx's while he was in Berlin, but their ways had parted as Marx had moved further away from his Young Hegelian origins. The tone of the book was strongly sarcastic, the text was replete with words flagged in quotation marks, the ironic use of exclamation marks, and short and long extracts from other publications, and it was presented in a rather cluttered structure of nine chapters divided into many parts and subdivisions. A flavour of the type of criticism of Bauer's ideas that it contained can be gleaned from the following passage, laden with sarcasm:

> Criticism achieves a height of abstraction in which it regards only the creation of its own thought and generalities which contradict all reality as 'something', indeed as '*everything*' ... Everything that is real and living is un-Critical, of a mass nature, and therefore 'nothing'; only the ideal, fantastic creatures of Critical Criticism are '*everything*'.[9]

Basically, Marx and Engels were accusing the Bauer circle of disappearing inside their own idealist abstractions, as the final sentence of the book made very clear. One section of the book, on French materialism, did (more serenely) indicate how Marx viewed materialism as the philosophical complement to socialism, and traced the lineage of materialism back through Pierre Bayle, John Locke and Thomas Hobbes, to its English progenitor Francis Bacon and French origins in Cartesian metaphysics. This empiricist tradition was a very different one from Marx's own Young Hegelian ancestry, but the detailed discussion of it in 1844 showed that Marx was already reaching well beyond the confines of German intellectual traditions at this time.

The Holy Family was certainly not one of Marx's great works, and if it is read in its entirety today it appears full of the philosophical minutiae of the period that lack any greater relevance. It did provide a clear indication that Marx's ongoing cerebral development would periodically produce 'casualties of the ideological war', as his once-close friend Bauer was publicly savaged in print. Marx was absolutely convinced that his own intellectual evolution was correct, at every single stage of its unfolding, and he gave no ideological mercy to those whom he left behind in the process. But how were the two undoubtedly talented polemicist co-authors of The Holy Family suited as friends, in character and temperament?

PHYSICAL APPEARANCE AND CHARACTER

Engels' nickname for Marx was 'the Moor' because of his dark appearance, which in the language of the time was described as 'swarthy'. In a poem of 1842 Engels described Marx as follows:

> A swarthy chap of Trier, a marked monstrosity.
> He neither hops nor skips, but moves in leaps and bounds,
> Raving aloud. As if to seize and then pull down
> To Earth the spacious tent of Heaven up on high,
> He opens wide his arms and reaches for the sky.
> He shakes his wicked fist, raves with a frantic air,
> As if ten thousand devils had him by the hair.[10]

The young Jenny von Westphalen referred affectionately to Marx as 'my dear wild boar' and 'my dark little savage'. In his youth Marx had flowing locks of thick black hair that turned grey in old age, a high forehead and full lips, and in adulthood he cultivated a long beard. His mind was described as 'piercing' and of rare intellectual calibre, as even many of his enemies sometimes admitted. His favourite virtue in men was listed as strength, his idea of happiness was to fight, and the vice he most detested was servility. According to one visitor his personal manners frequently violated all social conventions and he spoke with a sharp metallic voice. A police agent's report described him (perhaps a little tenden-tiously) as a highly disorderly and bad-mannered individual who rarely washed, combed his hair or changed his linen, and who held to very unu-sual working and sleeping habits. Marx's house was in 1853 apparently so untidy that 'a rag-and-bone man would step back ashamed from such a place'.[11] His study was usually thick with tobacco smoke and he was not averse to the odd glass of claret when it was available.

Reports of his character are somewhat divergent, with his daughter describing him as good-humoured, kind, sympathetic and patient, and sympathisers characterising him as honest, never hypocritical and free from vanity. Others have reported his disdain and contempt for oppo-nents, occasional outbreaks of petty spite, dictatorial tendencies and even intellectual arrogance. He was, however, always kind and caring with his children. Certainly no one could doubt Marx's sincere devotion to the cause of revolutionary socialism, but he undoubtedly saw himself as the theoretical leader of this movement, which in itself implied some form of hierarchical relationship between the sage and his followers. Marx was certainly not an egalitarian anarchist.

Another perspective on Marx's character may be gained by compar-ing it with that of his lifelong friend, Friedrich Engels. In his personal life Marx was unquestionably a family man, despite occasional lapses, and he savoured his role as the head of the Marx family throughout his adult life. This is in direct contrast to Engels, who was a lifelong bach-elor, despite a long-term attachment to one particular woman. In stark contrast to Marx, Engels was always immaculately dressed and his study was organised in an impeccable way. As any biographer of Marx would attest, Marx's handwriting was excruciatingly illegible, whereas Engels' was neat and clearly presented. In theoretical terms Marx was a perma-nent explorer, ceaselessly roving in whatever direction his studies were taking him, with less concern for a final resting place or with keeping to any single pre-established intellectual path. Engels was (in his later life at least) a systematising force and a codifier of Marxism, who worked to bring order to the Marxian project by publishing Marx's incomplete legacy in apparently finalised form.

One particularly notable difference between Marx and Engels in their early lives was that Engels did not begin his intellectual journey as a full devotee of Hegel in the way that Marx had done. In the preface to his passionate condemnation of factory conditions and proletarian suffering,

The Condition of the Working Class in England of 1845, Engels wrote a little sceptically of those German theoreticians who had arrived at communism 'by way of the Feuerbachian dissolution of Hegelian speculation', implying that an acquaintance with the real conditions of the proletariat might be more germane.[12] Engels' writing style was usually more 'straightforward' than that of his devoted friend and, in its early manifestations at least, was free from the Hegelian terminology that often pervaded the young Marx's capacious texts.

BRUSSELS

Even in Paris and after his momentous meeting with Engels, Marx could not escape the wrath of governments or censors. In January 1845 a biweekly publication that he had contributed to was closed down, and an order for his expulsion from Paris was issued. Marx's reputation as a political agitator was growing, and he quickly travelled on to Brussels, where he would remain for the following three years of his life. But just before fleeing Paris, Marx had signed a contract to write an innocuous-sounding book called *A Critique of Economics and Politics* – this work would never be finally completed, despite the fact that he would spend the rest of his professional life in the process of writing it. In one form or another, the 'critique of economics' would be his central intellectual goal from this point onwards.

In Brussels Marx continued his burgeoning study of economic and social development, composing the oft-quoted *Theses on Feuerbach* (as they were later titled by Engels) in 1845. These pithy aphorisms contained a version of the pragmatic theory of truth (thesis two), that the correctness of any idea or assertion could be proved only in practice. The most famous eleventh thesis emphasised the need to change the world rather than only to interpret it – on this point Marx's desire eventually came true (but be careful what you wish for). Thesis three, on the meaning of materialism, pitted the influence of general circumstances against individual action in a sophisticated and non-reductionist manner. Thesis four called for the destruction of the earthly family, both in theory and in practice, although whether Marx was thinking of his devoted wife Jenny at this point is debatable. The *Theses on Feuerbach* were not meant by Marx for formal publication, only for theoretical self-clarification, and were not available to readers until many years later, when Engels included them as an appendix to one of his own works.

In March 1845 Marx wrote a draft of an article discussing Friedrich List's *National System of Political Economy* of 1841, an article that was not published at the time of its composition. List is today viewed as the most well-known German economist after Marx, and is remembered as the theorist of protectionism as a means of encouraging a nation's industrial development. In his article Marx described List as a 'German idealising philistine' and suggested that he had not provided any original propositions in economic theory at all. Marx was heavily critical of List's conception of 'national economy' and the measures that he proposed for fostering a country's economic development, instead emphasising that:

> The nationality of the worker is neither French, nor English, nor German, it is *labour, free slavery, self-huckstering*. His government is neither French, nor English, nor German, it is capital ... the German philistine wants the laws of competition ... to lose their power at the frontier barriers of the country![13]

Marx's highly critical attitude towards List was in part conditioned by the fact that List was in turn critical of the analytical approach of the classical economist David Ricardo. Marx later felt some conceptual affinity with Ricardo with respect to his use of the labour theory of value, and hence List's country-specific approach to understanding economic phenomena grated with Marx's aim (in embryo) of providing a universal theory of capitalist production. List was, however, very close in approach to the methodology favoured by the German historical school.

In July 1845 Marx travelled to England (together with Engels) to conduct research for his proposed work on economics. Most commentators saw England as standing in the forefront of economic change at this historical juncture, and so it was a natural location for the study of contemporary economic theory. On their return Marx and Engels decided to compose a critical account of their old intellectual fraternity, the Young Hegelians. This was conceived as a method of making their recent intellectual progress clear, and to settle accounts with their previous philosophical colleagues, before moving onwards. The project resulted in the writing of a long manuscript entitled 'The German Ideology', which was subtitled 'Critique of Modern German Philosophy According to Feuerbach, B. Bauer and Stirner, and of German Socialism According to its Various Prophets'.

Marx and Engels worked on this project jointly through 1845 and 1846, but it was eventually abandoned while still incomplete. It would be many years before this collaborative effort saw actual publication. Despite much effort being devoted to finding a printer, the bulky manuscript was finally left to the 'gnawing of the mice' as censorship concerns had frightened off potential publishers. A significant part of 'The German Ideology' dealt with Feuerbach, but its most important legacy was that it provided the first detailed presentation of the materialist conception of history. This was one of Marx's most important and enduring contributions to human understanding, and was still sometimes employed in historical analysis 150 years after its first formulation.

It is difficult today to understand how significant and revolutionary (in an intellectual sense) the materialist conception of history actually was in the context of European thought in the mid-1840s. As Marx was fond of arguing at this time, European thinking was dominated by idealist phantoms such as religion and philosophical abstraction. In contrast, what Marx and Engels were saying with their materialist conception of history was that *all previous conceptions of how the historical process operated were fundamentally erroneous*. Not only this, but that the elements previously taken to determine historical progress not only did not have the generative power that had been assigned to them, but simply *did not exist at all*, and hence had no actual significance whatsoever. History had been a subject constructed on totally mistaken foundations, and thus the existing historical method deserved to be thrown unceremoniously into the dustbin of history. This formulation was in some regards an exaggeration of Marx's theoretical originality, but it was certainly not completely so.

In many ways the materialist conception of history was one of the most revolutionary ideas (as a pure conceptual change) that Marx would ever conceive. It brought together his interests in economics, politics and history in a particularly apt manner, and could have been conceived only by someone who was pursuing a multi-disciplinary approach to studying human society. It was the first end result of Marx's intellectual journey away from the idealist philosophy of history, as presented by Hegel, towards an engagement with the practical matters of real life conceived theoretically. However, given that 'The German Ideology' remained unpublished as a book for many years after its initial composition, the first opportunity that most historians had to actually understand Marx's innovation would be through a later version of the materialist conception of history as published in a completely separate work. Hence few reactions to this new conception of historical progress were documented in the mid-1840s, outside of those who had read the draft manuscript or who had discussed the idea with Marx and Engels in person.

Although 'The German Ideology' was not published in its entirety until the twentieth century (in 1932 in fact), chapter four of the second book, on the historiography of true socialism, appeared in a German journal in 1847. This part contained an amusing parody of the two authors' opponents, who were ironically referred to as 'saints' and 'prophets'. While discussing the suggestion that the whole individual might be contained in essence within a single attribute, Marx and Engels ridiculed this idea as suggesting that a man was contained in himself 'like his own pimple'. In fact much of the work was bitingly polemical in tone, just as *The Holy Family* had been two years earlier. It was also replete with colourful phrases used metaphorically, such as 'bones in this beggar's broth' and 'Sancho's ass'. Reading these polemical sections today, they appear in some contrast to the more theoretical part that dryly outlined the materialist conception of history.

As well as presenting a new approach to understanding historical change, 'The German Ideology' was destined to become well known as an important milestone because of a simple phrase that it contained that aptly summarised Marx's conception of human activity within a future communist society: 'hunter, fisherman, shepherd and critic'. The full liberation of all aspects of human potential would enable individuals to perform multiple work roles within the new society envisaged by Marx, this notion being a further development of ideas first outlined in the 'Economic and Philosophical Manuscripts' of 1844. How exactly this multi-tasking would operate in a complex economy was not really outlined by Marx in any detail, but as an inspiring vision it was a very potent suggestion. One extraordinary page of the manuscript copy of 'The German Ideology' (mainly in Engels' hand) was divided into two rough columns. The first contained the written text; the second contained dozens of different-sized sketches of human faces in profile, all looking from right to left, as if they were perusing the text in anticipation or judgement. It would be reading too much into these figures to suggest that they might be looking forwards to socialism.

At around this time (1846) Marx's personal financial situation began to deteriorate, the first of many financial difficulties that he would encounter throughout his adult life. In one sense Marx's ongoing financial woes were easily explained – he had no permanent full-time occupation. The royalties he periodically obtained from writing were nowhere near enough to support his family, and without continuous financial support from Engels (and other sources) it is certain that Marx would have found himself in very serious trouble many times in his life. On the other hand, it might be suggested that someone with the unquestionably brilliant intellect that Marx possessed should have been supported in some way through a permanent university attachment. Except of course that Marx's political infamy prevented this possibility ever being realised. Hence Marx was destined to endure bouts of relative poverty throughout his adult life – although compared with the conditions endured by some workers at this time his plight was relatively mild. Few workers could appeal successfully to a well-to-do benefactor to send them a financial pick-me-up in the post.

It was in Brussels that Marx and Engels started up a Communist Correspondence Committee, which in effect was the germ of the Communist International. Its basic aim was to enable discussion of socialist ideas and policies across England, France and Germany. It was Marx's first serious effort in practical political organisation, and other important members of the Committee included Philippe Gigot and Sebastian Seiler. Marx was particularly interested in creating connections with Parisian socialists such as Pierre Joseph Proudhon through the Committee, and he wrote to Proudhon in May 1846 with this aim in mind. Proudhon's carefully worded reply warned against posing as the apostles of a new religion, and expressed more sympathy for evolutionary socialism than for revolutionary action. Partly as a result of this cool reply, one year later Marx attacked Proudhon's new book (which was titled 'The Philosophy of Poverty') with a vengeance, in a work with the ironically reversed title *The Poverty of Philosophy*, which obtained immediate publication in French in 1847. Marx was apparently not someone who let personal slights go at all easily.

This book was important in that it contained Marx's first detailed published account of the opposition of use-value and exchange-value – an important distinction within Marx's mature economic theory. It also contained a discussion of the proportionality of labour time to commodity value, a detailed analysis of the division of labour, and an account of the relation between competition and monopoly. Most of the book was presented in the form of a critical discussion with Proudhon's ideas. The final section on 'strikes and the combination of workmen' provided Marx with the opportunity to present his teleological conception of the role of the working class as the universal class bearing the liberation of all humanity within the bounds of its actions. In response to this barrage of philosophical criticism, Proudhon branded Marx 'the tape-worm of socialism', which in a sense was an accurate characterisation of Marx's method of reaching inside the ideas of someone and then destroying their beliefs by consuming them and burrowing outwards.

In Brussels the issue of the less-than-perfect state of Marx's health had already begun to manifest itself: an issue that would significantly affect his later life, and would often be cited by commentators as a reason for the incompletion of his life's work. In a letter to Engels dated 15 May 1847 Marx wrote:

> About 12 days ago Breyer *bled* me, but on the *right* arm instead of the *left*. Since I continued to work as if nothing had happened the wound festered instead of healing up. The matter might have got dangerous and cost me my arm. Now it's as good as healed. But my arm's still weak. Must not be overworked.[14]

The reason for this bleeding was not explicitly stated, but the semi-quack nature of many health treatments at this time is well recorded. It might also be remarked about this apparent uncertainty, didn't Marx himself realise which of his two arms was being bled? A cynical reader might read an element of exaggeration into this letter ('Must not be overworked'), although Marx's health problems in later life were certainly real enough. But in 1847 Marx was on the cusp of a series of political revolutions in Europe that would rock the foundations of bourgeois society to its very core – for a brief moment at least.

CONCLUSION

It can be seen from the above presentation of Marx's youthful development that his early works – from the doctoral dissertation on Greek philosophy to *The Poverty of Philosophy* – were often a combination of brilliant polemic, original understanding, biting wit and unplanned intellectual exploration. This resulted in works that were sometimes inanely repetitive, frequently unfocused and meandering, sometimes amusingly droll, and now and again fundamentally original. Given Marx's spontaneous manner of work and uncompromising attitude to life, the style and structure of his writings followed quite naturally. But it is now possible to understand how Marx's writings sometimes remained unpublished in his own lifetime, accepting that there was often a political factor at work in this also. A publisher reading through the manuscript of 'The German Ideology' might easily miss the (relatively short) few paragraphs of genuine genius and instead become thoroughly anaesthetised by endless petty sarcastic criticism. There was, unsurprisingly perhaps, an element of immaturity in Marx's early works that some other great philosophers (such as David Hume, for example) had managed to avoid. Marx undoubtedly demonstrated great intellectual promise in his early years, and how he would realise this potential is the subject of the rest of this book. But before this task is begun, Marx's early writings deserve more careful examination in and of themselves.

2

EARLY WRITINGS

The special importance of the early (or formative) years of any famous intellectual is frequently acknowledged in the biographical literature discussing their life and impact upon the world. W. W. Rostow has posited the shared notion of a youthful 'sacred decade' of the twenties, when all the main themes and ideas that will be explored in later life are first articulated by any given individual thinker. In its halcyon twenties the human mind is sufficiently developed to be able to engage with major new concepts, but not sufficiently mature (or disillusioned) to be easily able to see beyond the initial impact or significance of something: life-long intellectual associations are thus frequently created. As Marx was born in 1818, his 'sacred decade' relates (approximately) to between 1838 and 1848, from the time of his long letter to his father recording the first detailed reading of Hegel, to the publication of *The Manifesto of the Communist Party*, written together with Friedrich Engels. It will be maintained here that this notion of a 'sacred decade' is especially true of Marx's life, and that to gain an understanding all of his later work an appreciation of his early work is absolutely crucial.

In Marx's case it will be suggested that the idea of 'intellectual path dependency' is particularly applicable – the notion that his early intellectual influences were not only the background against which he began to develop his own unique ideas, but that they also set the conceptual framework and laid the rail tracks of much of his later work and attitudes.

In fact, the underlying approach of Marx's early writings constituted an ongoing point of reference that he never entirely abandoned. How he used and modified his early understanding in the light of more substantial research in economics is certainly important in comprehending his later innovations, but the once-popular notion that he experienced some type of epiphany or 'revelatory break', as a result of which he discarded all of his early (unscientific) ideas, is thoroughly misleading. Marx's mature work on economics was the consequence of the development of ideas and themes that he had begun to pursue in the early 1840s.

MARX AND HEGEL

The most significant, yet impersonal, intellectual relationship that Marx had in his early life was with G. W. F. Hegel. In fact, Marx never discarded his deep and profound appreciation of Hegel's method. And, as this biography will aim to demonstrate, Marx was still employing Hegel's method in the final years of his life. Indeed, if Engels constituted Marx's most significant personal (or actual) intellectual relationship throughout his life, then it could reasonably be argued that Hegel was Marx's most significant impersonal (or abstract) intellectual relationship across his entire life, both in a positive, 'springboard' sense and in a negative, 'reactive' sense.

Marx's youthful devotion to Hegel is apparent from one item in a series of poems that he composed in 1837, which were dedicated to his father. One verse of the revealingly titled 'Epigram on Hegel' read as follows:

> Forgive us epigrammatists
> For singing songs with nasty twists.
> In Hegel we're all so completely submerged,
> But with his Aesthetics we've yet to be purged.[1]

Jenny von Westphalen referred to Marx playfully in a letter written in 1841 as a 'Hegeling gentleman', and conveyed her hope that Marx had been able to locate some Hegel clubs in which to participate.[2] Hegel is, of course, one of the great names of Western philosophy, as the two progressing trios of 'Locke, Berkeley, Hume' (the British Empiricists) and 'Kant, Hegel, Marx' (the German Idealists) clearly attest, and Marx's early submergence in Hegel was entirely understandable for a German student of his day. The fact that Marx himself moved away from his early interest in philosophy as a subject of study, to his more 'mature' concerns of investigating history and economics, should not be taken to demonstrate that he came to reject his youthful Hegelianism completely.

One of the difficulties in fully comprehending Hegel's influence on Marx is that this influence was greatest in relation to the underlying method being employed, while not necessarily in regard to the specific elements that were being considered at any given point. Hence, for someone looking for the continued mention of Hegel by name, or the use of his specific philosophical ideas in Marx's writings, the results might be disappointing. Some examples of the real nature of Hegel's influence on Marx are thus required. To take a very early case, Marx's doctoral dissertation, written in 1840–1, was entitled 'The Difference between the Democritean and Epicurean Philosophy of Nature'. This work counterposed the views of two Greek thinkers (Democritus and Epicurus) on aspects of the natural world in a characteristically contrary manner. Marx wrote that:

> ... the two men are opposed to each other at every single step. The one is a sceptic, and other a dogmatist; the one considers the sensuous world as subjective semblance, the other as objective appearance. He who considers the sensuous world as subjective semblance applies himself to empirical natural science ... The other, who considers the phenomenal world to be real, scorns empiricism ... the contradiction goes still farther ...[3]

Marx explained (in Young Hegelian fashion) that the duality of philosophical self-consciousness appeared as a double trend: the first side being critique, the second side being positive philosophy. In discussing the relevant conceptions of physics under examination, Marx's dissertation also contained phrases such as 'the point is negated in the line' and 'the atom is the immediate negation of abstract space'. Marx concluded that for Epicurus, atomistic philosophy was the natural science of self-consciousness, whereas for Democritus the atom was the objective expression of the empirical investigation of nature. The Epicurean conception of science as self-consciousness was something that had a clear affinity with Hegel's idealism.

The influence of Hegel on Marx's analysis of Greek philosophy was thus apparent in the contrasting method being employed even in this very early work, and in the foreword to his doctoral dissertation Marx credited Hegel with correctly defining the general aspects of the Epicurean, Stoic and Sceptic systems of thought. In his notebooks on Epicurean philosophy Marx had referred to Hegel as 'our master', despite acknowledging variant interpretations of Hegel's ideas. However, Hegel was not mentioned by name in any of the main sections of the dissertation at all. But, as always with Marx, the living spectre of Hegel hovered over the general approach that Marx had adopted of directly contrasting two opposing Greek thinkers in a dialectical manner.

Another possibly deceptive aspect of Marx's relationship to Hegel was that Marx's most substantial written work on Hegel was concerned mainly with criticising Hegel's political philosophy as revealed in *The Philosophy of Right*. This book was a rather conservative work that contained Hegel's idealisation of the Prussian state as the realisation of the Absolute Idea in the historical world. The Marx commentary on this book will be considered in more detail later in this chapter, but regarding the manifestation of the Absolute Idea, Marx wrote in his analysis that:

> Hegel's sole concern is simply to re-discover 'the Idea' ... in every sphere, whether it be the state or nature, whereas the real subjects, in this case the 'political constitution', are reduced to mere *names* of the Idea ...[4]

Of course Marx was highly critical of any writings that seemed to justify the existing political order in Europe, and hence Marx appeared to be being very critical of Hegel as a philosopher. However, this should not be taken to imply that Marx had the same negative attitude to Hegel's *Science of Logic* as he had expressed towards *The Philosophy of Right*. The former work was Hegel's most significant book on abstract dialectical logic, whereas the latter was merely one aspect of the political component of this logic as Hegel had presented it at one point in his life.

Marx never composed a substantial work on Hegel's dialectical method, in part because he actually held a great deal of respect for the form of this method of understanding. Marx tended to focus his critical fire on those published works that he disagreed with in a major way, and he did not expend intellectual energy writing hagiographies of those thinkers that he was basically in agreement with. Even *Capital* itself was a critique of something (political economy). The closest that Marx ever came to a serious work on Hegel's method was a section entitled 'Critique of Hegel's Dialectic and General Philosophy' in the 'Economic and Philosophical Manuscripts', which are discussed in more detail further on in this chapter. But although the heading of this section sounded as though it might contain an account of Hegel's general method, a large part of it dealt with the alienation of self-consciousness from itself, or Marx's Young Hegelian interpretation of the nature of human understanding.

Although appearances were sometimes to the contrary, Marx was at heart a supporter of the Hegelian approach in terms of the underlying methodology that he employed in his analysis of social and economic development, despite the fact that he had published a thoroughgoing condemnation of Hegel's political philosophy in his formative years. True to his own method of critique, Marx was not shy of using Hegel's method to criticise Hegel himself, as any dialectician would proudly demonstrate, but the negation of the negation brings you back to the point of origin (Hegel's method) once again, albeit at a higher plane of understanding.

MARX MOVES AWAY FROM PHILOSOPHY

Although Marx was thoroughly immersed in German philosophy in his youth, in the early 1840s he began to move away from the abstract concerns of philosophical understanding, and towards analysing the more concrete problems of real life. This was an important step in Marx's intellectual journey, and is most clearly seen in some of his journalistic writings from 1842. One of the longest articles that Marx wrote for the *Rheinische Zeitung* in 1842 was entitled 'Debates on the Law on Thefts of Wood', and Marx himself cited this article as one of the first to bring him into close contact with practical matters of immediate concern to everyday life. In discussing the legal norms surrounding the practices of gathering dead wood, Marx argued that aristocratic customs ran counter to the general law, and hence were unjust and should be ultimately abrogated. Marx later said that this article on wood theft, plus one other written slightly later on the position of local peasants ('Justification of the Correspondent from the Mosel' of 1843), had played a significant role in moving his focus away from purely philosophical and political questions and towards analysing economic conditions. In the latter article Marx highlighted a contradiction between the reality of the situation of vine growers and the inappropriate administrative principles that were used to manage this reality.

This practice-orientated aspect of Marx's early intellectual evolution has been readily acknowledged by many of Marx's commentators. However, another aspect of this evolution has been less documented. In a newspaper article, 'The Philosophical Manifesto of the Historical School of Law' of 1842, written a few months before the article on wood theft, Marx characterised the views of the author of a textbook on natural law (Gustav Hugo) as follows:

> ... he by no means tries to prove that the *positive* is *rational*; he tries to prove that the positive is irrational ... he adduces arguments from everywhere to provide additional evidence that no rational necessity is inherent in the positive institutions, e.g. property, the state constitution, marriage, etc, that they are even contrary to reason ...[5]

In the view of the historical school of law, institutions such as private property were simply conventions that evolved historically over time; they were not the outcome of any form of rational thought or deliberate human (or even spiritual) design. This conception clashed in the most fundamental manner with Marx's nascent Hegelian view of social economy, where historical development was seen as the outcome of a process of Reason propagating itself consciously across the world. Marx consequently mocked Hugo's conception of institutions as 'historical relics', and chastised the 'crude genealogical tree' of the historical school.

Marx believed that in taking an evolutionary approach, and in employing the notion of a natural animal state of human existence in corollary, members of the historical school of law were justifying the right of arbitrary power as represented in existing institutions. One such institution mentioned was the French pre-revolutionary government. Marx was of course highly critical of the existing structure of society, and he believed in his youth that this structure developed in a Hegelian fashion. This approach of historicised idealism dated from as early as 1842, and was presented by Marx explicitly in contrast to the method of the German historical school. It is necessary to re-emphasise that, as well as a historical school of law, in Germany at this time there existed a historical school of political economy, which also employed an evolutionary conception of social development. This historical school used a method that was in direct contrast both to the abstractions of classical British political economy and also to the utopian socialism of French thinkers such as Charles Fourier and Henri Saint-Simon. But it was from the latter writers that Marx was to obtain much of his socialistic sympathies, not from the quite different approach to socialism of the German historical school. This intellectual lineage would be of notable significance for Marx's later work in economics.

Despite Marx's significant move to study more practical matters, in 1842 he was not yet a full-blown believer in the communism of the period. But although he would not have described himself as a communist at this time, Marx certainly knew of such ideas. He wrote an article on communism for the *Rheinische Zeitung* in 1842 in which he stated that communist ideas did not possess even theoretical reality, let alone could they admit of practical realisation. He promised that the *Rheinische Zeitung* would subject such ideas to thoroughgoing criticism. Marx warned that:

> We are firmly convinced that the real danger lies not in practical attempts, but in the theoretical elaboration of communist ideas, for practical attempts, even mass attempts, can be answered by cannon as soon as they become dangerous, whereas ideas, which have conquered our intellect and taken possession of our minds ... are chains from which one cannot free oneself without a broken heart ...[6]

This latter sentence, implying that communism was an intellectual prison, has had many additional reverberations across the twentieth century. But in 1842 Marx could not possibly have known what doctrinal developments lay ahead – even for his own individual belief system in the near future, let alone for the wider world.

MARX ON RELIGION AND LAW

Throughout his early writings on philosophy and politics, Marx discussed a wide range of topics that were significant issues of the day. One such issue, with which the Marx family had a personal connection, was the 'Jewish question', or the issue of the rights of Jewish people to participate equally in civil and political life. Jews had suffered many centuries of persecution in Europe since their initial expulsion from Israel, and were often treated as second-class citizens. Yet, despite his own ancestry, Marx has sometimes been accused of being anti-Semitic. In 1843 he composed a well-known article called 'On the Jewish Question', in which he wrote the following:

> What, in itself, was the basis of the Jewish religion? Practical need, egoism ... The god of the Jews has become secularised and has become the god of the world. The bill of exchange is the real god of the Jew ... The *chimerical* nationality of the Jew is the nationality of the merchant, of the man of money in general.[7]

Marx concluded this article by suggesting that the emancipation of the Jews could come about only if society was emancipated from Judaism, as the essence of Judaism – huckstering – was the common practical reality of civil society.

It is apparent from these short passages that Marx certainly did hold some stereotypical conceptions of Jews as being natural hucksters. But, against this negative aspect, Marx supported the idea of the equality of rights for Jews in relation to civil campaigns of the time, for example in Prussia where Jews had possessed lesser rights than those of Christians. In addition to this, Marx's analysis of the Jewish question was linked to his conception of human beings as being trapped by the external forms of their wealth as represented in abstraction by money. In Marx's view, Jews were just as much a victim of these alienated forms of wealth as were adherents of other religions, despite the fact that he had associated them in stereotypical manner with the role of the money-conscious merchant.

Another theme of this article on the Jewish question was Marx's view that political emancipation through the state (for example through civil liberties) was only partial emancipation, in that any form of intermediate (or indirect) relation between people (such as religion or the state) was necessarily only an incomplete mediation of true human social intercourse. Marx characterised 'bourgeois' liberties in relation to owning wealth as being the liberties of egoistic man, and for him these were inevitably constraining liberties. What he proposed instead was emancipation from huckstering and money themselves, calling this the real self-emancipation movement of our time. This true emancipation would liberate all religions, including Jews, from the intermediary forms of their estrangement as represented in organised religion, and would enable all members of society (including Jews) to participate fully in every aspect of social life.

In the same year as the article on the Jewish question (1843) Marx wrote his early work that was most explicitly focused on engaging with Hegel's contribution to philosophy, entitled 'A Contribution to the Critique of Hegel's Philosophy of Law', which was over 100 pages in length. Although this work was quite substantial in scope, it was written in Marx's early style of quoting many passages from those individuals he was discussing, interspersed with his own detailed commentary and analysis. It contained an account of Hegel's conception of the state, civil society and the family, in particular the relationship between these institutions, and also a discussion of various forms of government such as democracy and monarchy. Various forms of property (such as landed property and the peasant estate) and their relation to political institutions were then considered, as were various national variants. This work was not really a finished piece, more like a series of thoughts on the topics presented, and it clearly showed Marx developing his ideas through an active engagement with Hegel's political philosophy.

Of particular significance was the introduction to this work, where Marx discussed what he called 'the possibility of German emancipation' through the formation of a class with radical chains, or a class that could not emancipate itself without emancipating all other spheres of society as well. Such universal class characteristics Marx saw in the proletariat, which he stated was coming into being in Germany as a result of increased industrial development. He wrote in his characteristically millennial (and *heavily italicised*) manner that:

> By proclaiming the *dissolution of the hitherto existing world order* the proletariat merely states the *secret of its own existence* ... By demanding the *negation of private property*, the proletariat merely raises to the rank of a *principle of society* which society has made the principle of the proletariat ... As philosophy finds its *material* weapons in the proletariat, so the proletariat finds its *spiritual* weapons in philosophy.[8]

Hence Marx had conceived his own brand of philosophical analysis as being the ideational weapon of the proletariat as early as 1843, five years before the publication of *The Manifesto of the Communist Party*, and one year after describing communism as not admitting of practical realisation. In this passage Marx also demonstrated his antipathy towards the private ownership of property, which was to become one of the most central tenets of Marxism over the next 150 years. These various ideas received much more detailed elaboration in a very significant work that Marx wrote in 1844 in Paris.

THE 'ECONOMIC AND PHILOSOPHICAL MANUSCRIPTS'

The 'Economic and Philosophical Manuscripts' (or 'EPM' for short) of 1844 are often presented as the first systematic attempt by Marx to engage with 'bourgeois' political economy, or (in other words) with the long tradition of classical economics. However, the EPM were not published until many decades after they were written, not until 1932 in fact. It was Friedrich Engels who had first published on this topic, in his *Outlines of a Critique of National Economy* of 1844. In this work Engels presented competition as the underlying cause of all economic woes within capitalism, such as grinding poverty and continuous crime, yet it was also seen as the mainspring that drove all economic activity. Competition acted to set capital against capital, labour against labour and landed property against landed property, as well as each element against the other two. Engels argued that the extension of competition into every sphere of human life could be overcome only through a fusion of opposing interests by means of the abolition of private property.[9]

Marx was impressed by this analysis of national economy, and he wrote a summary of Engels' article in which he notated: 'The separation of capital from labour ... The split between land and the human being. Human labour divided into labour and capital'.[10] This type of analysis was taken much further in the EPM themselves, which are often regarded as the single most significant work of the early Marx by far, and were composed from April to August 1844. Just before Marx wrote the EPM he had written some 'Excerpts from James Mill's *Elements of Political Economy*', which provided one of his first serious engagements with economic theory. Marx's approach was to overlay his own socialist ethical beliefs upon the existing tenets of political economy. For example, he wrote that:

> Credit is the *economic* judgement on the *morality* of a man ... Thus the credit relationship ... becomes ... an object of mutual deception and exploitation. This brilliantly illustrates the fact that the basis of trust in economics is mistrust: the mistrustful reflection about whether to extend credit or not; the spying-out of secrets in the private life of the borrower ...[11]

Marx's attitude was that the capitalist financial system reduced human morality to the lender's rating of an individual. Marx neglected to ask whether, in any other field of human activity, the reality was any different from that in the economic sphere. In the political or personal realms, did universal trust reign supreme? Marx was implicitly comparing the existing money system with a utopian ideal that existed only in his mind – universal trust among all people – and he consequently found the credit system to be wanting. But what exactly was the perfected ideal that Marx was using in comparison?

This is where the EPM come into their own, as providing the first detailed outline of the utopian vision of communism that Marx was to maintain throughout his adult life. In addition, various key concepts were first presented in the EPM that would be of great significance to Marx's later writings, and also to the subsequent history of Marxist ideology. Some of these concepts were: the alienation or estrangement of labour, universal species-being, communism as naturalistic humanism, and the division of labour as an alienated form of human activity. Each of these ideas will be discussed in turn.

One of the most famous Marxian concepts that was outlined in the EPM was estrangement, which meant that something was divorced or separated from its true nature and real vocation. For example, according to Marx, workers in capitalism were alienated from both the products of their labour (which were owned by capitalists), and from their true natures as human subjects. In the abundant Hegelian language of the EPM Marx wrote that:

> *Estrangement* ... is the opposition of *in itself* and *for itself*, of *consciousness* and *self consciousness*, of *object* and *subject*, i.e. the opposition within thought itself of abstract thought and sensuous reality or real sensuousness.[12]

Marx conceived the history of estrangement in the EPM in philosophical terms, as the history of the manufacture of abstract thought, or thought that was divorced from real life. Hegel's philosophical system was the supreme example of this estrangement, in that Hegel had framed the Absolute Idea (the final result of the evolution of spiritual understanding) as the ultimate expression of the religious self-consciousness of humanity, all of which was conceived as abstract mental labour. In Marx's view Hegel's system was a direct inversion of the real situation, which was that human thought derived ultimately from concrete reality (materialism), not vice versa (idealism). Note, however, that Hegel's system was (for Marx) only an inversion of concrete reality, not a complete misrepresentation of it.

Throughout the EPM Marx was struggling to reassert the primacy of practical reality ('the economic') over abstract thought ('the philosophical'), and hence to move decisively away from his German idealist origins towards an engagement with the more worldly philosophy of real life and practical materialism. In the famous phrase, Marx was inverting Hegel in order to manoeuvre him 'right side up'; he was certainly not abandoning Hegel completely. One of the ways that Marx inverted idealist philosophy was to focus his analysis on everyday matters, such as the plight of ordinary workers. Applying the concept of alienation concretely, Marx emphasised the dehumanising conditions of many factories, and also highlighted the grinding poverty generated by the low wages that were often paid to factory employees. Capitalists appeared to treat workers as they did their inanimate machines, as simply tools for the furthering of their business interests, with no real concern for them as fellow human beings. Marx described this estranged state of labour in very poetic and sympathetic terms, bringing all his knowledge of the history of German philosophy to bear on this subject in a unique and memorable manner.

A rather more difficult concept to understand, but one no less significant for Marx's project of societal change, was the notion of universal species-being. In the EPM, Marx used the term 'species-being' to denote the fully developed humanity that he believed every individual person was capable of achieving but had in the past been prevented from realising by the prevalence of exploitative relations of production. Marx wrote that:

> The *real*, *active* relation of man to himself as a species-being, or the realization
> of himself as a species-being, is only really possible if he really employs all his
> *species-powers* – which again is only possible through the cooperation of man-
> kind and as a result of history ...[13]

This was Marx at his most utopian and visionary, implying that all and every human subject was capable of developing intellectual, emotional and physical powers that could approach those of the greatest geniuses of human history. But of course only within communism could all this human potential be fully realised. In addition, there was one other very important component feature of species-being, that of enabling the development of the all-round individual. Marx believed that human potential was mutually interactive, in that narrow specialisation in only one field of endeavour was necessarily restrictive of an exponential growth in species-powers. The species-nature of human beings necessitated the engagement in a diversity of activities that facilitated the growth of natural talents; hence the continued development of the division of labour (as promoted by capitalism) had acted to stunt natural human capacities. Communism would liberate the species-being of every individual person, thus promoting all human potential and the natural diversity of human talents.

This was a powerful and inspiring vision of possible human progress, one that has converted many individuals to believe in communism as a general political goal. It also demonstrated the classic symptoms of youthful naivety regarding the perfectibility of human nature, and also an inadequate consideration of the extraordinary practical conditions that might be necessary in order to achieve this nirvana on earth. Marx summarised his utopian vision of post-capitalist society in the EPM as follows:

> *Communism* is the positive supersession of *private property* as *human self-
> estrangement*, and hence the true *appropriation* of the *human* essence through
> and for man; it is the complete restoration of man to himself as a *social*, i.e.
> human, being ... This communism, as fully developed naturalism, equals
> humanism ... it is the *genuine* resolution of the conflict between man and
> nature, and between man and man ...[14]

Marx believed that once private property had been abolished, and all property was then held in common, the divisive conflicts between people that had their origins in the fight to control this property would be superseded, and the 'general good' would necessarily prevail. This passage also showed that the young Marx equated communism with humanism, and hence that the rigid hierarchical politics of Leninist 'democratic' centralism was a world away from the early Marx's youthful vision of the naturalistic liberation of humanity.

There is another important (and perhaps surprising) aspect of the EPM that is sometimes neglected by commentators. This was Marx's emphasis on human nature as being essentially sensuous, and hence his notion that the liberation of humanity was an essentially sensuous task. Marx wrote that:

> Only through the objectively unfolded wealth of human nature can the wealth of subjective human sensibility – a musical ear, an eye for the beauty of form, in short, *senses* capable of human gratification – be either cultivated or created. For not only the five senses, but also the so-called spiritual senses, the practical senses (will, love, etc.), in a word, the human sense ... all these come into being only through ... *humanized* nature ... The whole of history is a preparation, a development, for '*man*' to become the object of sensuous consciousness and for the needs of 'man as man' to become [sensuous] needs.[15]

Communism was thus conceived by Marx in the EPM as the full development of individual human sensuality in all its various forms. This might help to explain the otherwise puzzling notion that, according to Marx, one way that private property would be superseded was through the complete emancipation of all human senses. In communism these senses would be able to relate to material objects for their own sake, rather than only being able to experience these objects egoistically, as alienated trophies of ownership. Instead of only partially appreciating the few objects that were owned personally, every individual would be able to appreciate all objects fully through communal ownership, which in turn would assist in further developing the full sensuous capacity of every individual's universal species-being.

Again, this was a very powerful and emotive promise being offered by Marx as part of the communist package. It is important to realise, however, that elements of Marx's notion of species-being as articulated in the EPM were present in the works of a German philosopher that

Marx knew very well, Ludwig Feuerbach. In his major work *The Essence of Christianity* of 1841, Feuerbach had written that:

> Man has his highest being ... in himself ... in his essential nature, his species ... The yearning of man after something above himself is nothing else than the longing after the perfect type of his nature ... Individuality is the self-conditioning, the self-limitation of the species.[16]

Marx had corresponded with Feuerbach, and in one particular letter (dated 11 August 1844) he had praised Feuerbach for providing a philosophical basis for socialism, and for outlining the concept of the human species brought down from abstraction. Another component source of Marx's conception of species-being was Friedrich Schiller's idea of the aesthetic education of man, and the superior all-round personality that it claimed to produce. In highlighting these lines of influence on the philosophy of the early Marx, no charge of plagiarism is being suggested, as all the German thinkers of this period had studied each other's works in detail, and the critical approach that they employed required constant referencing to fellow theorists: both explicit sourcing and also implied allusions.

What Marx had provided that was original was the precise formula of the mix, the interpretative twist that was being brought to the various components under consideration, and also the intellectual use to which they were ultimately put. Neither Feuerbach nor Schiller had connected the notion of species-being with a future communist society in the inspiring manner provided by Marx. And neither Feuerbach nor Schiller had begun to move in the direction of criticising political economy by means of the Hegelian method of analysis. One of Marx's most characteristic achievements throughout his adult life was the originality of his mixing of the existing elements of philosophy, politics and economics, to produce something unique and powerful as the outcome.

Finally, that the EPM contains specific applications of dialectical understanding was apparent from the following passage discussing Hegel's *Philosophy of Right*:

> ... the act of superseding therefore plays a special role in which negation and preservation (affirmation) are brought together ... private right superseded equals *morality*, morality superseded equals *family* ... In *reality* private right, morality, family ... continue to exist, but have become *moments* ... which

mutually dissolve and engender one another. They are *moments of movement*.[17]

Marx saw these moments of movement (or acts of supersession) both as forces of separation and also as forces of unification. It would be supersession that would reabsorb alienation into itself, that would replace God with atheism, and that would mediate humanism within communism through the abolition of private property. There is no clearer indication in Marx's writings that communism was conceived by him as coming into being dialectically, and that an understanding of this process necessitated the use of Hegel's method. Consequently, Marx superseded Hegel only by reabsorbing Hegel's own estrangement from himself; that is, by rendering Hegel's method into its correct formulation through returning to itself, not by totally abandoning it.

'THE GERMAN IDEOLOGY'

After the composition of such an upbeat and wide-ranging exploratory work as the 'Economic and Philosophical Manuscripts', Marx's next most significant early work was, with one notable exception, rather more prosaic in the vast bulk of its content. With the writing of a book-length 'settling of accounts' with their philosophical past, Marx and Engels were aiming to elevate themselves to the next level of understanding regarding the importance of practical matters in determining human consciousness. Appearing almost as a by-product of this more general aim, the materialist conception of history (or one version of it) was first outlined in detail in 'The German Ideology' of 1845–6. Along with the 'Economic and Philosophical Manuscripts', 'The German Ideology' was the most important work of the early Marx that was not published at the time of its initial composition.

What, then, in detail was the materialist conception of history that has become so well known today? Marx and Engels proposed a 'stages' view of the development of all human societies in which the mode of production of material goods (and also life expression) was the determining factor in the nature and progress of social and individual organisation. By 'mode of production' was meant the structured manner in which products were actually made for human consumption, or the social relations that surrounded the process of manufacture, not the specific techniques of manufacture themselves. It was consequently the forms of development of the division of labour that determined the relations of individuals to each other in ordinary life, not any ideological tenet such as religious consciousness or political belief. The latter were merely alienated reflections of the former. The various historical stages of ownership of property that were outlined by Marx and Engels in 'The German Ideology' were as follows: tribal ownership, ancient communal ownership, feudal ownership and (by extrapolation) capitalist ownership. This last stage was only implied as existing at this point; it was not specifically outlined in detail.

Tribal ownership corresponded to hunting and gathering, with only an elementary division of labour relating to both family and tribe. Ancient communal ownership developed through tribal unions, and involved a more extensive division of labour relating to town/country and also slave distinctions. Marx and Engels described this form of ownership as 'communal private property'. Feudal ownership was determined by the sparseness of the human population and military conquests, and was based upon a peasantry in subordination to noble landowners through serf bondage. Craft guilds were the associated forms of small-scale industry.

A mechanism of transition between these various sequential stages of property ownership was proposed in 'The German Ideology' as follows. When the productive forces within a given stage began to clash with the means of social intercourse, a class was called forth that would bring about a revolution in the form of ownership, thus moving society onwards to the next stage of its evolution. Put another way, class conflict was ordained as the 'transmission belt' of historical change, which itself was conceived as technological development occurring at first within and then alongside the social relations of production, which themselves were generated by the specific form of the division of labour in operation. This in essence was the materialist conception of history, at least in its very early formulation.

At one point in the book Marx and Engels posited that, at its most fundamental level, the division of labour they understood as being determinate of social relations corresponded to the division between material and intellectual labour. At a later point they posited that the division of labour within the family was the first expression of this separation, but

it was clear that, as formulated in 'The German Ideology', the materialist conception of history had various forms of this division at its centre.
Overcoming the division of labour in itself was thus the fundamental
mission of communism conceived as the last and final mode of social
production. Marx and Engels summarised this theoretical innovation as
follows:

> This conception of history thus relies on expounding the real process of pro-
> duction ... and comprehending the form of intercourse connected with and
> created by this mode of production ... as the basis of all history ... each stage
> contains a material result, a sum of productive forces, a historically created
> relation to nature and of individuals to one another, which is handed down to
> each generation from its predecessor ...18

The reference to the basis of comprehending 'all history' in this passage
might reasonably lead the reader to conclude that Marx and Engels were
attempting to provide a universal theory of historical change that was
applicable to all times and all places. This implication would later provoke some controversy between Marx's own followers, and even lead to
significant splits in matters of party political strategy.

Even so, the materialist conception of history was a powerful and
original model of historical development for the time it was presented.
Without question, elements of the model had been discussed by some
historians before this time, but what Marx and Engels provided that was
original was the manner in which the various constituent elements
(political, technological and economic factors) were connected, and what
was posited as being the underlying driving force of social change. They
had gone beyond mere description of historical events to providing a
bare outline of a workable model or analytical explanation of the historical process itself, of how progress was generated through the structured
interrelation of the various elements involved. This was one of their
greatest and most enduring intellectual achievements, and it was first
conceived when Marx was 27 years old. It would also turn out to be
hugely controversial and even sometimes infuriatingly ambiguous, but
these aspects of the materialist conception of history are for later
consideration.

CONCLUSION

The early Marx was unquestionably a man of his time, being naturally and thoroughly immersed in the German philosophical debates of the 1840s. Today this is a fact accepted by most commentators on Marx as a matter of course. However, it is important to understand that Marx's early writings were little known up until the 1930s, as the 'Economic and Philosophical Manuscripts' remained unpublished in Marx's own lifetime. This meant that Marx's most successful disciples in political terms (to date) – namely his Russian followers such as V. I. Lenin – had not read Marx's most important early work as they were enthusiastically campaigning for the overthrow of capitalism in Russia before 1917. Thus the Hegelian, humanistic, holistic Marx was unknown to them; they knew only what was usually presented as an austere 'scientific' Marx, as shown by his later writings such as *Capital*.

This also meant that Marx's early utopian vision of communism, as entailing the liberation of the sensuous species-being of every individual, was simply not known at all by his own followers in the last decades of the nineteenth century or the first decades of the twentieth century. Perhaps never have such serious practical and political consequences resulted from the lack of an accessible publication of the most important early work of a major European thinker. It was no accident that the early Marx was championed as a hero most vociferously during the student uprisings across Western Europe in 1968, when personal (as political) sensuality was placed centre stage. In the next chapter, attention is turned towards Europe 120 years previous to this renaissance of the early Marx, on the cusp of 1848. It starts by examining Marx's own role in the popular uprisings that appeared to confirm the beginnings of his own desire for the imminent collapse of all reactionary governments.

3

THE SPECTRE OF COMMUNISM

In this chapter and the next, attention will be focused on a period in Marx's life that witnessed significant political activity and also saw great efforts being made to analyse the current events that were unfolding across Europe. From this perspective, the period around 1848 was one of the most optimistic times in Marx's life, and this optimism can be seen in the enthusiastic tone and raw energy of much of his journalistic writings at this time. If the abstract philosophical ideas of Hegel explicitly dominated the early period of Marx's life, then with the revolutionary events of 1848 his political baptism into the practical realm of human endeavour was finally completed. However, the optimism of 1848 would not be maintained indefinitely.

THE COMMUNIST LEAGUE

In August 1847 Marx decided to transform the Communist Correspondence Committee operating in Brussels into a branch of the already existing Communist League, a secret society that had as its central aim the propagation of the idea of the socialised community of goods. The Central Committee of the Communist League was based in London, and Marx attended a congress of this organisation towards the end of 1847 in which he publicly presented his own principles of communism in heated debates. At the conclusion to this congress Marx and Engels were allotted the important role of preparing a 'manifesto' of the ideas of the Communist League as a statement of general aims and objectives. Fulfilling this task would produce one of the most famous and powerful statements of extreme left-wing political affiliation ever to be written – *The Manifesto of the Communist Party* – and go a long way towards establishing Marx's reputation as the unchallenged philosopher-general of communist ideas in Europe in the second half of the nineteenth century. An indication of the key significance of this document is that at the beginning of the twenty-first century, a true first edition would be worth in the region of £100,000 (or $200,000), which is in the same league in terms of monetary value as a first edition of Issac Newton's *Principia Mathematica*, the *Principia* being a good candidate for the most important book ever written.

However, in no way could all the ideas that were contained within this portentous statement of communist aims be solely attributed to Marx. He had been provided with rough drafts for the manifesto from the League itself, and he had also received initial versions from Engels and Moses Hess. One early draft written by Engels was called 'Principles of Communism' and was presented in the form of various questions and answers. What Marx did provide was the final published formulation of *The Manifesto of the Communist Party* (which was written in German but published in London in February 1848), and hence the structure and underlying approach was that of Marx more than any other single individual. The text began with the famous declaration that the spectre of communism was haunting Europe (the word 'spectre' being quaintly translated in the first English version as 'hobgoblin'), and in 1848 revolutions did break out in various cities in Europe. Given this looming context, the League's declaration of principles was not meant as an abstract or academic account of the topic under review, but first and foremost as a document of immediate political agitation and socialist propaganda. It provided an analytical sketch of historical developments relevant to the political crossroads of the time, but this analysis was necessarily simplified and tendentious, in that its aim was to win people over to communist beliefs, not to paint a fully accurate picture of past times. Hence it was designed primarily as a tool of political indoctrination.

In terms of its specific political content, *The Manifesto of the Communist Party* aligned communism as an ideology directly with the interests of the proletariat as a whole. The party of communists was said not to form a separate party opposed to other working class parties, although how ideological differences with other socialist groups were to be dealt with was not fully explained. The basic aims of communism were declared to be the overthrow of the capitalist order of society by force, the taking of political power by the proletariat, then the abolition of private property and finally the replacement of the capitalist mode of production itself. Marx and Engels thus declared all-out warfare against the existing political and economic order of society, with little concern for the consequences of this violent overthrow for the individuals who might participate in revolutionary action.

The Manifesto of the Communist Party is still today a startling document in terms of the simplicity of its aims and the undeniable power of its analysis, but – as with many apparently rationalist declarations of intent – the devil was in the (unspecified) detail that lay hidden behind the various sweeping statements of noble purpose. Exactly how would social ownership replace the 'bourgeois' form of individual property holding? What would happen to those unfortunate people who (by chance) were born into the middle and upper classes of society after the communist victory? And how, precisely, would the proletariat form themselves into a governing party? Marx and Engels had at this time provided only a relatively brief sketch of a future communist society, much of which was contained within Marx's unpublished 'Economic and Philosophical Manuscripts' and hence was very abstract in nature, but they were both thoroughly convinced about its superiority in every possible way to capitalism.

One noticeable element of *The Manifesto of the Communist Party* was how much of it was taken up with criticising different approaches to socialism that Marx and Engels deemed to be politically erroneous. Among the extensive list of false socialisms were: feudal or aristocratic socialism, petty-bourgeois socialism, German 'true' socialism, conservative socialism and utopian socialism. Special vitriol was reserved for Christian socialism, which was characterised as the ideological 'holy water' with which priests consecrated the phoney bleating of the aristocracy. Workers reading through this document must have been grateful to Marx and Engels for showing them the correct path through all this pseudo-socialist mire. That is, if these workers understood the Hegelian origins of the techniques of criticism that were being employed. In this respect the notion of 'practical reason' received a mention vis-à-vis the French revolution of 1789 while German socialism was being criticised, but the fact that this was an allusion to the second of Immanuel Kant's three *Critiques* was not explained.

Undoubtedly, in terms of its writing style and long-term generative effect, *The Manifesto of the Communist Party* was a brilliant polemical classic. It was packed with memorable and inspiring phrases such as 'the history of all hitherto existing society is the history of class struggle', 'the free development of each is the condition for the free development of all', and 'the icy waters of egotistical calculation'. It finished with the rousing slogan for united action: 'proletarians have nothing to lose but their chains'. If the three volumes of Marx's *Capital* were sometimes described as dry and turgid (although this characterisation really applied only to volume two), then *The Manifesto of the Communist Party* was literary gold. And its central prophecy appeared to be on the verge of being fulfilled, as revolutions began to manifest themselves before it was even published.

THE 1848 REVOLUTIONS IN EUROPE

The series of revolutions that spread throughout Europe, reaching a peak in 1848, were a significant set of historical events – especially so for Marx and Engels. There was initially an outbreak of conflict in Switzerland at the end of 1847, which was followed by demonstrations and an insurrection in the south of Italy and a severe economic crisis in Belgium at the beginning of 1848. Then the February revolution broke out in France in 1848, with barricades springing up in Paris. The King of France (Louis Philippe) was subsequently forced into exile. Engels described this feverish outbreak as follows:

> At midday on Tuesday [22 February], all Paris was on the streets. The masses were shouting: 'Down with Guizot, long live the Reform!' ... On Wednesday morning ... the revolt began again with renewed vigour. A large part of the centre of Paris lying to the east of the Rue Montmarle was strongly barricaded; after eleven o'clock the troops no longer dared venture in there.[1]

Francois Guizot was an important French statesman who had controlled domestic affairs from 1840 to 1848. In June a rising of Parisian workers followed on from the February events in response to unsatisfactory political progress. In Germany, revolution was looming early in 1848 and an abortive uprising finally occurred in May 1849, the same year as an attempted revolution in Hungary. In Poland and Bohemia questions of territorial emancipation also flared up, and long-standing issues of national autonomy were raised within many of the uprisings that took place in this period.

These various spontaneous outbreaks of revolutionary struggle were all suppressed in one way or another, either immediately or after a period of time had elapsed, but it appeared to the casual observer that revolutionary ideas and actions were spreading like wildfire across the continent of Europe. The political aims of the revolutionaries concerned were undoubtedly not fully socialistic in spirit, but socialists were certainly an important segment of the insurgent forces that were involved. One of the most significant political questions raised for socialists by this sequence of events was that of developing the most appropriate strategy and tactics, or of selecting which particular alliances they should make, and which they should shun. Marx, of course, had much to say on this issue as the events themselves unfolded.

The Manifesto of the Communist Party was first published in February 1848, and with the beginning of the 1848 revolution in France also occurring in February, the timing of the publication of this statement of principles could not be described as anything other than perfect – except for the fact that it was first issued in German, a language that few French workers could read. It was also timely only from the point of view of communist advocates. From the perspective of the Belgian government, Marx's provocative presence in Brussels appeared to be courting danger, and hence he was issued with an order to leave Belgium immediately.

Marx embroidered the experience of his expulsion from Belgium as follows. On receiving the order to leave the country within 24 hours, he was arrested on the pretext of lacking proper documentation. On Jenny Marx's return to an empty house she was taken to a nearby police station, charged with 'vagabondage', imprisoned alongside common prostitutes and propositioned by guards: these details were later disputed by the warden involved. By the time both Jenny and Karl were released their allotted 24 hours were up, and they had to depart from Belgium without the opportunity of properly assembling all their personal belongings.

By now Marx was familiar with this sort of rough treatment from the authorities. Taking advantage of the political conjuncture that appeared so pregnant with possibilities, in March 1848 he immediately travelled to Paris with his family, where he witnessed first-hand the chaotic aftermath of the fighting at the barricades and the occasional fluttering of a red flag. He also observed columns of the workers' militia marching in the streets to popular acclaim. Much later Marx would describe the 'childish enthusiasm' with which he greeted the revolutionary situation in 1848, but this was the first time that he had experienced the environment of a large-scale revolutionary insurrection first hand, and he did not falter or flinch in political terms at what he saw. He was personally fearless in the face of his political dreams apparently becoming a reality.

In Paris Marx became very active in organisational terms, developing good personal relations with Alexandre Ledru-Rollin and Ferdinand Flocon, two ministers with progressive attitudes in the Provisional Government. A political club to be employed as an educational meeting place for the working class was also created. In tactical terms Marx advised French socialist forces against attempting to intervene as guerrilla volunteers in political developments in Germany, as he believed that they would be needed again within France. His advice was not heeded and revolutionary troops heading to Germany were heavily defeated. He also participated in meetings of various progressive political societies, although a large proportion of his organisational activities was focused on the community of exiles in Paris. Some of the political exiles forming an alliance with Marx in France were Wilhelm Wolff, Karl Schapper and Joseph Moll. Wolff became an associate editor of the *Neue Rheinische Zeitung*, which is discussed below, and was a close friend of both Marx and Engels.

While Marx was in France he kept a close watch on events in Germany, and at the end of March 1848 he and Engels composed a short political declaration entitled 'Demands of the Communist Party in Germany'. The main goals that were outlined in this document were as follows:

1) The declaration of a unified republic.
2) The implementation of universal suffrage.
3) The arming of the people.
4) The abolition of feudal obligations.

5) The nationalisation of feudal estates and peasants' mortgage payments.
6) The creation of a state bank to replace private banks.
7) The separation of church and state.
8) The introduction of progressive taxation.
9) The creation of national workshops guaranteeing employment.
10) The implementation of universal free education.

This programme could (on first glance) be seen as making concrete for the projected German revolution the more abstract ideas that had been presented in *The Manifesto of the Communist Party*. But it would be more accurate to describe these 'Demands' as being partly of a constitutional democratic nature, rather than being truly communist. In 1848 Germany was still to a significant extent feudal in structure, and had yet (within Marx's historical framework) to fully accomplish the 'bourgeois' revolution before it could even begin to contemplate the proletarian one. It was also still divided into regional mini-states, but many socialists were hopeful that the distance between the two social revolutions could be nimbly negotiated by careful political strategy.

THE REVOLUTION IN GERMANY

In April 1848, following direct signs of impending revolution in his country of birth, Marx decided to return to Germany, accompanied by his family and Engels. They carried along with them copies of the 'Demands' discussed above and also copies of *The Manifesto of the Communist Party*. Overall the political situation in Germany was not as advanced as it had been in France, in part because the existing structures of autocracy were somewhat stronger. In Cologne, where Marx decided to base his activities, he attempted to organise workers' groups so that they could participate directly in the political events that were unfolding. He did this through an organisation called the Democratic Society, which participated in elections to the newly created National Assembly for Germany in Frankfurt, and which agitated among workers.

In adopting this semi-parliamentary strategy Marx was disagreeing with the position of many socialists in Cologne, who were against the idea of participating in any elections that were being held with a restricted franchise. The most prominent opponent of electoral participation was Andreas Gottschalk, a leading member of the Communist League. The dispute between Marx and Gottschalk over strategy became heated and intense, with the former accusing the latter of ignoring the reality of the situation in Germany. Marx favoured the idea of pursuing an alliance between the bourgeoisie and the proletariat as being appropriate for the given circumstances, but Gottschalk campaigned for proletarian aims alone. This conflict was also connected to organisational questions. Marx believed that the secretive Communist League, a branch of which had already existed in Cologne on his arrival, was redundant in such heightened circumstances since it was now possible to conduct open propaganda among the workers. This dispute was de facto resolved when Gottschalk was arrested for incitement to violence in July, spending the next six months in jail.

By June 1848, Marx was criticising the manner in which the law on elections to the German National Assembly had been formulated – by a provincial body that was based on the old feudal estates system. This body was called the United Diet and it was characterised by Marx as the political pet of the absolute monarchy. He wrote in this regard that:

> The dear faithful 'United Diet' creates unlawfully the law of indirect elections. The law of indirect elections creates the Berlin chamber, the Berlin chamber draws up the Constitution and the Constitution produces all successive chambers from here to eternity.[2]

Basically Marx viewed the whole arrangement in Germany in mid-1848 as a political frame-up of monumental proportions, suggesting that the revolutionary golden eggs had been stolen by the regressive constitutional arrangements that had emanated from the initial revolutionary impulse. As the events on the ground developed further, the Berlin Assembly would, at the end of 1848, fizzle out as an effective political force when anti-revolutionary forces pushed for victory, suggesting that Marx's characterisation was accurate. However, by the summer of 1848 he had been actively campaigning alongside and within the revolutionary events in Europe for some months, and hence the failure of socialists to successfully influence the final constitutional outcome was not something from which he could totally divorce himself.

At this point the issue naturally arises of what influence the publication of *The Manifesto of the Communist Party* can be said to have exerted on the 1848 events themselves. Most commentators agree that the text's influence in 1848 was very limited outside a small group of communist supporters, and hence that most (if not all) the revolutionary uprisings that were observed in this period would have occurred whether or not Marx and Engels had published their memorable polemic at this particular time. Throughout 1848 they were more often than not chasing the tails of emerging revolutions rather than directing their lead. The influence of the *Manifesto* in later periods is of course a very different matter, and various re-issues and translations were printed as the second half of the nineteenth century progressed.

On his return to Germany Marx reapplied for Prussian citizenship, as he had previously found it necessary to relinquish this national right. According to the report provided by the Cologne Political Inspector in response, Marx was 'working on a book on economics which he intends to publish and he proposes to live partly on the proceeds of his writings and partly [on] the personal property of his wife'.[3]

The application was eventually rejected on the grounds that Marx had renounced his right to citizenship in 1845, not for the over-optimistic idea that book royalties might go a long way towards sustaining him financially.

One of the most significant activities that Marx was involved with in Cologne was making preparations to publish a German newspaper with an appropriately radical slant, by gathering financial backing from various wealthy subscribers. The result of this effort was the *Neue Rheinische Zeitung*, which was first issued in June 1848 with Marx as editor-in-chief. The editorial board also included Engels, Wilhelm Wolff and other members of the Communist League. The paper was eventually suppressed in May 1849, but before this occurred Marx had contributed a number of articles that allow an insight into his immediate political priorities at this crucial moment in time.

THE *NEUE RHEINISCHE ZEITUNG*

This publication, which was subtitled 'The Organ of Democracy' (the term 'democracy' was meant in the socialist sense of equalised property ownership), was designed as a daily newspaper, but circumstances sometimes intervened against its regular issue. It was intended to provide its readers with up-to-date information on revolutionary activities, taking a consistent socialist and internationalist perspective. Partly because of this controversial approach, members of its editorial board were periodically summoned to court attendance, and a warrant for the arrest of Engels and Heinrich Burgers, another editor, was issued in October 1848. Without any intended irony, Engels' religion was listed in this warrant as 'evangelical' and his occupation was given as 'merchant'. The two men's crime was to take flight from an ongoing court investigation. One such investigation involved Marx being accused of insulting the Chief Public Prosecutor in print.

A major part of the problem for the authorities was the obvious political slant that was provided in many of the newspaper articles. Marx himself was only an occasional contributor, as he was heavily involved in managing the newspaper, but in one important article entitled 'The June Revolution' he described the events of the first half of 1848 in France in colourful terms. He declared that:

> The *February revolution* was the *nice* revolution, the revolution of universal sympathies, because the contradictions which erupted in it against the monarchy were *undeveloped* ... The *June revolution* is the *ugly* revolution ... because the republic has bared the head of the monster by knocking off the crown which shielded and concealed it. *Order!* was Guizot's war-cry ... *Order!* thundered his grape-shot as it tore into the body of the proletariat.[4]

Marx judged that the real business of the National Assembly that had come out of the February revolution was to undo the gains that had been made by the workers during the February events. This attempted retreat had eventually produced the June barricades, which pitted workers against owners and divided France into two nations in a very stark manner. According to Marx this was a civil war of labour against capital, demonstrating that conflicts proceeding from the underlying nature of 'bourgeois' society had to be fought out to the bitter end. In this class war, workers were tormented by hunger and were called thieves, incendiaries and galley slaves by the press. Marx consequently mocked those who rallied for fraternity or the brotherhood of antagonistic classes while sections of the proletariat were burning and bleeding on the streets.

As the events of 1848 progressed, Marx's analysis of the political situation remained as sharp and as tendentious as ever, although his initial enthusiasm became dented by intimations of oncoming defeats. In September he wrote a short series of articles for the *Neue Rheinische Zeitung* under the general heading of 'Crisis', which described the counter-revolutionary struggles that were being waged against the newly elected government bodies in Berlin and Frankfurt. In one of these articles he explained that:

> Every provisional political set-up following a revolution requires a dictatorship, and an energetic dictatorship at that. From the very beginning we blamed Camphausen for not having acted in a dictatorial manner, for not having immediately smashed up and removed the remains of the old institutions ...[5]

Ludolf Camphausen was the liberal Prime Minister of Prussia between March and June 1848. By implication, the success of the counter-revolution in Germany was due to the failure of the National Assembly in Frankfurt to act in a decisive way against the old forces of the Crown and the aristocracy. After a period of dual power, the Crown had eventually opposed the Assembly, and this tension would (Marx warned) soon be followed by the latter's disbandment and the restoration of royal control. The lesson of acting immediately to destroy all oppositional forces after a successful revolution was one that the Bolsheviks did learn thoroughly from an analysis of the politics of this period.

As the *Neue Rheinische Zeitung* continued to publish its rich tapestry of analysis, events on the ground in Germany were developing at a fast pace. In the autumn of 1848 the government soldiers based in Cologne heightened their repressive measures, provoking mass meetings and continued protests. A warrant was issued for Engels' arrest, charging him with conspiracy to overthrow the government, and martial law was eventually declared. This dampened down revolutionary prospects across Germany, and in December the Prussian Assembly in Berlin was finally dismissed. The National Assembly in Frankfurt proceeded to choose a new Emperor, who refused the offer of the crown, and the Assembly subsequently collapsed. In a mixture of two-thirds disappointment and one-third despair, Marx modified his political analysis as a result of these apparently regressive developments. He now believed that a purely democratic revolution, as might be accomplished by a strong bourgeoisie producing victory for a new social order in Germany, was impossible.

THE TIDE TURNS AGAINST REVOLUTION

As always, Marx outlined this tactical shift in analytical terms. In a short series of articles from the very end of 1848 entitled 'The Bourgeoisie and the Counter-Revolution', he described this class as being like 'a damned old codger' who found himself condemned to mislead the youth into the channels of senility.[6] Marx now analysed the role of the Prussian bourgeoisie as merely passive recipients of political power, and he described the German revolution itself as a 'stunted after-effect of a European revolution in a backward country'.[7] Instead of a bourgeois victory leading to a new type of society, as had been the outcome of the 1648 English and 1789 French revolutions, the 1848 events in Germany were seen only as an anachronistic attempt to resurrect a society that had previously expired. Since he believed that the bourgeoisie lacked initiative and was inclined to political betrayal, Marx predicted that only an absolutist counter-revolution or a successful social republican revolution were possible outcomes. The latter was of course the favoured option, but external assistance might well be required in order to achieve it. The previous hope that an alliance between the proletariat and the bourgeoisie could decisively overthrow the autocracy had dramatically faded.

This was quite a blow for someone who had nailed his own red flag to the mast in such a decisive manner, and a new approach to the situation was evidently required. Continuing the tactical revision, Marx consequently articulated, in an article from the very beginning of 1849, a more internationalist analysis of the prospects for national revolutions in Europe. Describing Great Britain as seemingly 'the rock that breaks the revolutionary waves', he suggested that future social upheavals in France would be thwarted by Britain's economic dominance across the world. His evaluation was that a revolution that occurred across the whole European continent, but without England's participation, would really be a storm in a teacup. The only way of overcoming this political impasse would be the outbreak of war on a global scale, which could break the bourgeoisie of 'old England' and facilitate the creation of a workers' government across Britain. Hence the strategy that was now required was an uprising of the French proletariat followed by a world war, in which England would at first lead the counter-revolutionary armies, but through a subsequent rising of English workers would be thrown to the head of the international revolution. In this way revolutionary success could be achieved across all of Europe simultaneously.

This particular coordinated programme of communist action might appear far-fetched and unlikely from a more neutral perspective, and might even be characterised as expressing the desperation of oncoming defeat. Throughout the various political strategies in this period it is apparent that Marx was constantly looking for what might be described as a 'fulcrum point' or a point of leverage, from which specific revolutionary actions could be further articulated to achieve the ultimate aim of a general communist victory. When one particular strategy faded into impossibility, he immediately revised his tactical recommendations to take account of the new situation, but with the same underlying goal kept consistently in view. This meant that, as actual revolutionary processes in specific countries had run their natural course, Marx was sometimes forced to look for ever-more implausible scenarios to realise his desired aims. This might seem reasonable for someone involved only in socialist politics, but Marx claimed to base his strategies on an objective theory of historical development in a more rigorous and consistent way than did most conventional politicians. Whether his theory of history could coherently yield such dramatic and swift changes in socialist political strategy is debatable.

Of more immediate concern to the functioning of the *Neue Rheinische Zeitung*, Engels had previously fled the country to escape the conspiracy charges that were made against him, returning to Germany only at the beginning of 1849. But in February the earlier charges made against Marx and his two co-defendants were actually pressed in court. At the trial they were quickly acquitted of libel and then, after Marx had provided reasons why law should be based on the common interests of society rather than vice versa, they were acquitted of conspiracy. Marx concluded his speech about the libel charge with the rousing call that the first duty of the press was to undermine the existing state of political affairs, for which he received applause from the audience.[8] His second speech warned that, with regard to the struggle between the Crown and the National Assembly, only naked power could decide between two conflicting authorities. Marx had made no attempt at all to tone down the intensity of his political views for court consumption.

Despite the relief of a legal victory, the added attention of a public trial was unwelcome and, in March, Marx received a visit from military officials demanding that he name an author who had reported on army affairs for the *Neue Rheinische Zeitung*. He refused, and the officials eventually left, but Marx had nonetheless felt the need to keep a gun in his pocket during the incident. Financial problems were also beginning to mount at this time, and, as the editor-in-chief of the *Neue Rheinische Zeitung*, he was forced to travel around Germany periodically to gather funds to support his own newspaper. Despite the dedicated efforts of Marx and Engels to organise for victory, the death knell of the German revolution rang out in May 1849, with various final outbreaks of proletarian rebellion being suppressed by military force, and a proposed draft constitution that was rejected by a newly emboldened King. At this point the workers received precious little support from their supposed revolutionary allies, the bourgeoisie.

In the same month as the demise of the German revolution, an order was issued for Marx's expulsion from Prussia. The report sent by the Cologne authorities to the Minister of the Interior on this issue in March is worth quoting at length:

> ... the newspaper of which he is editor continues with its destructive tendencies, deriding and ridiculing all that men normally respect and hold sacred, and urging the overthrow of the existing constitution and the establishment of a social republic, and its effects are all the more damaging since its impertinence and humour constantly attracts new readers.[9]

Following Marx's expulsion in May, the *Neue Rheinische Zeitung* was forced to close its operations. The final issue was impertinently printed in red and sold especially well, since it constituted a memento mori of the German uprisings. It advised against any further organised street protests, which would easily be crushed. Marx decided to head back to Paris in the hope of participating in further revolutionary action in France, but in reality the political surge was waning there also. The Marx family found themselves in particularly difficult circumstances financially at this time, and in July 1849 they received notice of their forced eviction from Paris. It was decided that their next destination would be England. One of the most exciting periods of Marx's life from a political perspective was over.

LONDON

Marx arrived in London in August 1849, with Jenny and the children following a short while later. They stayed initially in Chelsea, but after being evicted because of financial problems they moved to Dean Street in Soho in April 1850. This was a particularly hard time for the Marx family, as they had young children to support but no source of earned income with which to provide for them. Marx certainly did not plan to remain in London permanently when he first arrived, but it would turn out to be the home of his family for the rest of their lives, barring various temporary journeys overseas. One of the most significant events to follow Marx's arrival in London was that he obtained a pass to the reading room of the British Museum in June 1850. Britain had not been convulsed by revolutionary outbreaks to anything like the same extent as many of its continental neighbours. After 1848 it had begun to experience a period of economic prosperity following a financial crisis in 1847, with the Great Exhibition following in 1851.

Throughout the winter of 1849 and early 1850, Marx devoted a significant amount of time to attempting to establish a journal that could continue the function of campaigning for revolutionary socialism, as his newspaper had done in Cologne. He was successful in raising some funds for this purpose, and in March 1850 the *Neue Rheinische Zeitung – Politisch-Oekonomisch Revue* first appeared. However, delays in distribution and the dramatically changed context compared with the revolutionary upsurge of 1848 meant that sales were low, and the last issue appeared in November 1850. Marx himself had contributed a series of articles to this journal in which he analysed the French revolutionary events of 1848–9 from a more remote perspective; these were issued separately at a later date under the title *The Class Struggles in France*. Engels described this effort as the first attempt by the author to explain an episode in contemporary affairs through the materialist conception of history, and hence this work has a special significance in the Marx canon. The content will be discussed in detail in the following chapter; suffice to say here that Marx drew to a significant degree on both his personal experience of French politics and his journalistic writings of the period.

Marx's initial studies in the British Museum in 1850 focused on the immediate economic situation in Europe and the prospects for a further revolutionary outbreak. Over time he became more pessimistic about the chances of a new revolution in the near future, as he believed that economic prosperity usually acted to dampen down political conflicts. In addition, reaction was taking a strong hold in France. However, he was sure that a new economic crisis would certainly break out some time in the future, and he believed this would be the cue for renewed class conflict and another chance for proletarian success.

Towards the end of 1851, Louis-Napoleon Bonaparte seized political power as Emperor in France, this event completing the turn to reaction that Marx had outlined in *The Class Struggles in France*. Directly as a consequence of this, Marx composed a series of articles re-examining the revolutionary events of 1848–51 entitled *The Eighteenth Brumaire of Louis Bonaparte*. Marx's interest in this topic was not unique: other well-known authors such as Victor Hugo and P. J. Proudhon also wrote accounts of Louis Bonaparte's rise to power at this time. *The Eighteenth Brumaire* covered some of the same ground that was analysed in *The Class Struggles in France*, but it continued the story of the 1848 revolution to its final reactionary denouement. Again Marx was flexing his newly acquired theoretical muscles by claiming to apply the materialist conception of history to contemporary events. Both of his detailed analyses of 1848 and its consequences have become classics of political history, demonstrating his undoubted talent for combining astute insight with vivid description of the general sweep of events as represented through individual action. However, few commentators have attempted directly to evaluate his analysis of French society in terms of its stated aim of applying the materialist conception of history in concrete form, and this will be attempted in the next chapter.

On his arrival in London, Marx had quickly rekindled his political activities within the Communist League, becoming a member of the London Central Committee and then its president. One of the tasks undertaken by this organisation was to attempt to reconstitute the Communist League in Germany. In terms of its ideology Marx asserted that the League should organise both openly and secretly as the party of the proletariat, and should not allow itself to become sidetracked by the democratic faction of the bourgeoisie. It should support the bourgeois factions against the old aristocracy when necessary, but it must retain an independent capacity for acting to support proletarian aims both politically and militarily. During any immediate outbreak of revolutionary struggle, terrorist actions in support of the proletariat should be compelled, and the vengeance of the people on hated individuals and symbolic buildings should be directed rather than condemned.[10] In this respect Marx wrote an 'Address of the Central Committee to the Communist League' in 1850 outlining his proposed strategy, which clearly included violence in support of political aims.

THE POVERTY OF THE PHILOSOPHER

The minutiae of Marx's involvements in the Communist League in London were very involved and will not be examined in full detail here, but some incidents are worth discussing for the light that they throw upon Marx's polarising character. In 1850 the League had desired additional military representation, and a candidate appeared on the scene in the form of the Prussian Lieutenant G. A. Techov. Techov spent an evening with Marx discussing possible membership of the League, and he subsequently wrote his impressions of this meeting in a letter. Techov described how Marx had first consumed port, then claret, then champagne, eventually becoming very drunk, and discussions had followed in which Marx's intellectual superiority became very apparent. However, Techov's evaluation of Marx's underlying motivation was quite startling:

> The only people he respects are the aristocrats, the genuine ones ... In order to prevent them from governing, he needs his own source of strength, which he can find only in the proletariat ... In spite of all his assurances to the contrary, personal domination was the aim of all his endeavours.[11]

It might reasonably be considered that one evening's shared company was not really enough time to get to know someone properly, and many others have provided a directly contradictory account of Marx's underlying motivation, but Techov was certain of his judgement. But what was Marx doing drinking champagne and claret when his own family were living in such dire straits?

Personal tragedy had struck the Marx family more than once in this period, with one son, Guido (born in October 1849), and one daughter, Franziska (born in March 1851), passing away the year after their births. The immediate cause of their deaths was grinding poverty, with the neighbourhood around Dean Street being subject to various epidemics and general squalor. Jenny Marx described her daughter's death as follows:

> At Easter our poor little Franziska fell ill with severe bronchitis. For three days the poor child struggled against death and suffered much ... I went to a French fugitive who lives near us ... [He] gave me two pounds and with that money the coffin in which my child could rest peacefully was paid for.[12]

The Marx family survived in this period only through a combination of permanent indebtedness, continued pawning, dribs from his journalism and assistance from Engels, with (as temporary respite) relaxing Sunday strolls on Hampstead Heath. They were sometimes forced to send out actual begging letters pleading their case, and Marx was genuinely worried that Jenny might be pushed over the emotional precipice by their worsening situation. Marx's own health also took a turn for the worse: he suffered ongoing bouts of haemorrhoids alongside mounting political disillusionments, and he characterised the poverty that his family endured in this period as 'nauseating'.

To add personal insult to the injury of ill health, in the summer of 1851 Jenny's own maid, Helene Demuth, gave birth to Marx's illegitimate son Frederick. The newly born infant was sent immediately to foster parents and a concerted effort was made to conceal his real paternity, but the image of Marx as the devoted family man was forever dented by this affair. It seemed fine for Marx to rail against 'bourgeois' morality in theory, and to ridicule the 'bourgeois' family as an institution of female oppression in his writings, but his own treasured family was the centre of his everyday life, and Marx was genuinely worried that Jenny might be broken by his extra-marital effort. There is no evidence that Marx was a serial philanderer, but one betrayal can be enough to break forever a heartfelt trust.

In this period Engels returned to Manchester to work again in the family business, partly so that he could assist Marx financially. One of Engels' intellectual responses to the ultimate failure of the 1848 revolutionary events was to write an account of the German revolution of 1525 entitled *The Peasant War in Germany*, which was published in 1850. In the preface to this work Engels discussed the parallels between Germany in 1525 and the much more recent events of 1848–9, which mainly focused on the crushing of a series of local revolts by a royalist army. The opening section promised an escapist counterweight to the slackening of the revolutionary struggles that had been recently witnessed, with attention directed towards the traitorous classes of 1525 conceived in direct parallel with those of 1848. As the title of Engels' book indicated, focus was being turned away from the proletariat and towards the German peasantry – a tacit admission that, in Germany at this time, the workers were not the political force that *The Manifesto of the Communist Party* had initially made them out to be.

CONCLUSION

The spectre of communism had risen and then fallen over continental Europe between 1847 and 1849, with Marx actively participating in these events in a number of countries and by means of various organisations and numerous publications. In personal terms, Marx had become a permanent political exile, forced to flit from country to country on governmental whim and revolutionary impulse. He found a more permanent home only after the revolutionary surge had waned. This new home was in London, which was ironically the capital city of his political nemesis – international capital. And, while the various outbreaks of revolution early in 1848 had been sweet nectar to the communist cause, their eventual crushing left a bitter aftertaste that remained on the palates of revolutionaries for many years to come.

However, Marx's more permanent legacy from this period was his substantial writings on political change, which constituted a consistent body of analysis of current affairs written from an overtly communist perspective. These writings also claimed to illustrate Marx's approach to understanding historical development at a more fundamental level. The next chapter will venture to comprehend in more detail his aims and achievements in this controversial area of human activity.

4

POLITICAL WRITINGS, 1848–1852

It is perhaps a little incongruous that a political figure of the stature of Marx is most famous for a work of economic theory – the three volumes of *Capital*. But, as the previous chapter has indicated, Marx was very active politically in certain periods of his life, and he also wrote substantial analyses of political affairs that deserve more detailed scrutiny than was possible in previous chapters, when his individual role in the events themselves were being considered. Attention in this chapter will first be focused on the bold programme for revolution from 1848 that Marx wrote and published jointly with Engels. An analysis of Marx's own political ideas from this period will then be presented in more depth.

THE MANIFESTO OF THE COMMUNIST PARTY

Although the title of this work is frequently presented in contemporary discussions as *The Communist Manifesto*, it is more accurate to render it as *The Manifesto of the Communist Party*, indicating that it was meant not only as an outline of a general social philosophy but also as a programme of a nascent political party. It was Engels who modified the title in 1872, on the grounds that the context had radically changed.[1] This is especially significant when it is considered that there was no such thing as a mass-membership communist party in existence around 1848, Marx being instead a member of the Communist League, a much more amorphous grouping. And, as the previous chapter has demonstrated, Marx had abandoned the Communist League during the height of the 1848 events as being an inappropriate tool of direct revolutionary propaganda, suggesting that the most suitable organisational form of communism was still undecided.

In terms of the amount of space occupied within its pages, *The Manifesto of the Communist Party* was first and foremost a declaration of principles in abstract terms, but it also included a very significant set of practical policy proposals that Marx and Engels envisaged would be implemented by communist revolutionaries when they first obtained the reins of state power in various specific countries. These policies were (in slightly simplified form) presented as follows:

1) The abolition of landed property.
2) A heavily progressive income tax.
3) The abolition of all rights of inheritance.
4) Confiscation of the property of all emigrants and rebels.
5) The centralisation of banking and credit in the hands of the state.
6) The centralisation of the means of communication and transport.
7) The extension of factories owned by the state.
8) An equal liability of all to labour.
9) The gradual abolition of the distinction between town and country.
10) Free education for all.

In addition, it was explained that, in the course of further developments some time after socialists had taken power, all production would be concentrated into something called 'an association of the whole nation'. Exactly what his association was, and how it would function, was not specified, nor was the length of time before it would come into existence indicated.

It is striking what was and what was not contained within these ten policies. Two key components of the projected socialist economy were to be immediately centralised under state control – banking and the means of transportation (policies 5 and 6). Other industries were omitted from this initial centralisation drive, with only an extension of state factories being proposed (policy 7). There was no mention of implementing any type of planning system within these ten policies. Prior to outlining this programme, Marx and Engels had given as the ultimate goal of communism the centralisation of all instruments of production under state control, but this was presented as occurring only by degrees, i.e. as not being accomplished all at once. It is worth noting a difference between the idea of state centralisation and the idea of the concentration of economic control into an association of the whole nation. In the conception of political power articulated within *The Manifesto of the Communist Party*, the state was simply a tool of class domination, and hence centralisation was seen only as the initial form of socialist economic control, corresponding with the political dictatorship of the proletariat. This would be replaced at some point in the future by the enticingly named 'association of the whole nation', where (presumably) everyone would participate in managing the economy equally. This meant that within fully developed communism there would be no separate caste or group that controlled economic policies apart from the nation (or group of nations) as a whole.

There is a very significant issue that is still unresolved today regarding whether it is actually feasible to have economic control by an association of the whole nation, but what is beyond any doubt is that this was not what happened in Russia after 1917. In the USSR state centralisation was never superseded by the proposed universal association of producers; instead a government bureaucracy was created that wielded the equivalent of 'bourgeois' powers of economic control. How it used this power is not the point at issue, since Marx and Engels had projected that in communism all separate class functions would be abolished. It can be concluded from this that either what they had proposed was always impossible to achieve, or that Soviet communists had (for whatever reason) not followed what Marx and Engels had outlined for them in 1848. Only by employing ideological contortions of the most extreme and untenable kind is it possible to suggest that the leaders of the USSR fully implemented all the policies that were presented in *The Manifesto of the Communist Party*. It is clear from reading this document that they did not.

As noted in the previous chapter, Engels had in October 1847 written an early draft of *The Manifesto of the Communist Party* that was entitled 'Principles of Communism', and which was presented in the form of a series of questions and answers. Of particular relevance to the ten policies just outlined was question seventeen: would it be possible to abolish private property at one stroke? Engels provided a very clear answer to this question: 'No ... the proletarian revolution ... will transform existing society only gradually, and be able to abolish private property only when the necessary quantity of the means of production has been created'.[2]

This answer was of crucial significance to practical policy-making, yet it was not found in such a clear formulation within *The Manifesto of the Communist Party* itself. The answer implied that a proletarian government would retain some aspects of private property after it had come to power, and it would use them to assist in developing the productive forces. Only when these forces had been developed to a sufficient degree would all private property be finally abolished. Hence the ultimate abolition of private property should (for Engels) be contingent on economic circumstances. When the Bolsheviks won state power in Russia in 1917, this Engels draft was not readily available to them, as it had only just been published in an obscure London-based magazine in 1914–15.

Another very significant question posed in the 'Principles of Communism' was question nineteen: would it be possible for the revolution to take place in one country alone? Engels' answer was again very clear. The communist revolution had to take place simultaneously 'in all civilised countries, that is, at least in England, America, France and Germany'.[3] It was conceived as a worldwide revolution and would be international in scope. The idea that a communist revolution could take place in one country by itself, and especially in a 'non-civilised' country (by which Engels meant less developed), was so completely against the whole approach being outlined by Marx and Engels early in 1848 as to not even be considered by them in any respect at all. The absurdity of the notion of conducting a successful communist revolution within one less-developed country alone is made all the more apparent when Engels' answers to questions seventeen and nineteen are considered together. He was stating that, if a revolution was successful in a group of advanced countries such as the UK, the USA, France and Germany together, then some elements of private ownership would still have to be retained in order to further develop the productive forces, before full communism could be achieved. This conception was so thoroughly ignored by the Bolsheviks after 1917 that it would be fully accurate to describe the October revolution as the revolution against the 1848 policies of communism.

Turning to the more analytical aspects of *The Manifesto of the Communist Party*, it provided at the outset a rousing sketch of the communist conception of class functionality within capitalism. In the first section (section I), the bourgeoisie were portrayed as playing 'a most revolutionary role in history', as relentlessly tearing aside all feudal ties that had previously restrained naked commercial interests. They were described as constantly developing the instruments of manufacture, a process that in turn acted upon the social relations of production in a dynamic way, and they were seen as stripping the halo from all political and religious illusions. It was this class-conceived positive evaluation of the political role of the bourgeoisie that Marx and Engels had taken with them into the revolutionary upheavals of 1848.

But to their great disappointment they found instead that, as the events of 1848 unfolded, the German bourgeoisie did not act out the class function that had been allotted to them within the pages of *The Manifesto of the Communist Party*. In effect, the bourgeoisie refused to play along with their assigned class position. It was the concomitant recognition of the overly simplistic analysis of class allegiance presented in early 1848 that led Marx to revise his political strategy away from the notion of supporting an alliance with elements of the bourgeoisie. Instead, he moved towards supporting a revolutionary war across Europe that could involve the English proletariat in fighting within an all-out class conflict on a supra-national scale.

There are other related discrepancies within this document that are worth considering in more detail. In the final section (section IV), it was declared that at the time under consideration (i.e. early in 1848) communists should turn their political attention chiefly to Germany, because Germany was ripe for the bourgeois revolution to take place, and that this would be immediately followed by the proletarian revolution. The reason given for this predicted instantaneous shift of revolutionary gear was that the German revolution would take place in more advanced conditions than had all previous bourgeois revolutions. However, on deeper reflection this hypothesised shift might be seen to contradict the materialist conception of history, in which the different modes of production took some considerable period of time to work their way through from beginning to end. The idea of telescoping entire historical eras was not something that Marx and Engels had really discussed in any detail in earlier works, yet their political strategy for Germany in early 1848 was apparently based upon this idea.

A few years earlier, in 'The German Ideology' of 1845–6, it had been suggested that, in order for revolutionary collisions to occur within a specific country, the contradictions between the forces and the relations of production need not have reached their ultimate peak within that country itself. Competition between less-developed and more advanced countries could be sufficient to produce such contradictions in the former type of countries, the example supplied being that of the latent proletariat in Germany.[4] But the events in Germany throughout 1848 meant that Marx would have to revise this conception of the nature of class conflict in less-developed states, at least in terms of his notion of the political role of the bourgeoisie. This revision might also have consequences for a precise formulation of the materialist conception of history itself.

This episode could be interpreted as one example of Marx's value-laded analysis of current events contradicting his more considered theory of historical development. Throughout Marx's writings there was often an essential tension between his passionate desire for revolutionary change and his more objective analysis of exactly how societal progress occurred. In the heat of the political moment it was often the former desire that won through, to the temporary detriment of the internal logic of the latter. This was borne out by the fact that, as described previously, revolutionary uprisings did break out across Europe in 1848, but none of them was followed by an immediate shift to the predicted proletarian revolution. As Marx's own analyses of the period from 1848 to 1851 would later brilliantly portray, the direct outcome was political reaction rather than continued revolution. Moreover, Marx and Engels' suggestion that Germany was in a more advanced condition than other European countries in comparable periods was also disputable. In his political predictions, Marx sometimes illicitly substituted what he wanted to take place for what a more considered version of his own theory of history actually stated was likely to occur.

CLASS TECTONICS

Despite these various political inconsistencies and outside the heat of the moment, Marx had a genuine talent for dissecting the structure of class interrelationships, or for analysing the development of inter-class and intra-class conflicts and alliances – what might more generally be called class tectonics. 'Class tectonics' can be defined as the study of how class blocs are constituted, how they manoeuvre, and how they collide with each other across the national and international political landscape. Although Marx is most famous for pitting 'the bourgeoisie' against 'the workers' as the two basic constituent elements of capitalism, as was presented in *The Manifesto of the Communist Party*, in his in-depth writings on political affairs he sometimes demonstrated a more sophisticated and nuanced understanding of the shifting sands of class structure than any such simple duality would allow. For example, in 1850 Marx identified the following classes and sub-classes as existing in France: the aristocracy of finance, the industrial bourgeoisie, the republican bourgeoisie, the republican petty-bourgeoisie, the property-owning classes (for example the landowners), the upper middle classes, the industrial proletariat, the lumpen-proletariat, and the peasantry. These various terms were not always clearly defined, and there was some overlap between them. But their meaning usually became apparent from their use within the text, and the number of terms implied more complexity than simply 'ruling' versus 'working' class.

At a more fundamental level, Marx claimed to provide a general theory of historical development in which class tectonics played a significant role. Yet, perhaps a little strangely, it was not Marx who had previously conducted a detailed empirical study of the working class *in situ*, but Engels. His book *The Condition of the Working Class in England* (published in 1845) was a pioneering work of descriptive social history, and it drew upon Engels' own experience of working for his father's textile company in Manchester between 1842 and 1844. As the title would suggest, the book provided evidence of the terrible living conditions endured by many working people at this time, especially in large cities such as London. In this book Engels identified three different types of proletarian drone – the industrial, the mining and the agricultural proletariat – and he predicted a growing divide between these three subgroups and the callous bourgeoisie. However, Engels' political analysis was not developed in strategic terms in 1845, and hence the consequences of this growing divide were only hinted at.

In terms of approach and style, there was a large difference between Engels' book on the working class from 1845 and Marx's own analyses of class in his political writings from the period around 1848. Engels' approach was predominantly empirical, aiming to provide a vivid picture of everyday working class life in all its degradations. Marx's approach was more dynamic and conceptual, aiming to analyse the general processes of class conflict within and across nations. Engels' work came across as more human and engaging, whereas Marx's work seemed as brilliant and hard as a diamond. Both Marx and Engels had, before jointly composing *The Manifesto of the Communist Party*, outlined a more complex class structure than just proletariat versus bourgeoisie, but the messianic nature of a raw statement of principles had meant that such subtleties were easily lost in political translation.

THE CLASS STRUGGLES IN FRANCE

Marx's first major work of political analysis after *The Manifesto of the Communist Party* was *The Class Struggles in France*, which was first published in parts across three issues of the *Neue Rheinische Zeitung* in 1850. Engels re-issued it much later as a separate pamphlet. It is worth emphasising that the title, although given by Engels to all the separate articles linked together, referred appropriately to 'class struggles' (plural) and not 'the class struggle' (singular), so as to be clear about the subjects under consideration. More than two classes were involved in the struggles that were to be documented. In *The Class Struggles in France* Marx's stated aim was to demonstrate that, although the period 1848–9 appeared to contain the defeat of the revolution, in fact it witnessed only the defeat of pre-revolutionary ideas from which the revolutionary party had yet to liberate itself.[5] Thus Marx's analysis was an attempt to rescue the apparent failure of the revolution by supplying a different interpretation of the significance of what had eventually occurred.

In his political writings of this period and within his conception of class tectonics, Marx often identified individual leaders as being representative of specific classes or class alliances – or, as he expressed it in 1848, as being 'nothing but the mouthpieces of a class'.[6] For example, in France under Louis Philippe, who was the monarch from 1830 to 1848, the aristocracy of finance had controlled the government, and King Louis was just their agent of political control. This aristocracy of finance included bankers, stock exchange leaders, mine owners and landed proprietors. The 'middle' industrial bourgeoisie were part of the official opposition, and the petty bourgeoisie and the peasantry were excluded from political power. Marx subsequently identified the Provisional Government, which resulted from the barricades in February 1848, as a compromise between the various classes that were involved in French society.

Within this new government, Marx assumed that specific individuals had a direct relation to social classes. For example, Alexandre Ledru-Rollin and Ferdinand Flocon represented the republican petty-bourgeoisie, Louis Blanc and Alexandre Albert represented the working classes, Adolphe Cremieux and Jacques de l'Eure represented the dynastic opposition, Louis Cavaignac represented the republican bourgeoisie, and so on. Hence Marx was considering these various individuals only as ciphers that represented specific class interests. This conflation of individual and class allowed the possibility that, in advocating the need for class conflict (or even in celebrating it), struggle against specific individuals would actually be the result. From this position it was only a short step to believing that, in order to abolish classes, as was Marx's ultimate aim, specific individuals had to be 'abolished'. Class struggle was clearly not for the faint-hearted.

But what had provoked the outbreak of revolution in this period in the first place? Marx's analysis of the immediate causes of the 1848 revolution in France was that simmering political discontentment, ultimately generated by the grinding plates of class tectonics, had been brought to a head by two economic events of global significance. The first was the crop failures of 1845 and 1846, which had produced rising prices of many basic necessities. The second was the industrial crisis in England in the autumn of 1847, which had resulted in commercial collapse across Europe. Bankruptcies and a struggle over food had thus acted as incendiary factors that provoked the rising of the barricades in February 1848.[7] The underlying cause was of course the class system of power itself, which would inevitably be transformed through political conflict.

According to Marx's analysis of the immediate situation, the February revolution had been won by the working classes acting with the passive assistance of the bourgeoisie. However, only a 'bourgeois' republic was the outcome, and the workers had subsequently to be defeated in order to secure this form of rule. He explained:

Just as the February republic with its socialist concessions had needed a battle conducted by the proletariat united with the bourgeoisie against the monarchy, a second battle was necessary in order to sever the republic from these socialist concessions ... The real birthplace of the bourgeois republic was not the *February victory* but the *June defeat*.[8]

The defeat in June 1848 referred to a period of conflict that had begun with legislation favouring piecework and the expulsion of some workers from Paris. A workers' insurrection was the outcome, which was defeated only by an armed assault after five days of intense fighting. The consolidation of the capitalist republic then proceeded, with the republican bourgeoisie securing political power. This victory did not last long, however, as on 10 December 1848 the peasantry secured an electoral victory that ushered in Louis-Napoleon Bonaparte's rule and the beginnings of the royalist restoration. Marx described this event sarcastically as a 'peasant insurrection', with the peasants desiring an end to taxation and an end to the republic of the rich. On 20 December Louis-Napoleon was declared President of the republic, and he subsequently restored the tax on salt that had provoked the peasants' anger. He also began a campaign against the Constituent Assembly, which eventually resulted in his own crowning as Emperor. The course of 'bourgeois' revolutions evidently did not always run very smoothly.

The preceding account of *The Class Struggles in France* is of course only a brief summary of some of its basic features. But without question this was a predominantly descriptive work of political journalism, albeit of great clarity and penmanship. Thus there might be noted one significant absence in Marx's account of the 1848 revolution, namely any detailed discussion of how developments in the economic base of French society had generated the changes to the political superstructure that were being discussed. It was, as explained previously, Marx's contention in his materialist conception of history that the ultimate driving force of historical change was a conflict between the forces and the relations of production, which in turn produced subsidiary forms of this conflict such as class tectonics. But in *The Class Struggles in France* Marx did not explain how the underlying conflict over production manifested itself in the events of 1848–9, nor did he show explicitly how it had caused the political shifts that were being observed. To do this he would have had to analyse how technological changes in the forms of production in Europe at this time had begun to cause unrest in the social relations of production, or in the class structure surrounding the manufacture process. Instead, what Marx provided was only a political and constitutional account of developments within the superstructure of French society, not any substantial account of changes relating to the economic base. But Marx would return again to an analysis of the 1848 revolution in his next major work of political history, as described below.

THE EIGHTEENTH BRUMAIRE OF LOUIS BONAPARTE

Between December 1851 and March 1852 Marx composed a series of articles that were first published in a New York journal, and subsequently re-issued as a long pamphlet of nearly 100 pages. The unusual title of this pamphlet – *The Eighteenth Brumaire of Louis Bonaparte* – referred to a historical analogy that Marx was making with the first French revolution in 1789. The eighteenth brumaire was a date in 1799 (expressed in terms of the republican calendar) of a *coup d'état* that resulted in a military government, a second version of which he was implying had occurred in France in 1851. The beneficiary of this second *coup*, Louis-Napoleon Bonaparte, was the nephew of Napoleon Bonaparte. Louis-Napoleon was the President of the French Republic from 1848 to 1851 and, following this, the French Emperor until 1870.

Marx's pamphlet was another brilliant dissection of the political events under review, written in an engaging and readable style that revealed him at his polemical best. It was also highly partisan and heavily politicised in approach, with the author clearly favouring some of the participants against others. In no way could it be described as a neutral or an objective account of the political history under review, and it was not meant to be so. The basic aim of the pamphlet was to demonstrate Louis Bonaparte's rise to political power in terms of the shifting class tectonics that had (according to Marx) underpinned it. The approach employed was thus to tie changes in the political superstructure of French society with a series of class struggles that he believed had generated them at a more fundamental level.

In this regard *The Eighteenth Brumaire* contained a summarised periodisation of the ongoing results of the class conflicts that Marx was analysing, as expressed across the period of 1848–51. This is reproduced in simplified form as follows:

I.   First period – prologue to revolution.
     From 24 February to 4 May 1848. Characterised by a facade of universal brotherhood.

II. Second period – the foundation of the bourgeois republic.
     1. From 4 May to 25 June 1848. Characterised by the combined struggle of various classes against the proletariat, and then the eventual defeat of the latter.
     2. From 25 June to 10 December 1848. Characterised by the dictatorship of the bourgeois republicans.
     3. From 20 December 1848 to 28 May 1849. Characterised by the fall of the republican bourgeoisie.

III. Third period – the lifespan of the parliamentary republic.
     1. From 28 May to 13 June 1849. Characterised by the defeat of petty-bourgeois democracy.
     2. From 13 June 1849 to 31 May 1850. Characterised by a parliamentary dictatorship.
     3. From 31 May 1850 to 2 December 1851. Characterised by a struggle between the parliamentary bourgeoisie and Bonaparte, followed by the eventual victory of the latter.[9]

This chronology was clearly divided into three basic periods of events, with the second and third periods being further sub-divided into three sections, i.e. I, II (1,2,3), III (1,2,3). The third part of the third section was also further sub-divided. This periodisation can, without too much forcing, be interpreted as mimicking Hegel's pattern of dialectical logic transferred to the political realm, with triadic progressions developing within triadic progressions.[10] An explicit reference to Hegel had occurred in the opening sentence of *The Eighteenth Brumaire* in order to highlight the historical analogy that was being made. It famously began: 'Hegel remarks somewhere that all facts and personages of great importance in world history occur, as it were, twice. He forgot to add: the first time as tragedy, the second as farce.'[11]

The triadic structure that Marx was employing to summarise the sequence of revolutionary power shifts was not necessarily a conscious arrangement of the events of 1848–51 along Hegelian lines, but the dialectical understanding of reality was so deeply ingrained into Marx's way of thinking that it could manifest itself without any conscious effort or deliberate plan. In a newspaper article from the beginning of 1849, Marx explicitly referred to the sequence of revolutionary defeats across 1848 as 'the cycle of the three restorations', although this related to a shorter period of time than was covered in *The Eighteenth Brumaire* as a whole.[12] What he was attempting to highlight through this manner of presentation was that political events were characterised by continuous movement and change. The struggles between the various classes were ongoing and continuous, not static or fixed. Any victory (or indeed any defeat) would be only transitory, and would sooner or later be overtaken by further conflict, the outcome of which would again provide a new (if only a temporary) point of departure for yet more ongoing class-related developments. It was the unity of Being and Nothing as Becoming in the political arena.

In more concrete terms, Marx's analysis of Louis-Napoleon Bonaparte's rise to power in *The Eighteenth Brumaire* as a triadic progression went as follows. The prologue to revolution (period I) was characterised by the revolutionary events of February 1848, followed by a provisional government in which all the classes and elements that had been involved in these events coexisted, but in a confused and temporary form. The foundation of the bourgeois republic (period II) was characterised by the emergence of a National Assembly as the form of government representing the republican section of the bourgeoisie, and excluding proletarian representation. A new constitution proclaiming universal suffrage and giving powers to the Assembly to remove the President was declared. However, the republican bourgeoisie were subsequently outflanked by the royalist bourgeoisie, which included the large landowners and industrialists.

The lifespan of the parliamentary republic (period III) was characterised by a motley mixture of many contradictions. Marx's melancholic description of these contradictions is worth quoting at length:

> ... constitutionalists who conspire openly against the Constitution; revolutionists who are confessedly constitutional; a National Assembly that wants to be omnipotent and always remains parliamentary ... royalists who form the

patres conscripti [senators] of the republic ... an executive power that finds its strength in its very weakness ... a republic that is nothing but the combined infamy of two monarchies ... inane agitation in the name of tranquillity ... heroes without heroic deeds, history without events ... If any section of history has been painted grey, it is this.[13]

This last sentence was a direct allusion to Hegel, who famously characterised philosophical understanding (symbolised as the Owl of Minerva) as painting its grey-on-grey only after the event (Owls spread their wings only after dusk). This meant that theoretical analysis inevitably trailed behind actual historical developments, a characterisation that also applied to the strategy outlined in *The Manifesto of the Communist Party*. In general Marx characterised this third period of class conflicts as demonstrating revolutionary paralysis, which had resulted ultimately in the crowning of a new Emperor.

It was central to Marx's analysis of events that Louis Bonaparte had been able to win ultimate power through his ability to organise the lumpen-proletariat into a secret society by means of a network of loyal agents. Marx described the constituent members of this secret society in colourful terms as follows:

> ... vagabonds, discharged soldiers, discharged jailbirds, escaped galley slaves, swindlers, mountebanks, lazzaroni [Italian reactionaries], pickpockets, tricksters, gamblers, maquereaus [procurers], brothel keepers, porters, literati, organ grinders, rag pickers, knife grinders, tinkers, beggars – in short, the whole indefinite, disintegrated mass...[14]

It might be asked at this point, what has happened to any left-orientated sympathy for people who, through unfavourable circumstances, have been forced into adopting modes of living that were frowned upon by the 'higher' orders of society? Marx characterised these lumpen-people as 'scum, offal, refuse of all classes', and declared that they acted only to benefit their own interests at the expense of the labouring nation. But shouldn't they be understood (from a left-wing perspective) as being forced into this behaviour by difficult circumstances? This was an example of the selective application of sympathy for the less fortunate. Such sympathy was being denied to them because they had not supported the political outcome that Marx had desired. The general Marxian evaluation of groups that failed to conform to their allotted class attitudes was that they were 'de-classed'. The potential dangers of this type of characterisation – 'we know what you really want, not you' – would become surreally and tragically real in the USSR in the 1930s.

There is no doubt, however, that *The Eighteenth Brumaire* was one of Marx's literary masterpieces and his sharpest analysis of political events up until this time. It characterised Louis-Napoleon Bonaparte's contradictory yet ultimately self-serving nature as follows:

> Bonaparte would like to appear as the patriarchal benefactor of all classes. But he cannot give to one class without taking from another ... He would like to steal the whole of France in order to be able to make a present of her to France or, rather, in order to be able to buy France anew with French money ... But the most important feature ... is the percentages that find their way into the pockets of the head ...[15]

It ended poetically with a prediction that a statue of Napoleon Bonaparte erected in Paris in honour of his victories would topple when the imperial mantle fell on the shoulders of his nephew Louis. In fact, it was toppled in 1871 on the orders of the Paris Commune. In a new preface to *The Eighteenth Brumaire* written in 1869, Marx explained that his approach was designed to show how a mediocre individual was able to play the hero's role, against the approach of so-called objective historians, who had given Bonaparte too much personal capacity for initiative. Again, for Marx it was class position that had ultimately determined individual action, and not vice versa. *The Eighteenth Brumaire* can thus be interpreted as a hymn to the ultimate importance of the class bloc over that of the individual constituent.

Marx's various accounts of French history across 1848–51 appear today to be relatively modern in approach, and although no claim for scholarly detachment could credibly be made, it is relatively easy for readers over 150 years later to understand the framework that was being employed. Indeed, Marx explicitly presented his analysis of European class tectonics in opposition to some other accounts of French history available at the time. For example, Francois Guizot himself published a historical account of the English revolution in 1850, which Marx seized upon as epitomising the old-fashioned approach to history that he was attempting to overthrow. Marx wrote:

According to M[onsieur] Guizot, the whole Revolution is to be explained by the evil intent and religious fanaticism of a few disturbers of the peace who could not content themselves with a moderate freedom ... The great riddle for M[onsieur] Guizot, which he can only solve by pointing to the superior intelligence of the English ... is explained by the continuous alliance which united the middle class with the largest section of the great landowners ...[16]

Guizot's riddle was to account for the varying degrees of success of the English and French 'bourgeois' revolutions, which he did purely through ideological differences. Marx, on the other hand, cited differences in the class tectonics of England and France, in particular the middle-class compatibility of the large landownership system in England, compared with the destruction of large landed estates that had occurred in France after the 1789 revolution. Both explanations might actually be seen as containing an element of truth, but Marx was right to imply that his own explanation was more controversial in its day.

WAGE LABOUR AND CAPITAL

Political affairs were not Marx's only interest in this eventful period of his life. He published a particularly significant set of articles in the *Neue Rheinische Zeitung* in the spring of 1849 that were later issued as *Wage Labour and Capital*, the first developed presentation of his ideas on the relation between capital and labour. These articles had been first delivered as lectures in Brussels in December 1847. The Cologne Police Inspector's report was accurate with regard to Marx working on a 'book on economics' at this time.

In *Wage Labour and Capital*, which was only a small part of the aforementioned book in progress, labour was defined as being a commodity that was sold to capitalists, and wages were presented as the price of that commodity. An interesting aspect of Marx's analysis was that he viewed competition within capitalism as being three-sided, in that it occurred between buyers themselves, between sellers themselves, and also between buyers and sellers. Within this triad of forces, the side whose participants damaged each other the least were specified as the eventual victors. In an unpublished draft of a continuation of his analysis of wages, Marx judged that the positive aspect of wage labour was that it equalised everything on the same commercial basis, and hence it served to demystify the patriarchal relations of previous eras.

In Marx's analysis, wages were determined by the cost of production of workers, i.e. the cost of their maintenance through training and subsistence, although this was true only for the working class as a whole. He also articulated the idea that the wages of workers inevitably declined (at least in relative terms) as productive capital increased in capacity over time – what became known as the immiserisation thesis. This thesis, and whether it was meant in a relative or an absolute sense, became a topic of significant controversy much later, as it was obvious in the twentieth century that the wages of workers in Europe were not (on average) declining but were actually rising in a very significant way. Many interpreted this to mean that Marx had simply been wrong on this issue.

Engels later explained that *Wage Labour and Capital* was written by Marx before he had fully completed his study of political economy – which according to Engels was finished only by the end of the 1850s – and hence it contained some incorrect formulations of theoretical issues. The key change emphasised by Engels was that Marx had replaced the common term 'labour' with his own special term 'labour power', i.e. workers sell their labour power for wages, not their labour. Another change was that in the first printing of *Wage Labour and Capital* within the *Neue Rheinische Zeitung*, Marx appeared to use the terms 'bourgeoisie' and 'capitalist' interchangeably. In later separate re-issues, Engels replaced the former term exclusively with the latter. Did this textual modification have any special significance?

Marx had used the term 'bourgeoisie' in his political writings of this period to connote a social class, within his general conception of class tectonics. The term 'capitalist' was more commonly encountered in his economic writings, to connote the class of owners of the means of production. It would be possible to suggest that these two concepts were entirely identical, but it may also be argued that they were not. In the period around the 1848 revolutions, Marx's conception of class was strongly political in orientation, as he was analysing current affairs with both eyes kept firmly on the articulation of communist strategy. After 1850, when it became clear that the European revolutions had failed to produce the political outcome that Marx had desired, he turned his main scholarly attention to economic studies, or to analysing the nature of class within a framework of capitalist production conceived in predominantly economic terms. It is likely that the terminological shift from 'bourgeoisie' to 'capitalist' followed this evolution of central orientation from mainly political to mainly economic matters. This was not necessarily a fundamental break in approach, but it was a significant change of emphasis.

CONCLUSION

It is important to understand what was (and what was not) original in Marx's overall analysis of class tectonics. The concept of social class itself was certainly not Marx's invention, as he readily acknowledged. What was original was his claim to have connected the idea of class conflict with a more general theory of historical change, and to extrapolate how this conflict would resolve itself into socialism. In a letter from March 1852 explaining on this issue, he wrote:

> ... no credit is due to me for discovering the existence of classes in modern society ... What I did that was new was to prove: (1) that the existence of classes is only bound up with particular historical phases ... (2) that the class struggle necessarily leads to the dictatorship of the proletariat, (3) that this dictatorship itself only constitutes the transition to the abolition of all classes ...[17]

However, in many of the political writings examined in this chapter and the previous, Marx's conception of class itself was not always clearly defined. Class corresponded in some way with structural position in a social hierarchy, but the large number of classes and sub-classes that Marx had identified in his political writings might be thought to make a simple definition of class more difficult to obtain.

One way of understanding class in this respect would define it as involving domination or control, i.e. that those within the bourgeoisie had the power of control over those within the proletariat. In Marx's contemporaneous discussions of current developments, such as the 1848 revolutions in Europe, it was the political component of class-consciousness that was usually to the fore, especially in regard to the notion of collective class action. Yet in *The Eighteenth Brumaire* it was explained with respect to the peasantry that: 'In so far as millions of families live under economic conditions of existence that separate their mode of life, their interests, and their culture from those of the other classes ... they form a class.'[18]

This might be interpreted to mean that it was the economic and cultural conditions of everyday life that was the formative feature of distinct classes – what might be termed a social conception of class. But was Marx's conception of class really social and/or political in nature, in that the materialist conception of history posited that class tectonics flowed from a more fundamental feature of human societies?

At a much later date and in volume one of *Capital*, Marx did provide a basic definition of class as he conceived of it in this very different period of his life. He wrote:

> What constitutes a class? ... What makes wage-labourers, capitalists, and landlords constitute the three great social classes? ... the individuals forming them, live on wages, profit, and ground-rent respectively, on the realization of their labour power, their capital, and their landed property.[19]

Here class was being defined in mainly economics terms, as the outcome of different types of ownership, and only three examples were posited as existing. It could be suggested that Marx was emphasising different aspects of the same conception of class in his earlier political writings as compared with his later economic writings, and hence that there was no necessary difference between the two. It might also be argued that his notion of class evolved from the predominantly political conception in operation at the time of the 1848 revolutions to a more analytical view, as was presented in later economic writings such as *Capital*. It was the failure of the 1848 events to achieve any lasting socialist victory that sent Marx back to the philosophical drawing board with respect to his analysis of the most important features of human society and how they could be influenced to achieve his underlying political goals: part of this process related to the notion of class. The next two chapters will therefore begin to explore Marx's turn towards economics as it developed through the 1850s and beyond.

5

THE WHOLE ECONOMIC MUCK

The title of this chapter is taken from one of Marx's letters from the early 1850s that accurately described his own initial attitude to being forced (by what he saw as political necessity) to study the 'dismal' subject of economics in great detail. After the failure of the 1848 revolutions to secure any permanent socialist victories, in the Marxian view it would be economic factors that set the framework for future political strategy. However, as will be seen from this chapter and the next, Marx's wide variety of academic interests and political concerns continued to develop as the 1850s unfolded. Many commentators have described the early and mid-1850s as one of the most difficult and troubling periods of Marx's life, as he suffered from chronic poverty, the progression of various illnesses, and the difficulties of trying to maintain a family home in a foreign country. But this period was also a time of significant intellectual progress in his economic studies, despite the many distractions that arose to divert his attention away from purely scholarly pursuits.

RE-ENGAGEMENT WITH ECONOMICS

In 1850 and 1851 Marx devoted a significant amount of time to a resumption of the economics research that he had begun in the 'Economic and Philosophical Manuscripts' of 1844 but had placed to one side as the result of immediate political events and his own developing émigré status. It was fortuitous that his final port of destination, London, enabled him to gain access to one of the leading research libraries in the world (the British Museum) on a regular and prolonged basis. Here, it is reported, he selected a favourite desk to work at, which was next to the 'literature' open shelves. That part of the British Museum where Marx worked is no longer a functioning library, but the potent smell of the leather, wood and accumulated dust in the circular reading room was (until very recently) redolent of 'knowledge' in the most profound sense.

As an example of this research, in the first half of 1851 Marx read such economics authors as Adam Smith, David Ricardo and T. R. Malthus, the economics writings of philosophers such as John Locke and David Hume, and numerous additional works on factories, population, banking and credit. In the whole of 1851 he completed fourteen notebooks with quotations and commentary on money, industry, agriculture, ground rent and other related topics. He judged (perhaps rather prematurely) that economics as a science had made no progress since the time of Smith and Ricardo, although he admitted that much had been done by researchers in individual areas – by which he meant in specific fields such as the gathering of statistical data and the analysis of national legal developments.

In the second half of 1851, various publishing possibilities for this burgeoning economics research arose, although they eventually fell through. One publisher became initially interested in the idea of Marx writing a history of economic thought, but the negotiations came to nothing. Thus in these early stages of his economic studies the final form of their output was constantly in flux, partly because the author himself was continuously discovering new books and topic areas to study, but also because of the difficulties of finding a publisher who was sympathetic to the project. Both the dry subject matter itself, and Marx's personal notoriety, worked against easily securing a publisher. Economic theory from a socialist perspective was not regarded as an immediately popular choice by most of those involved in book production in the early 1850s.

In one of the largest temporal underestimations in the history of human understanding, in April 1851 Marx judged that his economics research would take only five more weeks to complete. Also at this time,

Engels and various other friends admonished Marx to 'hurry up' and finish with economics so that he could move on to other topics, but by June 1851 Marx had extended his timetable for another six to eight weeks. In the event this research was never completed in his lifetime; the previous estimate of five weeks stretching out to 32 years (and more required). Apparently, economics was not a subject matter that was so easily mastered, even if Engels 'mucked in' with some much-needed monetary assistance. As the final attempt of this period, in the summer of 1852 Marx submitted an idea for a book on 'Modern Economic Literature' to a publisher, but it was rejected. Pressures of political and family life then forced him to shelve his economics project for some considerable period of time, but a welcome turn of events led to a request from the USA.

THE *NEW YORK DAILY TRIBUNE*

In April 1852 Marx received an invitation from the editor of the newspaper the *New York Daily Tribune* to contribute articles on a regular basis on topics relating to contemporary world affairs. Initially Marx asked Engels to write a proportion of them, in order to preserve his own time for pursuing economic studies. Articles on Germany after 1848 were published in Marx's name, and even reprinted together in book form; only much later was Engels revealed as being the real author. Marx did write on certain topics in the *Tribune* himself, for example on England and on some other European countries, and these contributions were highly valued by the editor. They were so well regarded that sometimes they were printed as editorial comments rather than as authored articles, and more than 60 articles by Marx appeared in each of the years 1853 and 1854. Although the volume of contributions declined after 1854, the sheer number of them in total meant that they should be considered as an important source for understanding his attitude to many issues of the day.

The author himself expressed some contempt for the quality of his own journalism, describing it on one occasion as 'newspaper muck' that in the final analysis meant nothing, but it did provide him with an immediate impetus to follow contemporary events in a very detailed fashion.[1] The most obvious reason for the self-deprecating attitude towards journalism was that the writing of newspaper articles consumed a great deal of time that could have been used on researching what were regarded as more fundamental economics matters, an inconvenience that was frequently resented. But despite this negative attitude, many of the resulting articles were well written and demonstrated a talent for framing an issue in a clear and easily digestible (albeit rather one-sided) manner. Moreover, Marx did sometimes engage with various economic issues in his journalism that were at least of indirect relevance to his long-term research goals, and hence the time spent studying contemporary events in this period was not a complete distraction.

As an example of this journalistic analysis, in 1853 Marx and Engels published a number of articles dealing with issues that led up to the Crimean War (1853–6), and these articles provided a running commentary on aspects of the Crimean dispute. This conflict had formally begun in October 1853, when Turkey declared war on Russia after a Russian invasion of Moldavia and Wallachia, and continued with the creation of a British and French military alliance with Turkey in 1854. It ended with a Russian defeat in the Crimea and the signing of a peace treaty in March 1856. What was dubbed 'the Eastern question', or the involvement in European powers in the disintegration of the Ottoman Empire, was a major concern of international relations across much of the nineteenth century.

Both Marx and Engels wrote detailed accounts of the developing situation regarding the Eastern question. In one article from the *New York Daily Tribune* entitled 'Turkey' (dated 22 March 1853), Marx and Engels explained that the country at the heart of the conflict was composed of three basic parts – African, Asiatic and European – but that the Slavonic component formed the 'great mass' of the population that was subject to the rule of the Turk. Hence the political point under debate was always Turkey's ambiguous place in Europe.[2] In an article called 'The Real Issue in Turkey' (dated 12 April 1853), Engels outlined a general attitude to Russia as a national political force. He warned that Great Britain could not afford to allow Russia to gain control of the Dardanelles and the sea channel of Constantinople, as this would constitute a direct challenge to British economic interests. Turkish ports and trade routes constituted the principal means of commercial intercourse between Europe and Central Asia, and were also important military positions; hence their strategic significance was large.

According to Engels, Russia had been a conquering nation for a century before the revolutionary events of 1789, and if the possession of Turkey were to be added to its previous conquests this would be a calamity for the revolutionary cause. He concluded this article by emphasising that:

> The maintenance of Turkish independence ... [and] the arrest of the Russian scheme of annexation, is a matter of the highest moment. In this instance the interest of revolutionary democracy and of England go hand in hand. Neither can permit the Czar to make Constantinople one of his capitals ...[3]

Engels believed that Russia constituted an even more reactionary power than Great Britain at this time, and he clearly supported the British side on this particular issue. In a further article on this topic, later entitled 'Traditional Policy of Russia' (dated 29 July 1853), Marx highlighted that Constantinople was a 'golden bridge' thrown between the West and the East, and hence that (in a precursor to the 'clash of civilisations' approach resurgent much more recently), the struggle between Western Europe and Russia over Constantinople involved the question of whether Byzantium as an Empire was to fall before Western civilisation.[4] Describing Russian foreign policy as being composed of 'craft, cheats and subterfuges', Marx concluded that it could only be 'the Revolution' (i.e. an international socialist victory) that would finally overpower the barbaric elements of Eastern civilisation. Six months later, in January 1854, Engels echoed Marx's analysis in his own account of 'The European War', asserting that a sixth power could very soon assert its supremacy over the five great national powers of Europe, this omnipresent force being 'the Revolution'.[5]

The numerous newspaper articles on Turkey were representative in that they indicate that Marx and Engels often worked closely together as a team in their newspaper efforts, and hence the question arises of whether the designation 'Team Marx' is an appropriate label for their joint efforts analysing aspects of contemporary affairs. Within the hypothesised 'Team Marx', Engels frequently concentrated on military and strategic topics; Marx on financial and economic matters; although this division of labour was not in any way rigidly applied and both members of the team wrote on political affairs. Other topics that were tackled by 'Team Marx' in 1853 and 1854 included British parliamentary politics and agricultural affairs in Europe, and in this period Engels also translated some of Marx's articles written in German for English-language newspaper publication. This manner of collaborative working explains how it was possible for some of Engels' newspaper articles to be later reprinted under Marx's name. The question naturally follows, were there any differences in approach or conclusion within 'Team Marx'? No major political discrepancies can easily be detected in the many newspaper articles, and hence it is reasonable to conclude that they did see very much eye-to-eye on the significance of contemporary affairs, although the particular interests that they brought to bear were rather different. Even so, the designation 'Team Marx' might be seen as relevant only to their contemporary political writings, and was certainly not applicable to Marx's economic studies.

RUSSIA AND BRITAIN: A SECRET ALLIANCE?

In the Crimean War, Russia was one of the main protagonist nations, but Marx's interest in Russian affairs did not end with this specific military conflict; rather it expanded outwards from it. In fact it is accurate to suggest that the events around the Crimean dispute provided one of the most significant contextual boosts to Marx's early interest in Russian affairs. For example, in February 1854 Marx published a short article on 'Russian Finances during the War', in which he analysed the printing of inconvertible paper rubles as a means of war finance. He declared that this means had been used repeatedly to trick the Russian public into accepting paper notes instead of silver currency, which in turn had produced commodity price fluctuations and the accumulation of a huge government debt.[6]

More significantly, two of Marx's least well-known (yet quite controversial) book-length works originated from the time of the Crimean conflict in the mid-1850s. Marx explained their origin by revealing that, while digging in the British Museum in 1853, he had found a number of original documents which (he claimed) revealed a secret collaboration between the governments of London and Saint Petersburg that went back as far as Peter the Great. Marx believed that Britain had continually assisted Tsarist Russia (which he characterised as a thoroughly reactionary power) over a very significant period of time, and hence by association the British government was thoroughly implicated in support of this reaction. Marx subsequently authored two series of quite lengthy articles on this theme that were later published in collected form under the titles *The Story of the Life of Lord Palmerston* and *Secret Diplomatic History of the Eighteenth Century*.

Both of these works were initially published as a series of newspaper articles, the former in the *New York Daily Tribune* and the latter in the *Sheffield Free Press*, which were then reprinted in part as a number of separate pamphlets and in other newspapers. In the *Life of Lord Palmerston* from 1853, Marx accused the British Foreign Secretary and Prime Minister of consistently acting in the interests of the Russian government. An example of Palmerston recommending diplomatic tenderness towards the Russian government after they had recently committed atrocities was indicative of this presentation. Marx had, partly as a direct consequence of the Crimean conflict, spent some considerable time studying aspects of Russian history, and he wrote prophetically about Russia as a country in his *Secret Diplomatic History* from 1856 that:

> The overwhelming influence of Russia has taken Europe at different epochs by surprise, startled the peoples of the West, and been submitted to as a fatality, or resisted only by convulsions. But alongside the fascination with Russia, there runs an ever-reviving scepticism ... whether we consider her power as a palpable fact, or as the mere vision of the guilt-stricken consciences of the European peoples – the question remains the same: 'How did this power, or this phantom of a power ... rouse on the one side the passionate assertion, and on the other the angry denial of its threatening the world with a rehearsal of Universal Monarchy?'[7]

Marx himself believed that Tsarist Russia was a bulwark of backward-looking political institutions, and Engels later described Russia characteristically as the 'reserve army of European reaction'.

However, it is important to realise that at this time Marx's analysis of British–Russian relations was predominantly diplomatic in nature, and was focused primarily on associations between the respective political leaders and their associates. In his *Secret Diplomatic History* Marx did present some statistical data on British commerce with Russia, but only as a means of demonstrating that the Russian market was relatively insignificant for British exports. There was little analysis of the structure or organisational forms of the Russian economy itself. Russia was being judged by Marx mainly as a political entity, and as one element in the jigsaw of pan-European Imperial alliances related to issues in international relations such as the Eastern question.

Marx discussed the discoveries that he had made at the British Museum relating to British–Russian collaboration in a letter to Engels in February 1856. Here Marx alleged specifically that the Whigs had sold themselves to Russia, and that England had contributed significantly to turning Russia into a Baltic power during the reign of Peter I by means of direct aid. As an example of this assistance, Marx cited the fact that the English fleet had been placed at Peter's disposal in order to help him found Russian ports in the Baltic region.[8] In ideological terms the Tsar had been portrayed by the Whigs as 'a good Protestant' and hence as a useful ally against Catholic forces. Marx characterised the Whigs as representing the English oligarchy and hence the rule of a few great families. He judged that they were enlightened compared with the Tories and represented the cream of the aristocracy, but this does not help explain their apparent assistance to Russia. In order to understand Marx's reasoning more fully, a more detailed account of his analysis is required.

LORD PALMERSTON

The text of Marx's *Life of Lord Palmerston* was not a full life-story in the conventional biographical sense; rather it discussed various episodes in Palmerston's life that were germane to the case at issue. Nor did Marx accuse 'the noble lord' of directly receiving funds from the Russian government. Instead he discussed the instances of policy that demonstrated that Palmerston was 'the unflinching and persevering advocate of Russian interests'.[9] A key political issue in this regard had been Russian expansion into Turkish territories. In one example provided as evidence, revisions that were made by Palmerston to a treaty of commerce relating to Turkish trade were seen to favour Russian citizens against the British, and to increase the level of required export duties.[10] In response to this unfavourable turn, some English merchants had decided to trade under the protection of Russian companies. In addition, Palmerston had concluded a treaty with Russia that closed the Dardanelles to England during peace with Turkey. He had also acted to acknowledge the Russian usurpation of the Caucasus when many others had not. Hence, in Marx's view, the evidence pointed clearly to Palmerston being a stooge of Russian foreign policy, although Marx provided no convincing reason why this had been the case. Nor did he appear to acknowledge that in some instances that were discussed, the position of the Russian government as supported by Palmerston might have been partially valid.

Another component of Marx's set of Russophobe arguments, this time from the *Secret Diplomatic History*, was that, in pursuing an alliance with Russia, Britain was actually acting against its own best interests. This argument had two strands to it. First, Marx claimed that it had been against Britain's geo-political interests to assist Russia in becoming a stronger power in Europe, as in the long run Russia would eventually challenge Britain's own power itself. Hence those favouring British assistance to Russia in order to combat other European powers such as Sweden were taking a short-sighted position. Second, Marx suggested that it had not been in Britain's commercial interests to pursue an alliance with Russia, and he provided some figures to prove this thesis. For example, in 1730 trade with Russia amounted to only one fifty-third of the total value of all English trade, and by 1760 total commerce with Russia had increased by only £265,841 compared with 1706, which Marx declared was a trifling sum compared with the millions that were involved.[11] In fact, during the epoch that was being considered, the export of British manufactures to Russia was continuously declining. Hence Marx was suggesting that Britain's reactionary alliance with Russia had been a poor policy to pursue even from Britain's own economic perspective. Again, he provided no real explanation for this mistaken approach, other than that the specific companies involved in trade with Russia might have themselves benefited.

The judgements of many of the commentators on Marx's allegation of a secret alliance between Russia and Britain have been very sceptical. Robert Payne judged the thesis that Palmerston was in the pocket of the Russians as 'totally unfounded', and suggested that the evidence Marx had presented of a secret Russian–British alliance 'would scarcely convince a ten-year-old child'.[12] David McLellan considered Marx's views on these questions to be 'bizarre'.[13] Even the editorial in the part-Soviet-sponsored edition of the *Collected Works* admitted that Marx had 'somewhat exaggerated Palmerston's subservient role in relation to the Tsarist autocracy'.[14] Payne explained away Marx's dislike for Palmerston as the result of the latter being seen as the incarnation of British imperialism, and the allegation of a secret alliance as the result of his general conspiratorial view of history. However, these explanations seem inadequate in the light of Marx's acknowledged contributions to historical understanding in other areas of analysis.

Another point to consider is the success of these particular works. The pamphlet version of Marx's 1853 attack on Palmerston sold 15,000 copies and then was re-issued in a second edition, and it created something of a sensation.[15] Thus it was one of Marx's most successful publications from a sales perspective, especially so when it is considered that it was initially published as a series of newspaper articles, and hence the pamphlet version was not the first issue. The popular success of a work is of course no guarantee of a correct interpretation of the topic discussed, but even if Marx's views on this topic were mistaken, he was evidently not alone in his error. Moreover, his publications often contained analyses of individuals that he personally disliked, such as members of the aristocracy and other ruling elites, but rarely did they contain totally false interpretations of specific events as these two works apparently did. Indeed, as the previous two chapters have shown, his political writings on 1848 are known for their revealing insight into class tectonics, not for their mistaken interpretations of individual motivations. Could Marx really have been so totally wrong on the Russia–Britain question, and so wide of the mark when it came to interpreting the evidence that he had purportedly found? If so, why?

A biographer more sympathetic to Marx on this issue, Franz Mehring, implied that although the implication that Palmerston had actually been bought by Russia was taking the point too far, Palmerston was indeed sympathetic to the Russian cause, as was evidenced by his reluctance as Foreign Secretary to really wound Russia in any vital way during the Crimean campaign.[16] Mehring's interpretation implied also that Marx's appropriate concern for campaigning against Russia as the bulwark of European reaction led him sometimes to 'over-cook' his account of the diplomatic influence of Russia across Europe, and that this was part of the real explanation for Marx's paranoia on this issue. Hence Marx had seen a prolonged conspiracy when there were only various real but quite specific points of mutual contact and alliance.

Another point to question is the use of the word 'secret' in the title to the second of the two reissued volumes under consideration. The documents that Marx had used were all openly accessible to anyone studying at the British Museum, and were not classified as 'secret' in any administrative archival way. Some of the documents that he used were labelled 'confidential', 'private' or 'secret', but others were pamphlets that had been published apparently without censorship. Perhaps 'hidden diplomatic history' would have been a more appropriate (and less provocative) title – the original title of the series of newspaper articles was actually 'Revelations of the Diplomatic History of the Eighteenth Century'.

It has been suggested by some trying to make sense of Marx's Russophobe attitude in the 1850s that in attempting to link British with Russian political machinations in the past, Marx was really making a point for his contemporary audience, rather than one about historical alliances. He was trying to demonstrate the reactionary nature of British governments by linking them directly to the acknowledged central kingdom of reaction itself, Russia. There might be an element of truth in this idea, but Marx was certainly not afraid of openly accusing Britain of being politically demonic, so no subtle methods of propaganda were really required.

Another contextual factor that has been presented by commentators was the possibility of the outbreak of war between Russia and England in 1853 over matters in the Balkans, during which Palmerston had taken an appeasement line. Engels had noted this potential for war in a newspaper article from September 1853.[17] It has been suggested that, instead of a policy of appeasement, Marx desired the outbreak of open military conflict in order to stoke the flames of political revolution across Europe – this explaining his campaign to discredit Palmerston in the public eye, as the latter was trying to avert such a war. Perhaps it can be concluded that there was certainly a grain of truth in Marx's allegations of various political coincidences between Russia and Britain, although no evidence of a continuous conspiracy, and that, in addition, Marx's detractors have sometimes exaggerated the degree to which Marx himself alleged the conspiratorial aspect of the link in his actual writings, rather than in associated texts by other commentators.

In this regard it is necessary to explain that Marx's attitude to Palmerston and the British–Russian alliance had been stoked up at least to some extent by his contact with David Urquhart. Urquhart was a well-known British diplomat and an anti-Russia and pro-Turk campaigner, whom Marx had described on one occasion as 'a complete monomaniac'. Although Marx and Urquhart disagreed fundamentally on general political matters, Marx allowed Urquhart to distribute some of his writings on Palmerston, and hence there was common cause made on this specific issue. Palmerston had dismissed Urquhart from his diplomatic duties in Constantinople, and so this conflict had a definite personal component to it. It was Urquhart who had accused Palmerston of actually accepting money from the Russian government as payment for his loyalties, an accusation that Marx himself never repeated in print.

Little did Marx realise that the country that would first attempt officially to implement his revolutionary ideas in practice would be one that he despised (in political terms) so much.

LIFE IN LONDON

Poverty and various illnesses continued to afflict the Marx family as the 1850s progressed. In the spring of 1855, Marx's son Edgar died from gastric fever after a long period of poor health at the age of only eight, passing away in his father's arms. Marx wrote that this tragedy had deeply shaken his heart, and he reported that Edgar's mother was completely broken by the experience. This was a huge blow to the family that was difficult to recover from, and in 1857 another child was stillborn. Various maladies that had afflicted Marx periodically, such as liver problems, boils (apparently) and rheumatism, now grew in intensity, sometimes preventing any work from being done at all. This was not a happy time for Marx in personal terms.

Recent medical analysis of his illnesses has suggested that the liver problems that he suffered from cannot precisely be diagnosed, the most likely candidate being biliary colic. However, the well-publicised skin disease that was described variously as outbreaks of 'boils', 'carbuncles' and even 'furuncles' was in fact hidradenitis suppurativa. This condition originates from a blockage of certain ducts connected to hair follicles and is sometimes misdiagnosed as boils.[18] It manifests itself in certain affected parts of the skin as areas containing blackheads, lumps, spots and leaking pits of pus, grouped together as crops of 'boils'; the skin being prone to such outbreaks including the mammary, perianal and genital areas. Destruction of the skin in affected areas is sometimes the result. Outbreaks can be quite prolonged and severe, and match the descriptions provided by Marx in his many letters very accurately. Although the most obvious manifestations of this condition did not begin until the early 1860s, it is likely that Marx had contracted the disease before this time.

Even Engels, Marx's long-serving sympathetic ear on health matters, himself fell ill in the summer of 1857, temporarily preventing him from writing his due allotment of journalism as the other member of 'Team Marx'. In order to recuperate from his bout of poor health, Engels travelled to the seaside (near Brighton) for a period of relaxation in August 1857. Ever the faithful friend, he explained in a letter to Marx that:

> I had a hamper of wine sent to you from Manchester which will do your wife good: 6 bottles of Bordeaux, 3 of port, 3 of sherry ... Let me know the colour of the seals on the port and sherry so that I can keep a check on my wine merchant ... The Bordeaux bears the label Co. Destournel; I have just imported it.[19]

The wine in question was Chateau Cos d'Estournel in the St Estephe region of Bordeaux, which had just been elected a second growth in the 1855 classification of the Medoc still in operation today. This meant that it was priced just below prestigious first growth estates such as Lafite and Latour. This would have been an expensive gift to send, and indicates that Marx was very fortunate to have such a generous friend. In turn, Marx responded by relating that he had been reading up on the subject of Engels' illness, and he provided some advice on the correct medicaments that were to be administered as part of the cure. Apparently there was nothing that could not be solved by studying the appropriate literature on the topic.

However, temporary respite from the chronic financial problems then appeared. The Marx family received some inheritance money from Jenny's mother in 1856, and eventually moved out of the squalor of Dean Street to a more comfortable house in Grafton Terrace, Haverstock Hill, which was a palace compared with their previous abode in Soho. It was also close to Marx's beloved Hampstead Heath. Soon, however, they were forced to pawn various items of furniture due to the lack of any regular income, and by the end of the 1850s they had fallen back into the life of poverty familiar to them from Dean Street. Sometimes in the 1850s Marx was forced to feed his family on bread and potatoes alone, with the constant worry of where the money for the next day's meal would come from. He was even occasionally driven to borrow small sums of money from members of the downtrodden proletariat in order to survive.

In this period Marx and Engels were involved in various personal disputes on political and related matters. One such dispute arose with Ferdinand Lassalle in regard to interpreting German and other political developments, and it demonstrated that Marx's relationships with friends and colleagues were often inextricably connected to matters of social and political analysis. In this instance Marx had listened to accusations that Lassalle was using the socialist cause only for personal gain, and the frequent correspondence between them subsequently cooled. But this was the same Lassalle who would help Marx to find a publisher for one of his major books (see below). And Marx had previously been a little disingenuous to Lassalle, praising a book that Lassalle had written in a letter addressed directly to him, but then seeking absolution from Engels for his forced sycophancy. A pattern of making new acquaintances as he moved across nations and then falling out with them was repeated, with only a few very close friends (such as Engels) remaining for his entire life. Constantly struggling to maintain the 'correct' political line could, it seemed, be a lonely path to follow.

ECONOMICS ONCE AGAIN

Although various political developments (and his own desperate need for funds) had conspired to force Marx to engage with more contemporary topics between 1853 and 1855, a looming commercial crisis across Europe in 1856 turned his attention once again back to directly economics topics. In consequence he composed various articles for the *New York Daily Tribune* on the outbreak of these difficulties, such as was demonstrated by the Credit Mobilier case of financial speculation in France. Marx wrote a number of short but vividly written accounts of specific economic crises that focused more on their empirical manifestation than on their place in the theoretical scheme of capitalist production that he was engaged in developing.

For example, Marx published an article entitled 'The Monetary Crisis in Europe' in the *New York Daily Tribune* in October 1856, which connected the economic maladies being experienced in Europe with social and political convulsions that he claimed were imminent. He argued that the general bankruptcy facing the upper classes as a consequence of various speculative manias would be the harbinger of a social revolution analogous to that experienced across Europe in 1848.[20] Marx made a direct comparison with the economic crisis of 1847, which he suggested presaged the revolutionary events of 1848. A year later, in November 1857, he was gleefully reporting on the 'great symphonious crash of bankruptcy' that had burst upon the world, and which (he claimed) had laid to rest the idea that the introduction of free trade would bring an end to the era of commercial convulsions.[21]

Sometimes, however, Marx's journalistic writings did overlap more obviously with his economic theory. In 'The Causes of the Monetary Crisis in Europe' published in the *New York Daily Tribune* in October 1856, Marx compared the crisis as it was then breaking out in Germany with the previous monetary panic that had occurred in England in 1847. He suggested that the respite achieved by active financial measures was temporary in both cases:

> Similar results will ... be experienced in Germany, since at the bottom of the panic there was no scarcity of currency, but a disproportion between the disposable capital and the vastness of the industrial, commercial and speculative enterprises then in hand. The means by which the panic was temporarily subdued was the enhancement of the rate of discount ...[22]

This disproportionality approach to explaining industrial crises would turn out to be one significant thread within the Marxian tradition of political economy, but Marx's general work on economics would also suggest that other approaches might be equally valid, such as an under-consumptionist one. Evidence in favour of these explanations was sometimes found in the detail of specific events.

Other aspects of Marx's journalism can be seen as valuable background preparation for his more substantial work on economic theory. For example, in April 1857 he published an article on 'The English Factory System' where he outlined the rapid extension of this system of production that had occurred in recent years, by which he meant the growth of textile factories. He also explained that the law of concentration of production ruled in this sphere, and that this law operated in a regional manner. This meant that cotton manufacture was drawn to Lancashire, woollen production to Yorkshire, flax to Ireland, and silk manufacture to Cheshire, Derbyshire and so on. A division between industrial and agricultural regions within Britain also developed through the operation of this law, with areas such as Wiltshire and Dorset being divested of their manufactures, while many northern counties were strengthening their monopoly position.[23]

The outbreak of the economic crisis in the USA in 1857 resulted in the declining fortunes of the *New York Daily Tribune*, and as a consequence of this Marx's remuneration for his journalism was substantially reduced. He had been waiting impatiently for the onset of capitalist crisis for many years and, ironically, when it finally came it had an immediate effect on his family finances. But Marx was not at all distraught by this personal setback; quite the opposite in fact. When the crisis reached England he was overjoyed, writing to Engels in November 1857 that he had not felt so happy since 1849 as he did in the face of the current eruption of economic difficulties. It was, they thought at the time, a sign of impending political victories for the cause.

Thus, partly inspired by the outbreak of a crisis that he had long suggested might presage a new revolution, in 1857 Marx resumed his more in-depth economic studies with greater resolve. Between the autumn of 1857 and the spring of 1858, he composed the substantial manuscript now known as the *Grundrisse* (or 'Outlines of a Critique of Political Economy'), the first draft of elements of which formed part of his projected multi-volume 'Critique of Political Economy'. The main text of the *Grundrisse* was divided into two basic parts – the first focused on money, the second (much longer part) on capital – and it corresponded to only one of the subject divisions that he had initially outlined for his magnum opus on economics, although other related topics also appeared. The actual content of the *Grundrisse* will be considered in more detail in the next chapter, but in 1857 Marx presented a plan for the overall structure of his projected work on economics as follows:

1) The abstract characterisations of all types of society.
2) The categories of bourgeois society – capital, wages, landed property.

3) The bourgeois state and its categories – taxes, public credit and debt, population.
4) The international relations of production – exports, imports, foreign exchange.
5) The world market and crises.

This five-part scheme was soon revised and expanded into six parts. However, the first written draft of Marx's economic studies (the *Grundrisse*) was never published in his lifetime, even though it constituted an important mediating link between his very early writings on economics and the published version of *Capital* itself.

The completed rough draft that was the *Grundrisse* was around 800 pages in length, and the author was then faced with the daunting task of turning this manuscript into a more polished and complete work, as in March 1858 Ferdinand Lassalle had located a publisher that was interested in issuing a book on this topic. Marx's solution to turning the mammoth *Grundrisse* into a publishable text can be seen as either ingenious or cowardly, depending on one's point of view. He solved the problem in one bound by simply omitting all the material on capital (the longer part of the manuscript); instead, in the final version, he provided only an account of money plus some preliminary discussion of commodities. Marx broke the news with trepidation in a letter to Engels by warning him to 'take a grip on yourself' since the book contained 'NOTHING' (Marx's own emphasis) on capital, one of the main topics that the author was supposed to be investigating in his economics research that Engels had partly funded. And this was even despite the fact that the first section of the book was entitled 'capital in general'.

In writing these words of warning, Marx was obviously concerned that Engels, and his general readers, might be disappointed by his initial efforts. But he need not have been, as the published output contained (in the preface) one of the most famous short descriptions of historical development ever to be written. But – hold on a minute – wasn't it supposed to be a work of economic theory that Marx was publishing, not one on the theory of history? Characteristically, when the time came to send the final manuscript to the publisher, he did not have the funds to pay for the postage, remarking wryly that no one who had previously written on money was so lacking in it. Would publication of this long-presaged volume provide the financial solace that was desperately required?

THE *CONTRIBUTION TO THE CRITIQUE OF POLITICAL ECONOMY*

The first published account of Marx's economic studies, issued in German in mid-1859, was modestly titled *A Contribution to the Critique of Political Economy*. Although Marx had written a draft manuscript that contained a wide-ranging discussion of many of his developed themes of investigation, he chose instead to publish a much shorter account of the topics of commodities and money alone, as a way of gently introducing the reader to his unique approach, and also of solving the problem of needing much more time to prepare a publishable version of the entire *Grundrisse*. Consequently the topic of capital itself was left for a future volume, which Marx had promised to complete at a brisk pace. Today the *Contribution to the Critique of Political Economy* is famous only for the preface it contained (a detailed account of this is given in the next chapter), where Marx provided a succinct and powerful presentation of his materialist conception of history, but in fact it constituted the first published step on the road to *Capital*, even though it contained no actual analysis of capital.

In some ways the *Contribution to the Critique* gave a more direct expression of Marx's basic ideas than was contained in *Capital*. For example, in 1859 Marx clearly articulated a real labour theory of exchange value. He wrote that 'the conversion of all commodities into labour time is no greater abstraction nor a less real process than the chemical reduction of all organic bodies to air'.[24] Ignoring the fact that this particular chemistry was mistaken, the meaning of the metaphor was clear: that the exchange value of commodities was directly determined by the labour time necessary to make them. In other ways the 1859 *Critique* was directly comparable to the first few sections of *Capital*, both starting with the seemingly innocuous idea that capitalism was characterised by an immense accumulation of commodities.

By the time of the preparation of the manuscript for the *Contribution to the Critique*, Marx's projected scheme for all of his economics research had changed. The structure of version two of Marx's proposed work on economics was given by him in 1859 as follows:

1) Capital
2) Landed Property

3) Wage Labour
4) The State
5) Foreign Trade
6) The World Market.

Comparing the five-part scheme from the *Grundrisse* (1857–8) with the six-part scheme presented above (1859), it is clear that Marx has removed the idea of investigating 'the characterisation of all types of society' and simplified the division of the basic elements of economic understanding that was to apply. It is this six-part division from 1859 that is the more well-known structure often reproduced by commentators today, but in fact it was only one in an ongoing procession of draft structures that Marx was to articulate in the latter part of his life, as the intellectual horizons in front of him shimmied over time.

Another significant feature of the *Contribution to the Critique* was that there was supposed to be a second volume being prepared in a relatively short period of time, in order to continue the analysis. The publisher duly waited to receive the completed manuscript from Marx through 1860 and 1861, but it never arrived. The final ignominy was the critical reception that the first part received. Far from the flights of criticism that Marx had expected for his 'devastating critique of bourgeois economics', it was in the main simply ignored. Even some of his friends admitted that they were disappointed by his first published effort in this field. Apparently this economic muck did not attract that much literary attention after all.

MARX ON LESS-DEVELOPED STATES

In this period of his life, Marx also wrote some shorter journalistic pieces on contemporary developments in less-developed countries such as Russia and India, which had some significance for his more general economic analysis. For example, in December 1858 he wrote an article entitled 'The Emancipation Question', in which he discussed Emperor Alexander II's efforts to liberate the Russian peasantry from serfdom. Marx was of course sceptical that the emancipation of the peasants was the real goal of the Russian government, and he suggested that the nobility would have to resist this development if they did not want to witness the great majority of their order subsequently being ruined. He related a previous example, that in Russia in 1847 the collective associ-ation of serfs attached to a particular estate had been allowed by law to buy this estate when it was first offered for sale. To the astonishment of both the Russian government and the nobility, this possibility was actu-ally taken up on one estate after another. In order to halt this unwanted development, in 1848 this right was extended to individual serfs, accord-ing to Marx on a 'divide and rule' strategy – in order to encourage the break-up of the associations that had enabled the serfs to pool their cap-ital together.[25]

However, the logic of this apparent act of sabotage was then contra-dicted by Marx's own suggestion later on in the same article that Russian peasants had no conception of individual landed property at all, as the village community governed all aspects of their lives communally. If this was indeed so, then individual serfs could never have conceived of buying an estate on their own in the first place, and the additional leg-islation in 1848 would have been superfluous. Marx concluded the article by predicting that the Imperial Central Committee's proposals for the abolition of peasant servitude, which were in fact highly restric-tive in both scope and timing, would be a signal for a tremendous conflagration amongst the rural population of Russia. He predicted omi-nously that, following a peasant political victory, 'the reign of terror of these half-Asiatic serfs will be something unequalled in history', but that following this dramatic turning point, 'real' civilisation would replace the 'sham' that had been introduced by Peter the Great.[26] This judgement implied that, as early as 1858, Marx had suggested that a peasant-based revolution in Russia might eventually produce progres-sive results.

Russia was not the only less-developed country to attract his atten-tion at this time. In a short article from September 1857, Marx asked the very pertinent question: what was the value of India to Great Britain from the economic point of view? His answer could be seen as quite star-tling. He answered that there was an overall deficit of financial receipts from India reaching Britain, compared with British expenditure on India, at least when viewed from the perspective of the British Treasury. The cost of maintaining the British military presence and pursuing related wars was very large, and the East India Company itself had accu-mulated a sizeable debt. Marx suggested instead that the advantages of

Indian occupation accrued to individual British citizens, either in terms of dividends on stocks held, or with respect to occupying positions in the India service and in receiving benefits from India-related trade.[27]

A year and a half later, in April 1859, Marx returned to this issue in more detail and provided some figures to back up his argument. He related that according to official accounts, the net deficit of expenses against revenue for Britain between 1836 and 1850 had amounted in total to £13,171,096, or to nearly £1 million per annum. In more recent times this deficit figure had increased to £9 million in 1857 and to £12 million in 1858. These sums had to be measured against net revenue, which (in the very last set of official accounts) amounted to £23.2 million, and against the cost of maintaining the British army in India, which was estimated at around £20 million per annum.[28] The obvious question that these figures raised was: if the British presence in India was so uneconomical, what did this signify for Marx's conception of the logic of capitalist expansion? Why were the British in India, if not to increase national profits? Marx did not answer this question in his journalistic writings, but it was very important to his general understanding of economic affairs.

There are a number of possible answers to the question. First, as Marx himself had suggested, the British presence in India was certainly profitable for some individuals, if not for Great Britain as a whole. But this does not satisfactorily fit with the fact that Marx conceived of capitalism as a mode of production with a general regularity to it, or as a structure with an underlying systemic logic. According to this view, if geographical expansion into any specific area was not profitable for capitalism as a whole, then it should not occur. A second possibility was that capitalists themselves had miscalculated when they began their expansion into India. But if this was so, then their miscalculations had continued for a very long time. A third possibility was that capitalists were looking to the very long run, to a period when British returns from India were estimated to increase substantially, thus justifying their earlier losses. But again, capitalists were (in Marx's view at least) notoriously short-sighted when it came to profit-and-loss calculations. How come they were taking the long view on India?

A fourth possibility was simply that Marx was wrong, that economic factors were not always the defining ones in explaining imperial expansion. Perhaps the British presence in India was motivated primarily by ideological rather than financial reasons, or to bringing 'civilisation' to the 'ignorant natives'. But if this was so, then it had very serious consequences for Marx's account of the internal logic of capitalist production. Moreover, these two journalistic pieces were written at a time (from 1857 to 1859) when his attention was well focused on his economic works, and hence the link between the two should have been easy for him to see. Was this a contradiction at the very heart of Marx's conception of capitalist expansion?

HERR VOGT

At the very end of the 1850s an event of great personal significance to Marx (but of little long-term relevance to his theoretical work) occupied much of his time for around a year and a half. This event was a very public and vituperative dispute with Karl Vogt, a politician and lecturer who had taken legal action against various accusations made against him that Marx was involved in repeating, such as that Vogt was funded from reactionary sources. Vogt then published a book that accused Marx of forgery and blackmail. In response Marx spent a great deal of effort gathering materials to refute these allegations, which he published in 1860 as a long book entitled *Herr Vogt*. The acidic language of this volume is quite startling even today, with the *Daily Telegraph* being described as 'the great papered central sewer' that spewed out articles fashioned from social filth. Despite its colourful style this book sold poorly, and Marx was left with a significant financial loss on his counter-polemical efforts, even though it was later revealed that Vogt had in fact received funding from the sources that were specified. Perhaps, in Marx's restricted financial circumstances, writing an article in refutation of Vogt's allegations might have been a more sensible choice than an entire book.

But to be fair to Marx, he attached great importance to refutations of slander against the proletarian cause, and he saw a conspiracy of reaction designed to discredit his ideas in the eyes of the working class. Vogt was also something of a Russophile, so Marx's critique of Vogt's politics linked into his more general analysis of European nationalist movements. In this regard *Herr Vogt* contained a 30-page account of the expansionist tendencies of Russian rulers over a number of years, and it warned that if Russian geo-political aims (which Vogt appeared to support) were not thwarted, then many proximate states were in danger of losing great swathes of territory. Marx wrote that: 'Vogt's 'principle of nationality' ... should according to *his* views prove its worth by the absorption of Polish nationality, the disappearance of Magyar nationality and vanishing of German nationality in – *Russia*'.[29]

Marx highlighted how, in Vogt's scheme of territorial revisions, Germany would lose East and West Prussia, Silesia, parts of Brandenburg and Saxony, the whole of Bohemia, Moravia, and the rest of Austria apart from Tyrol. The consequent strengthening of the Russian Empire that would flow from these changes was something that Marx was strongly against, so it is clear how an apparently minor legal dispute with Vogt took on much greater political significance in relation to Marx's socialist sensibilities. A less passionate revolutionary would have seen that, in the grand scheme of things, the balance of effort should remain on the more fundamental economic studies, but Marx's enthusiasm for dealing with the minutiae of struggle was an important part of his fiery character.

CONCLUSION

In re-engaging with 'the whole economic muck', Marx had begun on the path that would eventually produced *Capital*, sometimes referred to as the bible of the working class. But the contextual origins of this economics research were much more prosaic than the status of this sacred text is sometimes afforded by sympathisers. Its origins lay in Marx's economic understanding of the 1850s, which was to a large extent concerned also with political and national topics, as has been demonstrated in this chapter. Moreover, the exact nature of this projected economics research was not at this time fixed in stone. Rather, it was constantly developing as circumstances changed and as Marx's knowledge of the subject itself expanded through continuous study. Exactly what this knowledge consisted of, as revealed in the *Grundrisse*, is the subject of the next chapter.

6

'OUTLINES OF A CRITIQUE OF POLITICAL ECONOMY'

This chapter will examine in detail the draft manuscript of Marx's economics studies that was written in 1857–8, with regard to both aspects of the content of this work and the intellectual impetus behind it, before exploring his first published book on political economy. The draft manuscript, referred to as the *Grundrisse*, was divided into three basic parts: an introduction written in September 1857, a chapter on money written in October 1857, and a chapter on capital written between October 1857 and March 1858. There was also a short account of the ideas of two particular economists (Frederic Bastiat and Henry Carey) written in July 1857 that was often later included as part of the printed manuscript. This work articulated the first major results of Marx's economic studies of the 1850s.

However, the *Grundrisse* was not published in its complete German-language form until 1939–41, which meant that Russian Marxists had no opportunity to read it prior to the Bolshevik success in 1917. They could consult only the much shorter *A Contribution to the Critique of Political Economy*, published in 1859, as a guide to Marx's first concentrated effort to study political economy at the end of the 1850s. The first complete English-language translation of the *Grundrisse* appeared as late as in 1973, and made for a stark contrast with the concomitant era of Brezhnevite stagnation in the USSR.

The *Grundrisse* was a very important text for developments in Western Marxism, as it was the first post-1848 publication to illustrate a rather different Marx from that conventionally displayed within *Capital*. As will be seen from what follows, the methodology used was very much on show, whereas in *Capital* it was submerged to a much greater extent. Western Marxists in the 1970s hailed the *Grundrisse* as a revelation, and as a missing link between the early Marx of the 'Economic and Philosophical Manuscripts' and the later, more austere Marx of *Capital*. By implication, the austerity of Soviet communism was seen, in contrast to the inspiring visions of the early Marx, as only one possible result of implementing revolutionary socialist ideas.

THE BACKGROUND

In the early 1850s, Marx composed draft manuscripts on various monetary and financial issues as part of his evolving study of political economy. These were entitled 'The Money System as a Whole' (1851) and 'Money System, Credit System, Crises' (1854–5), but they were not meant for publication, only as a means to enable the process of self-education. The manuscript known today as the *Grundrisse* of 1857–8 was consequently designed to begin the process of bringing together the various individual studies that Marx had undertaken up until this date, within a framework that he had designed to highlight his own particular interpretation of the subject matter. This effort would constitute a rough draft of part of the series of books that he intended to produce on the essential nature of capitalism, and as a parallel critique of 'bourgeois' political economy.

In 1859 Marx himself identified three contextual factors that had advantaged the resumption of his economic studies earlier in the 1850s: the materials on the history of political economy held in the British Museum, the vantage point afforded by London for the observation of bourgeois society, and (perhaps more surprisingly) the discovery of gold in California and Australia, which had allowed a new stage of capitalism to develop.[1] Although on first sight the second factor (observing 'bourgeois' London) might appear as a very obvious one, in fact it was much less so, given that Marx's method of study did not involve much empirical fieldwork at all. It is true that his general travels around London would have brought him into contact with both rich and poor neighbourhoods, but he did not make any systematic first-hand study of them – as, for example, Engels had done as research for *The Condition of the Working Class in England*. Marx's knowledge of economic matters was drawn overwhelmingly from books and other written sources, not from personal experience, except perhaps what information he had absorbed second-hand from Engels.

The third factor that was listed as providing inspiration – the discovery of gold deposits in the New World – was perhaps the most puzzling of all. What effect could a period of monetary expansion have on Marx's resolve to make progress on his economic studies? He had seen that the discovery of gold in California in 1848 and Australia in 1851 had stimulated the colonisation of new geographical areas, and it had also given a boost to financial activities within capitalism. In this respect Marx outlined in the *Grundrisse* that, if the supply of gold increased even without a decline in its cost of production, then an expanding market was the result, which in turn produced an increase in trade. By implication, the heightened activity within capitalism following the new discoveries of gold had spurred Marx on with his theoretical work. Of course, as was outlined in the previous chapter, the very opposite was also the case – that the commercial distress that broke out in 1857 had bolstered his economics research. But as a philosopher Marx took the Hegelian form of reasoning very seriously, as the following account of the *Grundrisse* will conclusively demonstrate. Readers are warned at this point that there is no way of easing their introduction to the *Grundrisse*, other than to tackle it head-on.

THE INTRODUCTION

In the introduction, Marx examined the general relation between production and consumption as economic categories, and also between exchange and consumption. He conceived of them in philosophical terms as moments of a dual identity, or in terms of the mutual interpenetration of productive consumption and consumptive production. The following passage was indicative of the approach taken, and gives the flavour of his analysis:

> The direct unity, in which production coincides with consumption and con-
> sumption with production, allows their direct duality to persist ... Each is
> immediately its opposite. At the same time, however, a mediating movement
> takes place between the two. Production mediates consumption, for which it
> provides the material ... But consumption also mediates production, by pro-
> viding for the products the subject for whom they are products.[2]

Marx argued consequently that 'bourgeois' economists such as J. B. Say
could see only one side of this dual interrelationship, i.e. that production
equalled consumption. This was translated into Say's Law, a well-known
law in economics stating that supply created its own demand, which in
turn produced the idea that the general overproduction of commodities
was impossible. But since (in Hegelian logic) any two categories that
were identical were also necessarily opposites, Marx (but not Say) could
conceive of circumstances in which production and consumption were
the very opposite of identical, even when accepting that they were identical. Hence, general overproduction was indeed possible, and Say's Law
could (in certain instances) be violated. Empirical reality tended to support Marx on this point, as how else could the wide spectrum of economic
crises within capitalism be explained?

This approach was further developed as follows. Outlining the three-
fold nature of the posited identity of production and consumption, this
unity progressed in triadic form as follows:

1) Direct Identity, when production was directly consumption and
   vice versa (perhaps, in modern terminology, when all markets
   cleared).
2) Mutual Dependence, when each appeared as the means of the other,
   were indispensable to each other, but were still external to each
   other: for example, when consumption created needs as internal
   objects, or when production created materials for consumption (perhaps, in modern terminology, through creative advertising).
3) Mutual Creation, when each provided the other with its object, and
   created itself as the other: for example, when production was determined by the needs of consumption (perhaps, in modern terminology,
   in complementary goods).[3]

These three moments formed the Marxian sequence:

Direct Identity – Mutual Dependence – Mutual Creation

Within their Direct Identity, consumptive production and productive consumption were the terms employed interchangeably, indicating an immediate unity or exact match between production and consumption. Within their Mutual Dependence, a movement occurred through which they were brought into dual interrelation, but in which the possibility of disequilibrium was first allowed. Within their Mutual Creation, each completed the nature of the other by providing the means for their own realisation, through moving onwards again towards unity.

Expressed in this way, it is obvious that Marx was directly employing the form of the triadic progression (such as 'Being – Nothing – Becoming') to model the relation between production and consumption. Even the specific elements within the triad were themselves broken down into three parts. For example, the results of the production process (individual commodities) were constituted from Material, Instrument and Labour, which were given as the three moments of productive consumption. At this stage of the argument being formulated, the use of a Hegelian framework seemed to point backwards to the type of account found in the 'Economic and Philosophical Manuscripts' of 1844. However, Marx concluded his account of this topic thus:

> The result at which we arrive is, not that production, distribution, exchange and consumption are identical, but that they are all elements of a totality, differences within a unity ... A definite [mode of] production thus determines a definite [mode of] consumption, distribution, exchange and *definite relations of these different moments to one another*.[4]

In this passage Marx has widened the framework of analysis to situate the various different forms of the unity of production and consumption within his materialist conception of history, or in relation to the various sequential modes of production. Thus the particular form of the unity of consumption and production expressed itself differently in relation to the historical epoch in which it occurred (as according to the Hegelian triad of 'Universality – Particularity – Individuality'). At this point Marx was looking forwards to a more sophisticated historicised account of the categories of production, or the categories that were more conventionally employed in the economics literature. His economic theory was beginning to ripen into its mature form.

THE CHAPTER ON MONEY

The chapter on money in the *Grundrisse* contained one of the first detailed presentations of the circuits of capitalist production, or of money as a means of circulation of goods. Marx presented these circuits in schematic form as:

M (Money) – C (Commodity) – M (Money)

This diagrammatic model (M – C – M) constituted something that many readers might find immediately recognisable from their previous encounters with *Capital*. Here is how this idea was described on its initial presentation:

> ... circulation appears to be *simply a never-ending process* ... The commodity is exchanged for money; money is exchanged for the commodity ... But on closer examination, it reveals other phenomena as well: the phenomena of closing the circle or the return of the point of departure into itself ... The buyer becomes a seller again, and the seller again becomes a buyer. So each is placed in a dual and antithetical determination, and we have the living unity of both determinations.[5]

A few pages later Marx drew an explicit parallel with the cycle of life (Death – Life – Death), or the constant dissolution of the individual into the elemental and its vice versa, with the constant monetisation of commodities and its own vice versa. He also described each particular stage of the process of monetary circulation as 'moments of the movement' being considered. It is evident that the circuits that Marx invented to represent the movements inherent within capitalism were explicitly modelled on the movement of the categories of understanding as presented in Hegel's *Science of Logic*. The content of the economics being presented was of course very different in tone from the categories of dialectical logic, but it was the underlying structure of reasoning that Marx was employing. Put another way, Marx's own thought processes while writing the *Grundrisse* naturally transformed the economics content under consideration into patterns of reasoning that mimicked dialectical processes.

Another issue that was raised in this chapter was the function of money (as the universal equivalent) of providing a way of equating the essentially incommensurable, or of facilitating commensurability between commodities with very different properties. Marx's answer to the riddle of how a yard of cloth 'equalled' a loaf of bread (at least in terms of exchange value) was that they both contained the same amount of socially necessary labour time. But money was being used here as the universal equivalent or measure of this work expenditure. The *Grundrisse* also contained some historical materials on the use of precious metals as money that Marx had obtained from various authorities in the field, as well as an account of their physical properties, but his presentation of this topic was rambling and his conclusions were rather opaque. He noted various issues that he wanted to pursue further throughout the text, this being a characteristic feature of many of his rough drafts, but Marx's analysis of metallic currency was not the most original part of his output. He was (after all) still learning about these questions while composing the manuscript.

THE CHAPTER ON CAPITAL

The main focus of the chapter on capital was of course an understanding of capital, but Marx had a special approach that needs to be carefully formulated. He was particularly concerned to develop an exact presentation of the concept of capital as the fundamental concept of modern economics, and as the single basic category of capitalist production. He specified firstly the General concept of capital, secondly the Particularity of capital, and thirdly capital as money, which might reasonably be taken as the Individuality of money. He wrote:

> *Capital* is [the] *direct unity* of product and money or, better, of production and circulation. Thus it itself is again something *immediate*, and its development consists of positing and suspending itself as this unity – which is posited as a specific and therefore simple relation.[6]

If, in general, capital was the direct mediator between production and circulation, then it took various particular forms, such as industrial capital and mercantile capital, in specific circumstances. The former appeared as production; the latter as circulation; but then in turn, mercantile capital mediated between industrial capital and the consuming public. Hence each mediating pair led into other such interlinked dualities.

Examples of such pairs of categories that Marx presented in mediation were: commodity brokers and wholesalers, manufacturers and agriculturalists, and financiers and the state, each positing the other in itself. The exchange value concept (more commonly known as 'market price') employed by 'bourgeois' economists was then defined as the essential mediator between poles of all opposing categories, the ultimate measure that equated them each as one. Finally, within the concept of capital, the two poles into which it formed itself were consequently use value and exchange value; the latter being the monetary expression of the former. But (according to Marx) certain specific laws governed the determination of exchange value within capitalism, and hence differing movements between these two poles were possible.

It is apparent that this type of analysis of the categories of economics was very different from that conventionally presented by most economists. Without an understanding of Hegel's philosophical method, Marx's reasoning might easily appear to be very obtuse, even confused, and lacking in the sort of features that were usually expected from economic analysis. Even accepting the link to Hegel, some commentators have still evaluated Marx's first draft of his economic studies as often impenetrable, or at the least as contributing little of interest to strictly economic understanding. Here is where an understanding of Marx's basic goals in undertaking his economics research is crucial. He was not, in these early stages, trying to investigate economic theory within the same framework as that of most other economists; indeed he accepted that the originators of classical economics had made valuable contributions to the subject, which need not be repeated by other theorists. He had accused 'vulgar' political economists of exactly this unnecessary repetition.

In his own work, Marx was attempting something quite different, namely re-setting the framework of economic analysis to take account of various previously unrecognised but very significant elements, such as the relation between the categories of economics and historical development, and between economics and class tectonics. The classical economists had failed sufficiently to investigate such topics, and this imbalance consequently needed redressing. One such topic that Marx believed was central to economic analysis, but that had been neglected by classical thinkers, was the structure of social relations.

SOCIAL RELATIONS

In the chapter on capital from the *Grundrisse*, Marx focused his attention on the idea of social relations as being a key constituent of the economic structure in all the various modes of production that he had outlined. He wrote:

> Society is not merely an aggregate of individuals; it is the sum of the relations in which these individuals stand to each other ... Being a slave or a citizen is a socially determined relation between an individual A and an individual B.[7]

Society was seen here as the set of social relations between all individuals in a given place and time; the totality of the specific interactions among all citizens. This approach might be interpreted as somewhat different from the central idea of class tectonics, in which the ownership rights possessed by classes (as groups) determined the social structure. In fact Marx was approaching the same problem (how to define a social formation) from different angles, but there was indeed a difference of emphasis between the two.

At another point in the *Grundrisse*, Marx wrote of 'secondary and tertiary relations' and of 'derived and transmitted relations of production'.[8] The example given was of international relations, or of relations between nation states, which were here being conceived of as a secondary set of social relations that were built upon the primary set of relations of production. Hence by implication each particular mode of production had a primary set of relations (the economic base) and also a series of higher-order relations that were related to it. Other examples of these derived relations might be gender relations, cultural relations and so on. This is extrapolating a little from the text, but in this conception social relations between individuals were the primary constituent feature of every given society, and precisely how the various types of social relations were conditioned and interrelated defined the nature of the mode of production in question.

In the *Grundrisse*, Marx defined property as the relation of the working subject to the conditions of production and reproduction, and he listed the Asiatic, Slavonic, Ancient classical and Germanic forms of property.[9] But in some other works, a mode of production was defined in terms of the specific manner in which the surplus product was extracted from the exploited classes, or from the various subordinate gradations of rank. In this regard, the well-known Marxian concept of 'surplus value' made one of its first appearances in the *Grundrisse*, to signify a surplus quantity in excess of that which was legitimately purchased by the capitalist. Marx argued that surplus value signified:

> ... that the labour time objectified in the product ... is greater than that present in the original components of capital. Now this is possible only if the labour objectified in the price of labour is less than the living labour time which has been bought with it ... [T]he capitalist ... must receive more value than he has given.[10]

What this in effect meant was that workers were being paid less by capitalists for their labour time than it was actually worth. This notion of surplus value was a key part of an economic theory of exploitation, but a full discussion of this issue will be left for a later chapter, when a more developed version can be considered. In the *Grundrisse*, Marx was still working out the specific elements of his critique of the economic categories.

The question then arises of how this incomplete text can best be judged. It is well known that Marx had reported to Engels in a letter from January 1858 that a colleague had recently sent him some books, which included a copy of Hegel's *Logic*; this gift was evaluated by Marx as 'of great use' in developing the method he was using at the time. Of course Marx knew Hegel's method by heart from his university days, and he did not really need reminding of its nature or significance in 1858, nor would he even in 1878. The once-popular myth that Marx discarded Hegel some time in the mid-1840s is clearly erroneous, and the *Grundrisse* is the single most important piece of evidence that can be cited against this myth. However, Hegel provided only the method that was being used, not the subject matter being discussed. The latter was taken squarely from the existing authorities on political economy.

Moreover, it must be said that, for all the splattering of memorable passages and sporadic intellectual originality, the *Grundrisse* was really a 'halfway house' between the idealism of German philosophy and the analytical abstractions of British political economy. It represented Marx's search for an approach to the subject that went beyond his youthful interests, but he had not yet found a mature resting place. In his later works on economics, Marx would take the conscious decision to reduce substantially the amount of Hegelian reasoning that was apparent on the surface of the text, in part to facilitate reader understanding. But there was also the sense that, as Marx's intellect matured, the need to secure his newly acquired knowledge upon Hegelian scaffolding was felt less and less, and consequently the triadic progressions made much less of an appearance. This does not necessarily mean that Marx was discarding Hegel in the absolute sense, only that he became more comfortable within the subject of political economy in its own terms as his study of it developed over time.

THE PREFACE TO *A CONTRIBUTION TO A CRITIQUE*

Apart from brief political slogans such as 'workers of the world, unite!', the most famous passage on historical change that Marx published in his lifetime was arguably found in the preface to *A Contribution to a Critique of Political Economy* of 1859. Whole legions of interpretations have been published discussing what this passage actually meant, and how it connected with other areas of Marx's work. Here is the first part of the passage in question:

> In the social production of their life, men enter into definite relations that are indispensable and independent of their will, relations of production which correspond to a definite stage of development of their material productive forces. The sum total of these relations of production constitutes the economic structure of society, the real foundation, on which rises a legal and political superstructure and to which correspond definite forms of social consciousness.[11]

Here was presented an original model of the general structure of society (or of social formations), in which it was stated that the relations of production formed the foundation (or base), above which arose an ideological superstructure. The implication of this positioning was that the economic base of society 'determined' (in some as-yet-undefined sense) or 'created' the superstructure that was appropriate to it. Note especially, however, that the economic base was defined as being composed of the relations of production, not the forces of production. The latter were conventionally defined as the level of scientific understanding and technique, together with their concrete manifestation in existing plant and machinery.

The question naturally follows: were the relations of production within this base/superstructure model identical to the social relations that Marx had claimed in the *Grundrisse* were the key constituent features of social formations? It makes more sense to answer this question in the affirmative rather than the negative, although some nuances of difference might be detected on further examination. Marx continued to outline his model in the 1859 preface as follows:

> At a certain stage of their development, the material productive forces of society come into conflict with the existing relations of production ... From forms of development of the productive forces these relations turn into their fetters. Then begins an epoch of social revolution. With the change of the economic foundation the entire immense superstructure is more or less rapidly transformed ... No social order ever perishes before all the productive forces for which there is room in it have developed ...[12]

Here was presented a structured model of the causes of social revolution, which were seen as originating from a developing conflict between the forces and the relations of production, the latter being torn apart by the former as new technologies clashed with existing social structures. As examples, Marx mentioned the Asiatic, Ancient, feudal and bourgeois modes of production as social formations, and implied that the sequential changes from one such type of society to the next were the social revolutions between modes of production that were explained by his model.

Marx described this approach as being the 'guiding thread' of all his studies, and located its initial impetus in his earlier inversion of Hegel's idealism. This inversion produced the notion that all intellectual developments were rooted in the material conditions of life. Marx characterised this new approach as 'realistic historiography', as opposed to the 'idealistic historiography' that he suggested had been prevalent previously. As was seen in Chapter 2, an initial account of a version of the base/superstructure model could be found in 'The German Ideology' of 1845–6, so clearly it had been germinating for some considerable period of time. The version contained in the preface to *A Contribution to a Critique* is regarded today as by far the most famous formulation, but it was certainly not the only one that had been provided.

In *The Manifesto of the Communist Party* Marx and Engels had presented a somewhat different sequence of modes of production than was contained in the preface to *A Contribution to a Critique*, which was simply: slavery, feudalism and then capitalism. Between 1848 and 1859 Marx had apparently discovered (or at least highlighted) a new mode of production (the Asiatic), accepting that the 'Ancient' and the 'slave' modes were really the same. It is tempting to see the addition of the Asiatic mode as (in part) the consequence of Marx's detailed study of less-developed countries such as Russia and India, both in terms of their political significance and the nature of their economic systems, as was discussed in the previous chapter. Engels had added a footnote to the 1888 English edition of the *Manifesto* in which he added 'primitive communism' as the first mode of production in the sequence, but this was well after his co-author had died.

The *Grundrisse* itself contained a section on pre-capitalist economic formations, where Marx distinguished between Romanic, Germanic and Oriental forms of property and land ownership. In the Roman form, individuals possessed private property as an essential feature of their citizenship. In the Germanic form, part of the land belonged in collective form; the other part was individualised. In the Oriental form, property existed only as communal property. He also distinguished the history of Asiatic societies, which demonstrated an indifferent unity of town and countryside, from other European histories, in which cities formed the central focus.[13] Hence by 1859 Marx had come to accept that historical development had not been universal across all countries; instead he realised that variant sequences of modes of production had developed in different national territories. The consequences for socialist political strategy of this modification to the universal sequence presented in the 1848 *Manifesto* were large.

In a more conjectural hue, Marx confidently explained while present-ing his base/superstructure model in its 1859 version that the material transformation of the economic conditions of production, i.e. changes in the relations of production, could be determined 'with the precision of natural science'. This indicated that he believed that his model uncov-ered historical regularities that could be described in a similar manner to the laws of motion of physical bodies. Marx had explained on another occasion that, through his work on economics, he had been searching for the 'laws of motion' of capitalism – that is, the laws operating within a specific mode of production. But it is apparent that he was also search-ing for the more general 'laws of motion' of historical change, or the laws operating between and across all the different modes of production, and that he believed these laws were akin to those of the natural sciences. This task was a 'very big ask', to use a modern colloquialism, and showed that Marx had set his sights very high indeed with respects to the scope of his research on realistic historiography. The assumption of similarity between the regularities uncovered by the natural and social sciences would be tested to the limit (and beyond) in the twentieth century.

CONCLUSION

With the writing of the *Grundrisse* in 1857–8, Marx had at last made a serious effort to engage with the existing themes of 'bourgeois' political economy. But he did so by employing a quasi-philosophical approach that was clearly indebted to his Germanic roots, and by frequently filter-ing the normative judgements made by political economists through his own socialistic sensibilities. The result was no less (but also no more) biased than the original texts that he claimed were 'ideological tools of class oppression'. Thus in his economic analysis Marx had not discovered an ultimate point of neutrality from which to present the 'real truth' about capitalism, only a 'bias-in-opposite' that was the mirror image of the bias that he claimed permeated British political economy. When the two were added together, ultimate neutrality might be glimpsed.

It can now also be asked in evaluation, did production and consump-tion within market exchange really form a 'dialectical unity' that moved through the triadic progression: Direct Identity – Mutual Dependence – Mutual Creation? In Marx's mind they certainly did, but what about in an actual capitalist economy? The best answer is perhaps the pragmatist one, which would reformulate the question thus: can some additional understanding be gained by thinking about the issue in this way? The answer to this question is yes, certainly, for Marx, understanding was aided through this means, and also, for some others (but not all), extra insights could be obtained through mental exercises of this type. But this is not the same as saying that production and consumption really were 'poles of a negative unity'. The reality or otherwise of Hegel's philosophical method is ultimately in the eye of the beholder.

Regarding the significance of the theory of history that Marx had articulated in the preface to *A Contribution to a Critique of Political Economy*, this would go on to become one of his most debated theories within academic circles, and one with a significant amount of explanatory value. Many later scholars have employed it in their own research, and various specific historical events have been fruitfully analysed using it as a basis for understanding the dynamic forces involved. This is not the same as saying that it is ultimately 'correct', only that it has proved operationally useful, but this was still a significant achievement. Its relevance to articulating socialist political strategy was somewhat less successful, given the reality of the twentieth century taken as a whole.

7

AN IMMENSE ACCUMULATION
OF RESEARCH

With the composition of the *Grundrisse* and then the publication of the *Contribution to a Critique of Political Economy* in 1859, Marx had reached a watershed in his life, in that his aim of writing a multi-volume attack on 'bourgeois' economics was now beginning to reach fruition. However, although by 1860 he had already accumulated an immense amount of material as a result of many years of research, there was still a long way to go in fully absorbing, sorting through and arranging these materials for final publication. In addition, Marx never stopped the process of learning new subject areas and researching additional topics within the field of political economy widely interpreted. Hence, in the first half of the 1860s, he continued the process of gathering materials that might provide assistance to his long-term goals.

In political terms, the early 1860s were a period of upturn in the fortunes of the socialist movement, with an insurrection in Poland in 1863 and the defeat of slavery in the USA. In relation to these events in 1861, Marx and Engels had both written numerous journalistic articles on the American civil war, and in 1863 Marx devoted considerable time to studying Polish history and politics. In the mid-1860s he also devoted a significant amount of time to his role as a leading figure in the First International Working Men's Association, which was a successor (of sorts) to the defunct Communist League. In preparation for the formal creation of the First International in 1864, Marx composed an inaugural address and also a set of provisional rules for this association, which demonstrated clearly his views on the political organisation necessary in order to secure proletarian aims. In this period, therefore, continuing his more abstract research on economics topics was by no means the only possibility that was available, as this chapter will document, but work on *Capital* was certainly his main theoretical focus.

MANNA FROM HEAVEN

In the early 1860s Marx's daily life was just as difficult in financial terms as it had been throughout much of the 1850s. He kept creditors at bay by various improvised means such as pretending to be out of the house (or even the city), hiding in the British Museum, threatening to declare bankruptcy, borrowing from the usual sources, and frequent visits to the pawnshop. The final ignominy occurred in 1862 when Marx was forced by financial desperation to apply for a menial job in a railway office, but was rejected because of his illegible handwriting. This was akin to Thomas Chippendale being rejected from a job in forestry because of his poor logging skills.

Such financial problems occurred alongside various health issues. Jenny Marx had contracted smallpox in 1860, and although she survived this serious infection with the help of a nurse, the disease left some characteristic pockmarks and impaired hearing. At one point she confessed poignantly to her husband that she sometimes wished herself buried in the grave with their deceased children. Marx's famous carbuncles also began growing in stature in this period.

These hard times not only affected the Marx family, as in January 1863 Engels' long-time partner Mary Burns died; although they were never married, she had been his loyal companion for many years. Marx responded to the tragic news in a letter with a mere 22 brief words of solace, before embarking upon a long plea regarding his own financial difficulties. Engels was thoroughly distraught by Marx's apparent lack of sympathy, and cool letters were subsequently exchanged. This was the only instance where 'Team Marx' came close to splitting up, but the damage was soon repaired by Marx's apology, and an explanation that a landlord's representative was actually harassing him while he was writing the letter in question.

However, after years of suffering dire poverty and constant financial worries, first in 1863 and then again in 1864 the Marx family received two measures of what must have seemed to them like manna from heaven, or what more ordinarily would be called their inheritance. In the summer of 1863 Marx's mother died, and after travelling to Trier to deal with the necessary administrative details, he received around £1,000 as his share of the estate. Then, in the spring of 1864, his long-time friend Wilhelm Wolff died, leaving Marx around £900 in his will. These were far larger lump sums than he was used to receiving from Engels on any one occasion, and allowed his family some definite respite from chronic poverty.

Consequently they moved out of Grafton Terrace to a bigger detached house in nearby Maitland Park Road, where they were to stay for the next decade or so. It was in this dwelling that Marx would complete the final version of volume one of *Capital*. His study in Maitland Park Road has been described as follows:

> Opposite the window and on either side of the fireplace the walls were lined with bookcases filled with books and stacked up to the ceiling with newspapers and manuscripts. Opposite the fireplace on one side of the window were two tables piled up with papers, books and newspapers; in the middle of the room ... stood a small, plain desk (three foot by two) and a wooden armchair ...[1]

However, the increased spending necessitated by this move to a more salubrious house meant that Marx was very quickly forced to write to Engels for further financial assistance. On one occasion in October 1866, Engels responded ever-patiently to his closest friend's request for help by reporting that he was 'tickled by your naivety in having bills outstanding against you without knowing the amount', and then by settling the bill in question.[2] Old habits (even of the revolutionary kind) still died very hard.

At around the same time as receiving these financial windfalls, Marx was affected in a serious way by outbreaks of painful boils (or carbuncles, as they were known at the time) on various parts of his anatomy, which were in fact manifestations of the skin disease hidradenitis suppurativa, as described in Chapter 5. This affliction began in its more advanced form in the autumn of 1863 and continued, off and on, for some years;

sometimes the infestations were so bad and awkwardly positioned that the subject could not sit or lie down. Jenny Marx described dealing with one especially horrific outbreak on Karl's back through a visit to a doctor in November 1863 as follows:

> ... when the swelling was the size of my fist and the whole of his back misshapen, I went to Allen. Never shall I forget the man's expression when he saw that back ... Lenchen had to hold Karl while he made a deep, deep incision, a great gaping wound from which the blood came pouring out ... Then began a round of hot poultices, which we have now been applying night and day every 2 hours, like clockwork, for the past fortnight.[3]

Although most of the outbreaks were not of this degree in size or seriousness, the condition evidently consisted of more than just a few itchy spots.

Marx kept Engels up to date by letter about the varying positions of his bodily outbursts, and their effect on his daily life. For example, he wrote to Engels in November 1864:

> I have had to stay *in bed* for almost a week on account of the carbuncle. The thing is now *healing up*. However, as the carbuncle is just below the breast, I still have trouble leaning forward in order to write.[4]

As prescribed 'cures' of the day Marx took opium and arsenic, which (unsurprisingly) had little effect on the illness in question. He reported alarmingly to Engels in June 1866 that a whole bottle of his arsenic supply still remained, as he had not taken it for several weeks since it was incompatible with his lifestyle.[5] In terms of real relief, he claimed that the best medicine had actually been the claret periodically sent to him by Engels. On one desperate occasion Marx even operated on himself with a razor to remove the offending growth. When the boils appeared around his more private areas he responded in characteristic intellectual fashion by studying pornographic poems.

Marx famously cursed that the damn bourgeoisie would pay for his carbuncles through the revolutionary consequences of *Capital*: it might be a little unfair to add, possibly – but only if it was ever finished. Such a curse suggested what he believed to be the real cause of this ailment. In January 1868 he wrote in a letter despairing that his doctors were not even able to distinguish carbuncles from furuncles, which was doubly incongruous: '... particularly here in England, the land of carbuncles, which is essentially a proletarian disease!'.[6]

Given that hidradenitus suppurativa was a skin condition that could afflict anyone, not just the working classes and not just those in the UK, Marx's analysis of the origins of his disease was inaccurate (although no more so than that of his own doctors). Even more unfortunately, this skin complaint was not the only illness that Marx developed as the 1860s progressed. He also suffered from bouts of sciatica, insomnia, rheumatism and tonsillitis, each of which was not in any way life threatening on its own, but which when added to the periodic bouts of skin and liver problems made for a near-continuous conflagration of minor illnesses.

THE AMERICAN CIVIL WAR

In the early 1860s and continuing his long-standing interest in current affairs, Marx began to write journalistic accounts of aspects of the American civil war. He had never travelled to America in person, but 'Team Marx' had a previous connection in that they had both published articles in the *New York Daily Tribune*. The new American-focused work was also for publication in a newspaper in Vienna, and in this period the material prepared for the *Daily Tribune* by 'Team Marx' fell into steep decline in terms of volume. Marx's contributions to this particular newspaper came to a final end in March 1862, although they still continued to be supplied to other current affairs outlets.

In their writings on the American civil war Marx and Engels wholeheartedly supported the Northern cause, and they conceived of the war as a struggle in support of a system of free labour against a system of slavery.[7] On one occasion Marx described it as a conflict between the highest form of popular government ever realised and the most abject form of slavery ever recorded. Although he might here have been exaggerating a little for journalistic effect, he did hold some American leaders (such as Abraham Lincoln) in rather high regard, describing Lincoln on one occasion as a 'single-minded son of the working class'. Marx was enthusiastic towards what he saw as a 'purer' form of bourgeois government in America compared with that prevalent in some European states, although this was only so in relative terms.

By the idea of a 'system of free labour' that they favoured in America, Marx and Engels of course meant freedom in the capitalist sense, or liberation from forced bondage, not the ultimate freedom that was promised under socialism. In their view the Southern Confederacy, in pursuing the war, desired the extension and perpetuation of slavery, as it was an economic law that the territorial confinement of slavery within its existing limits would inevitably lead to its extinction. They wrote that:

> The cultivation of the Southern export crops, i.e. cotton, tobacco, sugar, etc., by slaves is only profitable so long as it is conducted on a mass scale by large gangs of slaves and in wide areas of naturally fertile soil requiring only simple labour. Intensive cultivation, which depends ... more on capital investment and on intelligent and energetic labour, runs contrary to the nature of slavery.[8]

Thus the idea that the slave system could survive while it was confined to a small region of America went counter to the economic logic of slavery itself. Marx and Engels were also careful to demonstrate that the Northern states had been forced to oppose slavery in order to maintain the Union, and to assist in developing American economic hegemony, not ultimately for any idealistic reasons.

One issue might be seen to arise naturally from this economic conception of the civil war, but was not really fully articulated in their journalistic writings. Marx and Engels had, at the time of the *Manifesto of the Communist Party* in 1848, seen the slave mode of production as one of the most distant in historical terms and as predominating in the era prior to feudalism, for example in Ancient Greece. In the early 1860s, when capitalism itself was beginning to break up in Europe (at least as Marx claimed was occurring), what was the slave mode of production doing still remaining in a large part of the USA, where capitalism had been transplanted directly by European settlers? And how could the slave mode be replaced by capitalism, as was apparently going to happen after a Northern victory, when in Marx's previously outlined historical schema the next mode of production to appear after slavery was feudalism? How could this apparent 'leapfrogging' and 'mixing' of modes of production have occurred? The answer was quite simple, but had very significant consequences for Marx's previously linear account of historical evolution.

The answer was that a plurality of paths of historical evolution was apparently possible, and hence that one part of the globe was not necessarily fated to follow exactly the same sequence of modes of production as another had taken before it. However, once a plurality of paths was allowed in principle, this might open the floodgates to a whole range of different modal sequences to exist. It might even be questioned whether socialism would follow on naturally and inevitably from capitalism, as Marx had claimed on numerous occasions. Why should it, if slavery could coexist with capitalism? In Marx and Engels' writings on the civil war, it was even suggested that there were individual states in America where the systems of slavery and free labour had existed side by side, which formed the actual battleground of the war.[9] Hence this coexistence of conflicting modes was seen to occur not only on a national level, but also on a regional one. Was it really possible for different modes of production to exist (or coexist) in one individual part of a nation? If so, what was the relation between them? Answers to these questions were not always immediately forthcoming from 'Team Marx's' journalism.

One possible retort to this presentation of the issue might be that the slavery that existed in America was not at all of the same nature as that found in the Ancient (slave) mode of production. If this was really what Marx and Engels meant, then it was never fully explained as such. In the absence of a specific instruction to the contrary, the term 'slavery' used in two different instances might easily be interpreted as referring to the same underlying reality. The political consequences of a shift from a linear to a multi-linear schema of historical development will be explored in more detail in later chapters.

THE FIRST INTERNATIONAL

The Communist League had fallen silent in 1852, and the rest of the 1850s were a period when revolutionary forces (or those of a socialist bent) were often in retreat. But in the early 1860s there had been a revival of left-wing activities across Europe, especially linked to various international issues such as the American civil war and Italian unification. Partly as a consequence of such developments, but also partly because of increased displays of unity between European workers, a meeting was arranged in September 1864 at St Martin's Hall, Long

Acre, in central London, to formally initiate an international association among union leaders to promote working-class issues. For this meeting Marx aimed to compose an account of Polish affairs, giving full vent to his characteristic Russophobia, but this manuscript was never completed. Instead at the meeting he was elected corresponding secretary for Germany and also co-opted to write (with others) a declaration of principles for the new International. After some adroit manoeuvring to remove unwanted influences, Marx alone was left to draft the declaration, and the result was the *Inaugural Address and Provisional Rules of the First International Working Men's Association*.

Together with the Communist League, participation in the First International was Marx's most important contribution to direct political organisation. Members of the International came from a diverse group of leftist currents including Chartists, Owenites and Proudhonites. There was thus a significant difference between these two rather loose and relatively open umbrella groupings, which were devoted to campaigning on working-class issues and to agitating in support of socialist ideas in an international context, and the idea of a secretive underground party, or a small cell of supremely dedicated professionals whose specific aim was to take state power in Marx's name by any means necessary. Marx himself would not have recognised this latter type of party, and he never in any period of his life attempted to create such a clandestine clique. His own political manoeuvrings were frequently exclusive, but they were not solely focused on achieving supreme governmental control for the party. Only after his death did the Leninist notion of the need for a tightly organised revolutionary party, governed by the iron will of its leader, gain much greater ascendancy within European Marxism.

This contrast between organisational types is apparent from even a brief examination of Marx's *Inaugural Address*. This contained firstly an empirical account of the horrendous conditions faced by the working masses in the UK, which according to the author had not improved at all between 1848 and 1864, and secondly a call for the working classes (plural) to conquer political power. The *Provisional Rules* began with the concomitant assertion that the emancipation of the working classes must be the act of the working classes themselves, i.e. not the result of a tiny revolutionary party allegedly acting in their names. Some parts of it even sounded distinctly conservative: '... this International Association and all societies and individuals adhering to it, will acknowledge truth,

justice and morality, as the basis of their conduct towards each other ...
No rights without duties, no duties without rights ...'.[10]

The complete liberation of the working classes in an economic sense
was the ultimate goal, but in terms of its specific organisational purpose
the International's aim was to foster communication and cooperation
between working men's societies in different countries. As was com-
monplace for Marx in this period, the *Inaugural Address* also contained
reference to a 'barbarous power' (Russia) whose hands were (apparently)
in every cabinet of Europe, and he warned the working classes to master
the mysteries of international relations and to watch carefully the diplomatic acts of their respective governments. How they might find the
time or the energy for such intricacies, given that (as Marx outlined in
this very document) many workers were often subsisting on near-starva-
tion diets and labouring for very long hours, was not fully explained.

Despite such unrealistic suggestions, the First International developed in a relatively successful way in the years immediately following its
creation. For example, it assisted in various industrial disputes on the
side of workers, helped to prevent the use of non-recognised labour in
certain areas, and succeeded in attracting applications to join the
International from numerous unions and other left-leaning political
organisations. By April 1865 there were, on one estimate, around 12,000
members in the UK alone. Marx's individual role in all of this was significant, and in the mid-1860s he spent much of his time on International
affairs; he soon became the de facto leader. Thus, simultaneously with
his attempt to prepare *Capital* for publication, and suffering from various illnesses and ongoing financial difficulties, he was actively involved
in political organisation in support of working-class policies. These were
of course those working-class policies that Marx and his fellow
Internationalists favoured, but it would be a very harsh conclusion to
suggest that this grouping had provided no genuine assistance to the
working-class cause in any way at all.

However, by 1867 the progress of the International in the UK was
slowing, although in other European countries such as France and
Germany it was still proving successful. The height of its influence was
probably around the time of a congress of the International held in Basle
in 1869, where a resolution on the nationalisation of land was adopted.
Marx in the main tolerated the various different leftist currents within
the International, although conflicts over strategy did periodically arise.

One particular conflict developed with Proudhonists regarding the Polish question, which tapped into Marx's enduring hostility towards Russia, but the unimportance of narrow party politics to Marx at this time was apparent from a speech he delivered to a trade union audience: 'It is in the trade unions that workers educate themselves and become socialists ... Any political party, whatever its nature and without exception, can only hold the enthusiasm of the masses for a short time, momentarily ...'.[11]

After 1870 the International, which was not any type of political party, fell into decline, in part due to an association with the Paris Commune of 1871. These developments will be considered in more detail in later chapters.

THE PUBLICATION OF VOLUME ONE OF *CAPITAL*

As will be explored in detail in the following chapter, by the mid-1860s Marx had composed three substantial draft versions of *Capital*, from which a final version for publication could ultimately be distilled. This proved sufficient even for his restless mind, and in March 1865 an agreement with the German publisher Otto Meissner was made to print the outcome of Marx's economic studies. By February 1866 the author had reluctantly accepted the need to finish volume one and publish it alone, before the other volumes were completed. Finally realising the Herculean task of preparing various volumes for publication all at once, and feeling the pressure of a publisher's deadline, Marx had relented to the practicalities of the situation. A detailed discussion of the content of volume one will be provided in the next chapter.

The final manuscript was ready by April 1867, and Marx travelled to Hamburg to deliver it to the publisher in person, as usual with some necessary financial support from Engels. The author proudly described his forthcoming book at this time as 'the most terrible missile that has ever been hurled at the head of the bourgeoisie', apparently even trumping *The Manifesto of the Communist Party*. While in Germany Marx found the time to stay with Ludwig Kugelmann, a gynaecologist by profession and a socialist by inclination, and he described this brief period of respite as one of the most pleasant oases in the desert of life: he was probably experiencing the scholarly equivalent of post-coital release. The proofs began to appear in May, but Marx returned to England before this checking process was complete. He therefore continued to receive the proofs when he was back in London, the final pages being returned in August.

Marx wrote accurately to Engels that without his friend's continued sacrifices he would not have been able to complete this work. He thanked Engels very sincerely for all his efforts and then dedicated the book to Wilhelm Wolff, 'faithful champion of the proletarian cause'. It was receiving Wolff's inheritance in 1864 that had helped Marx to finish volume one, although in truth Engels had given much more (both financially and intellectually) over a longer period of time. The final result was published, in rather quick time, in September 1867, with 1,000 copies printed. The grandiloquent title was: *Das Kapital: Kritik der politischen Oekonomie, Erster Band, Buch 1: Der Produktionsprocess des Kapitals*, or in translation: *Capital: A Critique of Political Economy, Volume 1, Book 1: The Process of Capitalist Production*. Today this book is a relatively scarce title, but copies do appear quite regularly in booksellers' catalogues, priced at anything up to £25,000, which is much less than the price of a first edition of the *Manifesto*.

It must be said that international capitalism did not even begin to collapse on the issue of this publication, nor did the bourgeoisie tremble uncontrollably at the thought of it being read by workers. Indeed, the final paragraph of the book was rather muted, and simply pointed out that capitalism was based on the expropriation of the labourer from the means of production. There was never a real issue with censorship, and, given the political aims of the author, the immediate critical reception was relatively mild. The 'most terrible missile' appeared initially to produce only a puff of light powder, but first appearances can sometimes be deceptive. Engels worked hard to publicise the book in various reviews, and some of these appeared in print, but it was certainly a slow burner. It took fifty years for a nation state to come into being professing adherence to the book's principles, which, although undoubtedly a very significant achievement in political terms, was far longer than Marx himself had hoped or predicted. And, as the author himself later judged, the financial rewards from the book's issue were not enough to pay for the cigars that he had smoked while writing it. But of course this was not the real reason why it had been written.

One of the more unusual initial responses to volume one came from Ferdinand Freiligrath, a long-standing friend of Marx from the revolutionary days of 1848 who had later taken a job in a London bank.

On receiving a complimentary copy direct from the author, Freiligrath judged it as a sort of guidebook for merchants and manufacturers, reporting that many businessmen in the Rhineland were enthusiastic about it.[12] Whether this was quite the sort of enthusiasm that Marx had aimed to encourage is debatable, but from the position of the capitalist it might be possible to use the book to assist in increasing the amount of surplus value that was extracted from workers, as the mechanism of extraction had (apparently) been laid bare. The intended subversion of capitalism might itself be subverted.

What intellectual influences did Marx himself admit on *Capital* in the early 1860s? In January 1862 he had written in a letter that: 'Darwin's book is very important and serves me as a natural-scientific basis for the class struggle in history'.[13] The book in question was Charles Darwin's *The Origin of Species by Means of Natural Selection*, which was first published in 1859. It would turn out to be one of the most important books written by anyone in the nineteenth century. As an avid follower of new scientific developments, Marx had read Darwin keenly, and was only disappointed in the 'crude English method' that was employed. In another letter from a later date, Marx commented more sceptically that: 'It is remarkable how Darwin recognizes among beasts and plants his English society with its division of labour, competition ... and the Malthusian "struggle for existence"', the implication being that Darwin had projected capitalist social relations on to the natural world.[14] Ever since it was first proposed, the theory of natural selection has proved extremely controversial in left-wing circles, as it seemed to give credence to the (heartless) idea of the survival of the fittest, but Marx's early embrace of Darwin as support for his own approach has raised only sporadic comment.

The fact that Marx had travelled to Germany with the manuscript of *Capital* in person indirectly raises a question that is little considered by most commentators. Why did he choose to publish *Capital* first in German, given that an English edition would have reached a larger market (including North America) and would have been accessible to the workers in a country (Britain) that was considered more advanced in political terms than Germany? Although the title page of volume one also bore the imprint of a publisher in New York (L. W. Schmidt), this only related to the same German-language printing. By 1867 Marx's command of English was very good, given that he had been living in London for a number of years, and even before this his language skills were generally excellent. One part of the answer was that in practical terms it was easier to find a German publisher willing to publish such a specialised book, as most of Marx's previous works had been issued in German, but was there an additional factor at work also?

Marx had conceived of *Capital* in the intellectual tradition of system-building German philosophers such as Immanuel Kant and his own youthful mentor Hegel, not in the British empiricist tradition. Kant especially was famous for his trilogy of *Critiques* – of *Pure Reason*, of *Practical Reason* and of *Judgement*. In November 1867 Marx even referred to volume one of *Capital* as the 'first attempt at applying the *dialectical method* to Political Economy'.[15] Rather like philosophers from past eras who favoured Latin over the vernacular, did the author still have some intellectual loyalty to the traditions of his homeland? In fact, volume one was rather an eclectic mix of the two philosophical currents, as it opened with the more theoretical chapters on value and surplus value, where a commodity was seen as 'full of metaphysical subtleties and theological tricks', but then turned to a more empirical account of labour conditions and the working day. It was almost as if Marx was trying to synthesize German idealism with British empiricism as the first two moments of a triadic progression.

It should also be stressed that, despite possessing a reputation for being difficult for many readers to engage with, volume one of *Capital* is actually very well written and clearly presented, especially when it is considered as the first part of an incomplete trilogy. Its political sympathies were much more angular, with the continuous expression of hatred and contempt for people who (by absolutely no fault of their own) were born into political classes deemed 'reactionary'. In truth it is probably this element that has turned many readers away, as the writing style itself is very enlivening, but perhaps this polarising reaction was what Marx would have wanted. *Capital* might be said to be like the sandwich spread Marmite: most people either love it or loathe it. The author was no political compromiser after all.

LIFE AFTER VOLUME ONE

With the publication of volume one of *Capital* in September 1867, a major part of Marx's economics research was now seeing the light of day, after years of being locked away in the dark of near-illegible draft manuscripts. In April 1867 Marx responded to an enquiry from a member of the First International in a letter that revealed how much he believed he had given to this book in personal terms:

> Why I never answered you? Because I was perpetually hovering on the verge of the grave. Therefore I had to use every moment in which I was capable of work in order that I might finish the task to which I have sacrificed my health, my happiness in life and my family.[16]

The notion that he had sacrificed any modicum of happiness and all aspects of his family life to *Capital* was certainly an exaggeration, but he had unquestionably brought great difficulties on his close relatives and had lost some degree of potential happiness, in comparison with a husband and father who had held a steady job throughout his adult life. But on the other hand, for Marx at least there had been compensations in terms of the intellectual interests that he had been able to explore and the prestige that his writings brought to him and also his family, at least among socialist sympathisers. With the publication of volume one, this political prestige might be expected to grow even more.

In June 1867 Marx had sent to Engels some of the proofs of volume one, requesting Engels' advice about helping to popularise aspects of the book dealing with the concept of value. Engels' reply was quite revealing about the underlying structure of this work even as late as 1867, in the fourth and final draft:

> In these more abstract developments you have committed the great mistake of not making the sequence of thought clear ... You ought to have dealt with this part in the manner of Hegel's Encyclopaedia, with short paragraphs, every dialectical transition marked by a special heading ...[17]

First, it might be a little surprising that Engels dared to describe Marx's actual account as a 'great mistake'. Second, Engels was directly criticising Marx for being insufficiently Hegelian in his mode of presentation. This might also be surprising, as Marx has sometimes been regarded as a more devoted follower of Hegel's 'dialectical transitions' than Engels, especially with respect to the subject matter of political economy. In truth both Marx and Engels readily understood that *Capital* was rooted in the long tradition of German philosophy, even if its budding flowers were in the form of British economic history. Third, it is apparent that Engels had not read the final completed manuscript of volume one before the proofing stage, although Marx had corresponded regularly with Engels on specific matters as he was writing.

Another more personal matter that developed as Marx was feverishly trying to complete and then publish volume one was that his second daughter Laura had become engaged to a medical student, Paul Lafargue, in August 1866, and they were subsequently married in 1868. Lafargue was born in Cuba but later raised in France, and after the marriage he quickly assumed the role of a loyal son-in-law to Marx. But the courtship was protracted, and involved Marx investigating Lafargue (whom he sometimes referred to affectionately as 'my medical Creole', but then less so as 'a gorilla offspring' and 'Negrillo') by writing to a Parisian professor for a character reference. He then wrote a letter of warning to Laura's potential suitor, admonishing him not to become overwhelmed by 'unconstrained passion and manifestations of premature familiarity' in respect of his daughter, and asking for clarification about his financial position.[18] Declaring himself 'an avowed realist' on such matters, Marx warned Lafargue not to 'make poetry to the detriment of my child', by which he meant not to idle away their future on loss-making pipe dreams[19] – such as *Capital*: Marx was the first to admit the comparison.

The Marx family was, however, eventually won over to the prospective pairing, especially after it was revealed that Lafargue's parents had promised him a large sum on marriage. Their later good friendship was clear from a letter that Marx wrote to Lafargue's father in November 1866:

> My sincere thanks for the wine. Being myself from a wine-growing region, and former owner of a vineyard, I know a good wine when I come across one. I even incline somewhat to old Luther's view that a man who does not love wine will never be good for anything.[20]

Marx was referring to his father's small vineyard in the Mosel area, and he ended the letter by requesting some photographs of the Lafargue family. However, the courtship between Laura Marx and Paul Lafargue appeared, at least to many outside observers, as thoroughly 'bourgeois' in manner and execution.

Other details of Marx's personal affairs from the mid-1860s throw additional light on to his maturing character. Despite the family's continuous financial difficulties, in 1864 Marx's daughters organised a ball for fifty of their friends, following a long-standing tradition of English high-society life. Marx argued in his defence to Engels about his constant overspending that for his own household 'a purely proletarian set-up would be unsuitable' and would not enable his children to make the appropriate connections and relationships. Marx also advised Engels on investing money in the stock market in various instances, claiming to have made £400 on one occasion for himself. And once, in 1865, Marx travelled to Manchester to visit his closest friend but found him out fox hunting for the day.[21] Finally, in 1867, Marx was proposed as a constable of the vestry of St Pancras, a respected position in the area that might cement his family's 'bourgeois' status: he replied to an acquaintance that those making the offer should 'kiss me on the arse'.[22] It is unlikely that either party accepted this offer, especially given the location of some of Marx's ripening boils.

CONCLUSION

With the completion of volume one of *Capital* in 1867, Marx could genuinely claim to have finally made a substantial contribution to political economy with the composition of an enduring semi-polemical classic, even though this was the only volume of the work that was actually completed in his lifetime. The book could be described as economic theory written entirely from the perspective of the working classes, with the concomitant dismissal of all owners of business enterprises as inhuman vampires that sucked the lifeblood out of the proletariat, and with the middle classes being very much ignored (perhaps in small part because Marx was trying his hardest to live such a middle-class life himself). In fact it could reasonably be maintained that the hateful attitude to capitalists found in *Capital* mirrored exactly the attitude that the author claimed capitalists propagated towards workers, i.e. totally dehumanisation. Indeed, at one point Marx positively emphasised that he had dealt with classes within capitalism only as abstract categories, as representations of human atoms within a social matrix.

But here he was really playing a political trick (perhaps without even realising it himself), since volume one of *Capital* was replete with empirical facts that were designed to evoke sympathy in the reader for workers and respect for the dignity with which they bore their suffering, and disgust towards their employers, who were presented only as an economic caricature. Above all *Capital* was really a moral condemnation of capitalism, of how degrading it was to most of its occupants, and of how limiting it was to human development. Marx claimed that in it he had proved scientifically that workers were exploited by capital, but scientific techniques cannot be used to substantiate moral judgements. What exactly was substantiated in volume one of *Capital* is the subject of the next chapter.

8

VOLUME ONE OF
CAPITAL

Apart from *The Manifesto of the Communist Party*, *Capital* is probably Marx's most famous published output. It is one of those books that even today sharply divides critical opinion into fanatical supporters, impassioned opponents, and also those who don't care to think about it at all, which makes an objective analysis more difficult to present than usual. Volume one of this work certainly constituted the intellectual pinnacle of Marx's scholarly achievements. Most of the professional efforts of Marx's adult life before its publication were (in one way or another) devoted to securing its successful completion, despite his own disparaging comments about the unimportance of 'the whole economic muck'. But, as will be explained in this chapter and in those that follow, the author never did finally complete the work in the way that he had originally wanted to.

As has already been noted, in the first half of the 1860s Marx drafted various manuscripts that had a specific relation to what was eventually published as volume one of *Capital* in 1867. A detailed discussion of the actual content of this work considered as economic theory will be provided in the latter parts of this chapter, but first it is necessary to be clear about the sequential relationship between the various draft versions of what eventually became the first of three separately issued books. An account of this issue is provided below.

'Marx as a student in 1836';
Collection International Institute of Social History, Amsterdam

'The proponent of dialectical logic, G.W.F. Hegel'
Photo by FPG/Hulton Archive/Getty Images

'Marx's wife Jenny von Westphalen'
Collection International Institute of Social History, Amsterdam

'Marx with Engels and his three daughters'
Collection International Institute of Social History, Amsterdam

Das Kapital.

Kritik der politischen Oekonomie.

Von

Karl Marx.

Erster Band.

Buch I: Der Produktionsprocess des Kapitals.

Hamburg

Verlag von Otto Meissner.

1867.

New-York: L. W. Schmidt. 24 Barclay-Street.

'Marx at the height of his intellectual powers in 1867'
Collection International Institute of Social History, Amsterdam

'Marx's sometime co-author and life-long friend, Friedrich Engels'
Photo by Time Life Pictures/Mansell/Time Life Pictures/Getty Images

'The last known photograph of Marx in 1882'
Collection International Institute of Social History, Amsterdam

'An imposing statue of Marx symbolising his status as a heroic visionary'
AFP/Getty Images

THE DRAFTS OF VOLUME ONE OF *CAPITAL*

In addition to problems associated with its politically charged significance, *Capital* is a difficult work effectively to deconstruct, in that it was composed from numerous parts. First, it was (eventually) divided into three main volumes, and in one commonly issued version these volumes contained over 800, 600 and 1,000 pages respectively. But then volumes one and three were sometimes issued in two parts, and a so-called fourth volume (itself in three volumes) was later produced. To add to the confusion, there were three previous draft versions of major parts of *Capital*, prepared before volume one was published, much of which still survives today in manuscript form. And as the icing on the cake, apart from the three main volumes, which were published in the correct sequence over 27 years, the various other volumes appeared in print rather haphazardly over an even longer period of time, not always in any particular order.

To actually read through all these volumes is a major commitment of anyone's time, and, rather like the near-mythical person cited by one well-known economist who had actually read every word of Adam Smith's *Wealth of Nations*, the individual who has read *all* of the various versions and volumes of *Capital* is a very rare bird indeed. To complete the comparison, Smith's *Wealth of Nations* is a mere two long volumes. All the drafts and volumes of *Capital* add up (on one estimate) to ten substantial volumes. However, far from being a distraction from the content of *Capital*, the precise relationship between these changes and progressions in all the different versions of *Capital* can fruitfully be used as an important key to understanding the author's evolving aims. Put another way, the writing of Marx's main economics output had a complicated generative history that is important to understand if the changing content of the various volumes of this study is to be clearly comprehended.

Today this protracted history is much easier to understand than it was at the end of the nineteenth century, as there now exists an excellent multi-volume edition of Marx's voluminous works in English (containing both published versions and many of the drafts) that was prepared by Lawrence and Wishart. The following is the conventionally agreed order of composition. What is often referred to as the first version (or rough draft) of *Capital* was the economic manuscript that Marx wrote in

1857–8, which was divided into two basic parts – the first on money and the second on capital. This manuscript is known today as the *Grundrisse*, and it was discussed in some detail in Chapter 6.

What is often referred to as the second version (or rough draft) of *Capital* was the economic manuscript that Marx wrote in 1861–3, entitled 'A Contribution to the Critique of Political Economy', but which should not be confused with the 1859 book published with a very similar-sounding title. This draft manuscript, actually the proposed second part of the 1859 book that was never completed, contained a substantial section headed 'Capital in General', and then a very long discussion of the history of political economy. This historical part was eventually issued as the so-called fourth volume of *Capital* with the general title *Theories of Surplus Value*, itself first published in three volumes between 1905 and 1910. These historical volumes were written *before* the final draft of volume one of *Capital* was published or completed. Marx had of course devoted a lot of effort to analysing and criticising the work of previous economists, as at one point he had even wanted to write a *History of Political Economy* as the main focus of his efforts, but eventually this became supplementary material to *Capital*, or the history of the theory that was involved.

The third draft version of *Capital* was written in 1863–4 and this manuscript is now mostly lost, although one section of it, entitled 'Results of the Immediate Process of Production', has survived fully intact, together with various assorted fragments. The surviving section was divided into three parts: a discussion of commodities, an account of the production of surplus value, and an analysis of capitalist relations of production. Again, as with the *Grundrisse* (or first draft), this partial third draft was not published until well into the twentieth century.

The fourth version of *Capital* was the final version that was published by Marx in German in 1867, and this issue counts as the true first edition of volume one. However, the final decision as to what was included and what was excluded from the published version of volume one was not made until quite late in the day, at least relative to the number of years that had been spent on researching the book, with the author's incessant revisions continuing close to the manuscript submission date. Moreover, the story of the textual history of volume one of *Capital* in no way ended there, as Marx himself (and later Engels also) made some significant changes to the published versions of this work as it was re-issued and translated into other languages. This will be the subject of later chapters.

Obviously, as described above, there was much overlap and some repetition across the various versions of *Capital*, which was to be expected, but there were also some important differences. It also needs to be emphasised that the first three draft versions, outlined above, contained materials relevant to all three proposed volumes of *Capital*, not just to volume one. It was certainly true that not all the material that was projected to be used in later volumes was present in each draft version, but much of it certainly was. The decision to publish volume one separately, before the other continuing volumes were finished, was taken relatively late in the sequence of events being considered here.

It might be asked, therefore, why Marx did not from the very beginning simply concentrate on preparing the first volume of *Capital* only, i.e. draft and then polish the manuscript of this volume, and have it published, *before* proceeding to pursue work on topics from proposed later volumes? The answer was provided in a letter from Marx to Engels in July 1865:

> Now, regarding my work, I will tell you the plain truth about it ... I cannot bring myself to send anything off until I have the whole thing in front of me. Whatever shortcomings they may have, the advantage of my writings is that they are an artistic whole, and this can only be achieved through my practice of never having things printed until I have them in front of me *in their entirety*.[1]

It was not any type of error that Marx referred to *Capital* in this letter in terms of 'an artistic whole' rather than 'a scholarly whole' or something similar. *Capital* was designed like a cycle of novels or a series of narrative paintings, to relate the theory and history (or life story) of capitalist production over many centuries, with its form being just as important to the underlying message as its content.

It should be emphasised that this was for a long time Marx's *intention*, but since volumes two and three were still incomplete at the time of his death, the cycle was never completed by its true progenitor. Engels attempted to finish it by publishing the existing incomplete drafts of volumes two and three after Marx had died, but whether the author would have been entirely satisfied by how this was done will never be known. In a letter to Engels in February 1866, Marx commented about the existing version of volume one of *Capital* that: 'Although finished, the manuscript, gigantic in its present form, could not be prepared for publication by anyone but myself, not even by you'.[2]

Marx was not being in any way disrespectful to Engels in expressing this judgement, as both the structure and content of *Capital* as a whole was so complex that only someone who had followed every inflection of the endless revisions that Marx had made over many years could piece the jigsaw puzzle together. And, as was indicated in the previous chapter, Marx did not even show Engels the final version of volume one before it was delivered to the publisher, let alone all the numerous modifications.

What is known for sure concerning all the three volumes of *Capital* is that volume one was published in 1867, and that Marx had drafted at least some major parts of volumes two and three even before volume one was published. But Marx did not die until 1883, i.e. he still had 16 years remaining in which to complete the final manuscripts of volumes two and three, if he really wanted to. Yet he did not do so. And moreover, despite Marx's own warning that Engels would not be able to do justice to *Capital* using only a draft manuscript, Engels proceeded to publish volumes two and three as complete texts after Marx's death. It was true that Marx's written warning applied only to volume one, and that if anyone could finish *Capital* it was definitely Engels, but volumes two and three as eventually issued certainly did not have the final polish that Marx could have imparted to them, nor (arguably) did they satisfactorily complete the narrative cycle as he would have wanted them to. And this was not necessarily due to any editorial insufficiencies on Engels' part.

Why Marx failed to complete the 'artistic whole' of his economics research in the remaining period of his life is certainly the most significant mystery of his entire published output, and arguably of his whole political legacy. Illnesses and assorted difficult financial circumstances undoubtedly played a part, but whether this was the whole story will be investigated further in the rest of this book. Might there have been any *intellectual* reasons for Marx's inability to finish his magnum opus? This is a question that those with only sympathy towards Marx, and not the required sympathy plus hostility in harmonic balance, have been reluctant to ask.

THE SECOND DRAFT OF *CAPITAL*

As was explained previously, Marx wrote a second draft of *Capital* in manuscript form between 1861 and 1863, and this needs to be considered first of all in comparison with the *Grundrisse*. One of the biggest differences in approach was that, at least in relation to the historical part of the second draft, the language was somewhat less Hegelian than in the first draft. There were still some passages that contained use of the dialectical method, as will later be demonstrated, but they were rather more sporadic than in the *Grundrisse*. Put another way, the straight economics content was more often to the fore in the second draft than in the first.

The title that was later given to the historical sections of the second draft – *Theories of Surplus Value* – needs to be further explained. Marx used the term 'surplus value' as a more general term for profit, rent and sometimes interest, and hence the so-called fourth volume of *Capital* was really a historical account of the notions of profit and rent as previous theorists had propagated them. This sequential account began with the French physiocrats (such as Francois Quesnay), whom Marx evaluated as the true fathers of modern political economy, before presenting substantial sections on Adam Smith and David Ricardo. Interspersed were shorter accounts of other figures such as T. R. Malthus and J. K. Rodbertus. The published text as it now stands is not fully complete or polished, as the author did not prepare it for publication in his lifetime, but it often makes for easier (or more conventional) reading than the *Grundrisse*.

In theoretical terms Marx outlined that surplus value was an amount of labour that was being supplied to capitalists, but for which the workers providing it were not being paid. As he explained in the first theoretical part of the second draft: 'Surplus value *is* nothing but the excess labour provided by the worker over and above the quantity of objectified labour he has received in his own wage as the value of his labour capacity'.[3]

Hence, surplus value was basically organised theft. Previous economists had sometimes explained surplus value as being of physical rather than of human origin. For example, some had argued that it was a universal gift of nature, rather than the consequence of a certain set of social relations. In this view, profit arose naturally from the bounty of the soil instead of from the organised labour of workers. Marx emphasised the apologetic nature of this conception of surplus value, which in his view merely naturalised a historically specific system of production.[4] He also (at some points in the text) dismissed completely the idea that profit was either a legitimate reward for hazarding capital in production (entrepreneurial risk) or a payment for the supervision of manufacture (management capacity). In this view only the labour of the working class could create value, and hence by implication capitalists or managers deserved no reward for their efforts at all.

However, at other points in the same text Marx suggested something different, that the capitalist's labour of superintendence should be considered as constituting wages, albeit wage-work that was undertaken in relation to their own capital.[5] The implication of this idea was that capitalists did deserve some financial reward for their management efforts, although it would be much less than the full portion that usually accrued to them as profit. Even so, the normative judgement that capitalists were 'exploiting' workers by extracting some amount of surplus value free of charge applied to both of these cases.

In developing the idea of surplus value, Marx's aim was to prove scientifically that capitalists appropriated some part of the workers' labour without paying for it. In order to do this he employed algebraic formulae to represent the quantitative units involved; these techniques will be discussed in more detail in the following chapter. But it is clear that Marx had already come to a very definite conception of surplus value, and its historical precedents, in the rough manuscript of 1861–3. The first public presentation of this concept came in 1865 at a meeting of the general council of the First International, an address that was published much later, in 1898, as a pamphlet called *Value, Price and Profit*. But, as often was the case with Marx, the concept was developed in an earlier draft manuscript. On a lighter note, the text of *Theories of Surplus Value* contained numerous colourful dismissals of 'vulgar' political economy as 'belletristic piffle' and 'twaddle', and characterisations of the vulgar economists themselves as 'old windbags' and 'philistines'. No doubt the author hoped that, after *Capital* was finally completed, these ignorant bourgeois scallywags might come to see the error of their ways.

Numerous other topics were also analysed in the *Theories of Surplus Value*, such as the causes of business cycles and financial crises within capitalism. In volume three of this historical series, Marx discussed J. S.

Mill's version of Say's Law (which stated that supply created its own demand), a discussion demonstrating that the philosophical flavour of Marx's approach still remained in parts of the second draft. He wrote:

> One sees here how the direct identity of demand and supply (hence the impossibility of a general glut) is proved. The product constitutes demand, and the extent of this demand moreover is measured by the value of the product ... the same methods used to prove that supply and demand ... must balance each other. The logic is always the same. If a relationship includes opposites, it comprises not only opposites but also the unity of opposites. It is therefore a unity *without opposites*. This is Mill's logic, by which he eliminates the 'contradictions'.[6]

Without an understanding of Hegel's method this paragraph could be difficult to decipher. What Marx was saying was that Mill saw supply and demand as identical, without realizing that things that were by definition identical were therefore also opposites. Mill had thus neglected the *movement between* opposites/identities that was a key part of Hegelian logic. Supply and demand were indeed identical, but they were so by virtue of the movement between each pole of the opposition, and in this movement the possibility of non-identity arose. The contradictions of capitalism resulted in this possibility becoming a reality in certain circumstances.

Another example of the use of Hegelian reasoning with respect to cycles occurred in volume two of *Theories of Surplus Value*, where Marx wrote:

> ... purchase and sale – or the metamorphosis of commodities – represent the unity of two processes, or rather the movement of one process through two opposite phases, and thus essentially the unity of the two phases ... It is just the *crisis* in which they assert their unity ... Thus the crisis manifests the unity of the two phases that have become independent of each other. There would be no crisis without this inner unity of factors that are apparently indifferent to each other. But no, says the apologetic economist. Because there is this unity, there can be no crises.[7]

Consequently, for Marx, crises were an expression of the inherent contradictions of commodity circulation. Within capitalism goods and money were posited as identical, but this identity meant that they were also opposites: in the movement between identity and opposition the possibility of crisis was born. Put another way, in the ever-lengthening chain of payments, various types of economic disturbances required money to be immediately transformed from a measure of account into hard cash; monetary crises were sometimes the result if projected circumstances had not been fully realised. Thus, some passages in the second draft of *Capital* retained a strong Hegelian flavour.

THE THIRD DRAFT

The third draft of *Capital* was prepared in 1863–4, close to the formation of the First International. In what still remains of this penultimate draft, the 'artistic whole' aspect was emphasised at the very start of the manuscript. Here Marx wrote:

> The circular nature of our argument corresponds to the *historical development* of capital ... if the *commodity* appears on the one hand as the premise of the formation of capital, it is also essentially the result, the product of capitalist production once it has become the *universal elementary form of the product*.[8]

Products created by human labour obviously existed well before capitalism, but Marx argued that such products became commodities only within certain specific forms of the mode of production, or within specific sets of social relations. The commodities that circulated within capitalism were different in nature from the goods that existed in pre-capitalist social formations, in that they were absorbed into commerce in a much more essential and structured manner, acquiring an exchange value in line with the laws of commodity production. This was a process that had occurred historically, in the transition from pre-capitalist to capitalist modes of production.

Another aspect of Marx's analysis that was emphasised in the third draft was discussed under the twin headings 'the formal subsumption of labour under capital' and 'the real subsumption of labour under capital'. By the concept of 'subsumption' was meant the process through which labour was brought under the control of capital. The formal type of subsumption related to the takeover by capital of a mode of labour that had existed prior to capitalist relations, while the real subsumption occurred when a specifically capitalist form of production had already come into being. The former process preceded the latter in historical terms, and hence this distinction referred to the way that capitalism had emerged out of earlier forms of goods production. Marx was very concerned to demonstrate how capitalist relations had germinated in historical terms out of the existing conditions in previous economic systems, since his theory of historical development was (at least initially) based on the idea that this process occurred 'naturally', through the working out of essential tendencies within the economic systems themselves. The third draft showed this concern very clearly, and provided evidence of a link between Marx's political economy and the materialist conception of history.

One very significant component of the transition from the formal to the real subsumption of labour to capital was identified as the size of the manufactory units under consideration. Marx wrote:

> ... what appeared to be the maximum attainable in the mode of production of the guilds ... can scarcely serve as a minimum for the relations of capital ... This enlargement of *scale* constitutes the real foundation on which the specifically capitalist mode of production can arise if the historical circumstances are otherwise favourable ...[9]

At this point in the text there was also provided an account of how it was that the transformation of production by the conscious application of scientific techniques had produced the division of labour in manufacture, which in turn generated the productive power of socialised labour that appeared as the productive power of capital. According to Marx, 'bourgeois' economists had mystified this process, just as the increased scale and complexity of the real subsumption of labour to capital itself mystified the social relations inherent within capitalism. Here it was being implied that scientific advances had initiated the real subsumption of labour, i.e. it was caused by changes in human understanding interacting with economic needs, but of course the formal subsumption had existed previously.

The question might reasonably be asked at this point: why was Marx so interested in explaining the birth processes of capitalism, as opposed to merely its internal logic and operational laws? After all, the book he was planning to write would eventually be called simply *Capital*, not *On the Path to Capital*. Surely, as a socialist, Marx should have been more interested in investigating the exit forwards out of capitalism, rather than the transition into it? The answer (or a big part of it) is that the question of how capitalism was born was not only an abstract theoretical question but also very much a live and contemporaneous one for many countries of the world in the 1860s, just as it was much more recently for the former Soviet-bloc countries in the 1990s.

Many non-Western states such as India and China faced the question in the second half of the nineteenth century of whether they should encourage capitalist development or attempt to create an alternative non-capitalist growth path. Marx and Engels' initial assumption from the time of *The Manifesto of the Communist Party* was that capitalism was a universalising economic system, that once it was born in one part of the globe it would inevitably spread through its own internal logic to all other parts of the globe. As they wrote in 1848: 'The need for a constantly expanding market for its products chases the bourgeoisie over the whole surface of the globe. It must nestle everywhere, settle everywhere, establish connections everywhere.'[10]

As asserted in the *Manifesto*, the cheap price of commodities was the 'heavy artillery' that battered down all barriers to capitalist production. Hence the implication was that less-developed countries had no choice in the matter and instead should embrace their fate, which after all would be universal to all countries.

In terms of the spiralling expansion of capitalist relations after they had first been created, Marx wrote in a similar vein in the third draft that: 'Capitalist production is not merely the reproduction of the relationship: it is its reproduction on a steadily increasing scale ... so that it creates ever new supplies of workers and encroaches on branches of production previously independent.'[11]

The idea that capitalism expanded by means of reproducing its underlying relationship on an ever-widening scale was thus still present. Marx saw this spatial or geographical extension as an intrinsic function of capital as it replicated itself across the globe, both within particular countries and also between them. This feature of capitalism led naturally to the idea that there would eventually be a definite end point to expanded reproduction, i.e. the geographical limit of the earth's habitable surface. Once this limit had been reached, then capital could no longer spread outside of its own realm of dominance, and any laws of motion that operated within this realm could no longer be bypassed through relief mechanisms such as external outlets. But were there any limitations to capitalist expansion even *within* pre-capitalist social formations?

After the publication of the *Manifesto* in 1848 Marx had undertaken a much more extensive study of both capitalism itself and its various historical precedents, as part of his research for *Capital*. It can reasonably be argued that after this more prolonged period of study he became more cautious and ambiguous about whether capitalist development was an inevitable stage that all countries had to pass through. One element of the reasoning behind this shift was that Marx came to accept that the initial creation of capitalism was a more complicated and protracted process than he had first believed, and hence that transmitting capitalism across the globe was not quite as simple as had been implied in the earlier *Manifesto*. Capitalism still had its own internal logic once it was born, but initiating this logic out of something else was a different thing. Hence the third draft of *Capital* showed clearly the author's concern to explain the origins of capitalism *as an urgent political problem of the day*, and as one component of a scheme of progression of modes of production that was part of the materialist conception of history.

THE FINAL VERSION OF VOLUME ONE

Marx's most famous published work was self-evidently concerned with the nature and function of the essential 'stuff' of capitalist production – capital itself. However, the final version of volume one of *Capital* began not with a basic definition of capital, but instead with a 160-page account of the nature of commodities and money. The vast bulk of the remainder of volume one dealt with the notion of surplus value. There were only two parts that had any direct mention of capital in their headings: a short account of the transformation of money into capital and a section on the accumulation of capital. In fact the subtitle that Marx gave to *Capital* – 'A Critique of Political Economy' – might be taken to suggest that the book contained a critical discussion of existing economic theory. But this cannot be allowed to detract attention from the fact that Marx's economic theory was concerned fundamentally with capital. If the subtitle of volume one – 'The Process of Capitalist

Production' – was considered literally, this evidently meant analysing the process of capital-employing manufacture.

What conceptual arsenal did Marx bring to his newly constructed analysis of capital in the final version of volume one? Unsurprisingly, it was the logic of his respected mentor, G. W. F. Hegel, whose first explicit appearance can be found in a footnote on page 10 of the 1867 first edition. A specific reference to the Hegelian understanding of *Begriff* (the German word for 'concept'), and to Hegel's *Science of Logic* itself, can then be found in both the main text and the footnotes on pages 18 and 19. Consequently, despite the concept of capital taking some while to make an appearance, Marx's applied Hegelian conception of the process of capitalist production was nowhere more clearly expressed than in his understanding of capital itself.

Traditionally, most mainstream economists had understood capital in two distinct senses. First, as monetary capital, or as a block of money that was used for investing in the production process. Second, as physical capital, or as the plant and machinery that was used in the manufacture of commodities. However, for Marx capital was not limited to either of these two specific meanings. For him, capital was really a movement or a circulating process that progressed through different stages of production, i.e. it was a process of motion. Marx represented this movement in its commodity manifestation by the following formula:

$$M - C - M'$$
(Money – Commodity – Money')

The last form of M (or M') was here augmented by the addition of surplus value. In volume two of *Capital* Marx wrote:

> A part of capital exists as commodity capital that is being transformed into money ... another part exists as money capital that is being transformed into productive capital; a third part as productive capital being transformed into commodity capital ... capital is simultaneously present, and spatially coexistent, in its various phases. But each part is constantly passing from one phase or fundamental form into another ...[12]

So Marx understood capital as an intangible flow that circulated through the production process, constantly transmuting from one tangible form to another, but not being confined by any one particular manifestation.

Marx's formulaic representation of the circulation process, presented in more detail in volume two of *Capital* but introduced in volume one, was designed to demonstrate this conception clearly. He explained that the circuit of capital was made up of three distinct but interconnected phases. First, money was transformed into commodities, or $M - C$. Secondly, the productive consumption of commodities occurred, or $C...P...C'$, a process that involved the use of labour power to generate surplus value. Third, the new commodities that had been made in the production process were transformed back into money, or $C' - M'$. In total these three stages coupled together to constitute the circuit of capital as a whole:

$$M - C...P...C' - M'$$

The quantities C' and M' had both been augmented by surplus value. As the whole process was circular, Marx explained that the premises of the process appeared as its result, or as premises produced by the process itself. Each moment of the process was correspondingly a point of departure, a point of transit and a point of return. The formulae given by Marx were only isolated instances of the ongoing movement of capital through its circuit of motion, which in the real world was continuous and multi-phased. Hence capital was not a corporeal thing that could be isolated and examined under the economist's microscope; instead it was a form of motion that flowed through the capitalist system rather like invisible blood.

If the link to Hegelian logic being presented here still seems a little tenuous, consider the formula that Marx constructed to represent the motion of capital: $M - C - M'$. Then place this formula alongside Hegel's own formula for the syllogistic progression: $U - P - I$.[13] It seems unlikely that Marx, as a long-time Young Hegelian, would have been unaware of a direct formal similarity between these formulae, and the spiralling structure of movement that they both were designed to represent.

Marx's Hegelian conception of capitalist production was also apparent from how money was distinguished from capital in a quantitative sense. He wrote that:

> ... the sum of money required for an individual to be able to metamorphose themselves into a capitalist varies with the different stages and spheres of production; but this illustrates Hegel's law that quantitative changes pass into qualitative changes beyond a certain critical point.[14]

What Marx meant here was that money was transformed into capital when it was aggregated beyond a numerical boundary level, but that the nature of the individual monetary units within this process did not change. What was actually being altered was the set of social relations operating around the various amounts of money in question.

A quantity of money up to a certain level nestled within one set of social relations, where the individual was merely the holder of a certain amount of purchasing power; but a quantity of money beyond a certain level functioned as part of a different set of social relations, where the individual was able to buy and sell labour power itself, and hence to extract surplus value from the production process. A quantitative change in the amount of money in question was part of a qualitative change in the set of social relations functioning around the money in question, this being illustrative of one of Hegel's well-known dialectical laws. Moreover, the specific point at which money was transformed into capital itself varied under the different stages of development of capitalism, and also varied in different branches of production.

Another element that needs to be considered is that capital could exist outside of the capitalist mode of production, i.e. it could (and did) exist within pre-capitalist economic formations. For example, usurer's capital, a form of interest-bearing capital, was found in ancient Rome, and it corresponded to the predominance of petty production, i.e. of peasants and small craftsmen working individually. According to Marx, what distinguished interest-bearing capital within the capitalist mode of production from usurer's capital in ancient Rome was the different set of social relations in which it was embedded. Capital defined as a form of motion (the movement $M - C - M'$) might exist within various sets of social relations, but it was only within the capitalist mode of production that capital became the fundamental driving force of the entire economic system. Moreover, capitalism itself could come into being historically only through the employment of merchant's capital that had itself been created in pre-capitalist modes of production. Hence capital was not limited to capitalism, but capitalism was the only system in which capital became the primary element of production. The process of this becoming was part of Marx's explanation of how capitalism was created within pre-capitalist formations.

THE CONCEPT OF SURPLUS VALUE

Marx himself believed that his most important discovery in the field of abstract political economy was the concept of surplus value, and much of volume one of *Capital* was devoted to explaining its significance. The concept itself was an essential part of Marx's analysis of the 'laws of motion' of capitalism, and it is therefore necessary to discuss it in more detail. At root the idea of surplus value was used to claim a 'scientific' or numerical expression of his belief that the working class (or labour power in general) was being exploited within capitalism. The word 'exploitation' is an emotive and heavily laden word that requires careful definition if it is to be usefully applied. People routinely state in everyday conversations that they 'exploited' a particular situation to their own advantage, without necessarily meaning that moral conventions have been broken in any substantial way. Human beings routinely exploit the natural resources that they find around themselves, again without necessarily breaking any ethical code.

In the Marxian usage, the notion that the working classes were exploited meant something much stronger, that they were being deprived of what was rightfully theirs – the full fruits of their labour power. Capitalist production was (it was being alleged) based on the expropriation of the results of labour by the capitalist, something that Marx subconsciously believed was morally wrong. He set about proving this by creating a set of concepts that described the inner workings of capitalism, and then showing how the circulating motion of capital through these concepts over time resulted in the extraction of surplus value by the capitalist.

Marx used algebraic formulae to try to lay bare the mechanism of this exploitation. He divided capital into two categories, constant capital (designated by the symbol 'c') and variable capital (designated by the symbol 'v'). Constant capital was the amount spent on plant, machinery, buildings and raw materials that were used in the production of commodities. Variable capital was the amount paid to workers as wages in the production of commodities. However, if after selling the commodities thus produced capitalists only ever got back their initial outlay in constant and variable capital, then they would have no reason to actually produce commodities at all. They would do just as well to hold on to their initial capital. What made them eager to produce commodities was the possibility that they would get back more than they had initially expended. But from where did this potential increase arise?

Marx answered categorically that it arose from surplus value, or from an amount of labour power that workers were providing to capitalists free of charge. Hence in reality commodity value (C) was constituted from three elements: constant capital (c), variable capital (v) and surplus value (which Marx designated by the symbol 's'):

$$C = c + v + s$$

Surplus value was thus the key to understanding the inner workings of capitalism, in that all the focus of capitalists was directed to increasing the amount of surplus value that could be extracted from the labour of workers. And it was this process of extraction of surplus value that Marx deemed to be exploitative.

Was Marx right? Are workers really exploited by capitalists? Well, it all depends on what is actually meant by 'exploitation' in this context. Marx's analysis of capitalism in terms of c + v + s is intuitively plausible, and is indeed one way in which the value of commodities can be disaggregated. However, at the opposite extreme, the idea that workers should retain all of the profits taken by capitalists might itself be seen as unfair. After all, many owners of factories do spend at least some of their time helping to develop and promote the commodities that are produced, and the idea that they should receive no reward for this at all might seem unreasonable. Whether they should receive the *level* of recompense that many of them have done historically might be a more pertinent question from a moderate left-of-centre perspective. From a socialist perspective it could thus be suggested that capitalists take too large an amount of surplus value. But of course Marx was not a moderate socialist, he was a revolutionary, and his economic analysis also claimed to show how the intrinsic 'laws of motion' of capitalism compelled capitalists to try to take more and more surplus value. The idea that the logic of capitalism could be palliated in order to make it fairer to workers was something that went against Marx's entire approach.

CONCLUSION

Marx explained in the preface to volume one of *Capital* that England (by which he really meant Great Britain) was the national subject frequently used as the chief illustration in most of the book because it had been the 'classic ground' for the development of the capitalist mode of production. Comparing the 'purer' form in England with the less-developed case of his own homeland, he commented to his targeted German readers that:

> In all other spheres, we, like all the rest of Continental Western Europe, suffer not only from the development of capitalist production, but also from the incompleteness of that development. Alongside of modern evils, a whole series of inherited evils oppress us, arising from the passive survival of antiquated modes of production, with their inevitable train of social and political anachronisms.[15]

Marx was tacitly admitting that the 'pure' form of capitalism was only an abstraction deduced for analytical purposes, as real countries were usually mixtures of antediluvian survivals from older modes of production and the green shoots of newer ones. This admission harmonised with his journalistic writings on the American civil war examined in the previous chapter, where a 'mixing' of modes of production was also presented as developing, but it jarred with the idea of a natural sequence of modes, as was implied in the *Manifesto*.

As noted at the end of the previous chapter, volume one of *Capital* was partly a work of significant moral condemnation, and numerous passages on the nature of factory conditions in Britain illustrated this clearly. For example, Marx explained:

> ... certain London houses where newspapers and books are printed have got the ill-omened name of 'slaughter houses' ... young persons have to do heavy work in rope-walks and night-work in salt mines, candle manufactories, and chemical works; young people are worked to death at turning the looms in silk

weaving ... A classical example of ... brutalising effects on the workman from his childhood upwards, is ... tile and brick making ... Between May and September the work lasts from 5 in the morning till 8 in the evening ... Both boys and girls of 6 and even of 4 years of age are employed.[16]

The most obvious comparison with this empirical part of *Capital* was Engels' much earlier book *The Condition of the Working Class in England*. But despite numerous claims that Marx had proved scientifically that English workers were exploited by capital, the fact that children were forced to work from five in the morning to eight at night cannot be regarded as 'scientifically wrong', instead it is considered shameful from a humanitarian perspective. But in volume one Marx wanted to have his cake and eat it, by using illustrations of the moral degradation caused by mid-nineteenth century capitalism as an emotive call to improve working conditions, but then also claiming that his analysis of surplus value was 'scientific' and hence neutral and objective. Marx was (perhaps rightly) campaigning on the side of the working population when he wrote *Capital*; Isaac Newton was not 'campaigning on the side of light' when he undertook his optical experiments.

Even with all the above discussion, this chapter has provided only an introduction to some of the main themes and most important issues within volume one of *Capital*. Readers with a developing interest (either favourable or hostile) in socialist theory should of course read it for themselves. Marx and his various supporters were universally delighted that he had been able to finish (the first part of) his life's work, and in 1867 both Marx and Engels were sure that further parts of this work would soon follow. But Marx had a track record of leaving his multi-volume works incomplete – the promised second volume of the *Contribution to a Critique of Political Economy* of 1859 never ever appeared. To leave one multi-volume work incomplete might be thought understandable, but to leave two such works incomplete might be considered careless, or even a little suspicious. The next chapter examines Marx's attempts to develop further his research on the nature of capitalism, in order to finish the work that he had begun so promisingly in volume one, and to complete the proposed circle of socialist analysis.

9

THE TANTALISING MODEL
OF PARIS

In 1867 volume one of *Capital* had finally been issued, and what many regarded as the intellectual pinnacle of Marx's professional life sealed his fate within the very top level of economic thinkers of the modern age, although this evaluation was not universally accepted on its first publication. *Capital* stands today alongside Adam Smith's *Wealth of Nations* and Maynard Keynes's *General Theory of Employment* as one of the three most famous books on economics topics ever written, although it is not necessarily the most accurate in theoretical terms or the most well loved by mainstream economists. But despite such an intellectual achievement there was still something lacking in Marx's professional life that served on occasion to depress his general temperament – the lack of a clear political success for revolutionary socialist forces. In fact it would turn out to be only four years between the publication of volume one of *Capital* and a political event that could be claimed as the beginnings of such a success – the 1871 Paris Commune.

THE PARIS COMMUNE

The beacon of light that arose on the horizon in the later years of Marx's life was one that created a tantalising model for socialist political organisation. As an essential prelude to the tangible construction of this model, the end of the long rule of Louis-Napoleon Bonaparte as French Emperor was brought about by the defeat of France in the Franco-Prussian war of 1870 – a war that had lasted for around seven and a half months and ended with the military defeat of the French army by German troops. During 1870 Marx had composed two addresses to the First International concerned specifically with the Franco-Prussian war, in which he outlined his attitude to this particular battle and its significance for the working-class movement as a whole.

In the first address, written in July, the war was declared unjust, and consequently the International's position was set to oppose it. Marx suggested characteristically that in the background of the conflict loomed 'the dark figure of Russia', implying that Russian involvement aided reactionary forces. In the second address, written in September, just after the war had ended, Marx explained that the French republic had been proclaimed only as a measure of national defence, rather than as a matter of revolutionary principle. He advised the French working classes to 'improve the opportunities for Republican liberty' in order to assist in the operation of their own class organisation, although what this meant in exact terms was not specified.[1]

A new government of national security headed by Adolphe Thiers, who became the president of the French republic from 1871 to 1873, then followed, but an uprising in Paris led to the triumphant forces of the working masses assuming control of the city for around two months between March and May 1871. This particular period of French history (and the form of political control on which it was based) has consequently been named the Paris Commune. Like all such revolutionary experiments of the time it was brutally suppressed, with many thousands losing their lives in the process, but not before it had become a form of political organisation for many socialists to idealise. Of all the socialist experiments that were attempted in Marx's lifetime, the Paris Commune was the one that resounded the most, especially given the tragic fate of the participants. The resultant photographic images of Communards shot dead in their coffins was a potent reminder of the heroic sacrifices that were sometimes demanded of socialist revolutionaries.

However, the initial uprising itself had little direct connection either to Marx or to the International, although many anti-socialist campaigners painted in such a link when they could. In London, *The Times* reported on the following bizarre event in Paris in June 1871:

... on Monday evening a number of women known to have been in intimate relations with leading members of the Commune were arrested. At the residence of one ... was found a number of letters addressed to Citizen Franckel, by members of the International ... One of these letters referred to a remittance from the 'friends and brothers' of Berlin of a sum of 600,000f, payable at St. Denis. This fact was held to justify ... a strict inquiry into the connection of Karl Marx ... with the recent fearful events in Paris.[2]

Leo Franckel was Minister of Labour in the Commune government. In contrast to the rather tenuous reasoning presented in *The Times*, it is more accurate to recount that of the 92 members of the Commune's ruling council only 17 were actually affiliates of the International, and there was no concerted effort to control the Commune by International members.[3] For one thing the Paris Commune did not last long enough for such an operational mechanism to be fully formed, and for another the conflict itself militated against easy international contact, as military actions disrupted many lines of communication.

Marx did receive letters from (and even met with) delegates of the Commune in a few instances, but he was certainly not the puppet master directing the show. In a letter from June 1871 Marx explained that:

My relations with the Commune were maintained through a German merchant who travels between Paris and London all the year round. Everything was settled verbally with the exception of two matters ... I sent the members of the Commune a letter in answer to a question from them as to how they could handle certain securities on the London Exchange ... I sent them by the same method all the details of the secret agreement come to between Bismarck and Favre ...[4]

This protracted form of communication was hardly able to respond quickly to ongoing events, and Marx despaired in the same letter that the Commune had ignored all his advice on tactical matters. To the aforementioned Franckel, Marx had warned in May 1871 that the Commune was 'wasting too much time in trivialities and personal quarrels'.[5] In reality there were many more supporters of Blanquist and Proudhonist tendencies with the Commune's ruling Council than there were supporters of Marx and Engels.

However, Marx did follow the events in Paris closely, and he composed one of his most famous political works in response: *The Civil War in France* of May 1871. This was a work that was frequently quoted by many later followers as indicating the particular form of socialist government that the prophet had foreseen as arising. In fact it was written as another (more substantial) address of the general council of the International to its members, mainly as a guide to the events that were unfolding in France at the time. Like the best of his political tracts it was very well written, although it might appear a little distant to today's reader, simply because the personages and events being referred to are now only a faint collective memory. On its initial publication no author was formally indicated, but the true person responsible was soon revealed.

The title contained an important clue to Marx's attitude to the events that he was describing. Given the later importance attached to the Commune (or Soviet) form of government in the early part of the twentieth century, readers might have expected it to be called something like *The New Commune* or *Socialist Political Formations*. In fact the Commune itself was not mentioned in the title. Instead, Marx chose to highlight the conflict-related aspect of the events as a full-blown French civil war. This was part of his larger conception of the mechanisms of class tectonics, as the Commune was seen simply as a political outcome of the clashing plates of European class struggle.

THE CIVIL WAR IN FRANCE

The importance of the Commune as a form of political organisation was stressed repeatedly in *The Civil War in France*. Marx described it in the text as the positive form of the French republic and as the direct antithesis of the Empire. In the drafts he described it as the re-absorption of state power by society and as the political form of the social emancipation of the working classes. Thus he wrote:

> The Commune was formed of the municipal councillors, chosen by universal suffrage in the various wards of the town, responsible and revocable at short terms. The majority of its members were naturally working men, or acknowledged representatives of the working class. The Commune was to be a

working, not a parliamentary, body, executive and legislative at the same time
... the public service had to be done at *workman's wages*.[6]

Marx hoped that the Paris Commune would serve as a model for all the
industrial centres of France, and also for the country areas as rural communes, who would then send delegates to the nearest urban centres just
as district assemblies might send delegates to Paris. He characterised the
'true secret' of the Commune as the fact that it was a working-class government and a lever for uprooting the economic foundations of 'bourgeois'
society, and warned that it should not be mistaken for the old medieval
commune. He also emphasised that it would include the 'real purpose'
of choosing the people's own administrative functionaries, i.e. it would
be based on universal suffrage.

Marx included a few sentences expanding on the economic goals of
the Paris Commune. He outlined that one such aim was to abolish class
property and in its place to realise true individual property.[7] This was an
unusual formulation of the by-now-standard socialist notion of abolish-
ing private property. It could be interpreted as suggesting that property
would be redistributed from its existing unequal form of class ownership
to a new form of individual non-class ownership, i.e. that all individuals
within a socialist society would maintain equal holdings over equal
amounts of property. Marx also outlined that the economic form that
complemented the Commune as a political institution was 'united cooperative societies', which would regulate national production on a
common plan. Again this suggested something a little unusual, that
cooperative producers and consumers would unite together to set planning targets themselves within a Marx-type socialist economy. They
would not have such targets foisted on to them from above, even from
representative bodies such as the Commune itself.

Another key element outlined in *The Civil War in France* was the relationship of the Commune to the existing machinery of the capitalist
state. Marx clearly declared that the working class could not simply take
hold of existing state structures and use them for socialistic purposes. By
implication the capitalist state had to be destroyed, and new socialist
institutions developed. One significant example relevant to the experience of the Paris Commune was that of the military. Existing military
forces could not be relied upon to support socialist political institutions;
rather a people's army had to be created that was loyal to the new

government. Such a national army was indeed mobilised in Paris, and proved crucial to maintaining control for the relatively brief period of the Commune's existence. Similar strictures applied to various other political and state structures, such as the legal system and the judiciary.

However, Marx did not mention any specifically economic structures while discussing this total replacement of the 'bourgeois' state by a newly created proletarian one. This might have been because in previous writings he had specified precisely that a socialist government *could* assume control of the capitalist financial system and use it for its own ends. In fact the apparent simplicity of this takeover was used as an argument for how easy it would be for socialist forces to assume control of a 'mature' capitalist system, since the economic levers of the state had already begun the transformation into socialist institutions even before the political victory of the working class.

It is important to realise that Marx's account of the Paris Commune was thoroughly political in design and presentation. In no sense could it be described as an objective account. For a start, the writing itself was consistently glowing and reverential about the Commune, and hateful and disparaging about its opponents. For example, the heroic Parisians (who spoke 'all truth') were contrasted with the reactionary forces (who spoke 'all lies') based in Versailles. The latter camp was described as an assembly of ghouls eager to feed upon the carcass of the French nation – a brilliant political caricature, but certainly grossly simplistic. In addition, it might be seen as a little odd that Marx claimed in the text that the working class 'have no ideals to realise'.[8] Had not Marx spent his entire life developing the theoretical ideals that he believed the working class could realise in practice, i.e. the abolition of private property, the end of ruling-class domination, the emancipation of labour and so on? Had he forgotten his own life's work, or (more likely) was he waiting to see what the final outcome would be before nailing his flag of ideals to the Parisian mast?

It is also necessary to point out that Paris was not the only French city that experienced an outbreak of communal aspiration at this time. In various other French cities, such as Lyon, Communes made a brief appearance, although they were not nearly as developed or prolonged as they were in Paris.[9] However there was very little discussion of such regional complications in *The Civil War in France*, which presented a stark contrast between the Paris-based 'good guys' and the Versailles-based 'bad guys'. Reviewing the text today, the reader half expects an ending in which the Sith Lord Darth Thiers orders the Death Star to turn its awesome firepower away from Paris, swearing to crush the puny rebellion across the entire French Empire and admonishing the Jedi Knight Luke Commune-Walker to submit to the power of the dark side. Comparing this text with the author's other great political polemic, *The Eighteenth Brumaire of Louis Bonaparte*, much of the complexity of Marx's conception of evolving class tectonics has been sidelined, replaced instead by a simplistic support for Communard aims. It is accurate to say that Marx was usually more objective when all chances of a socialist victory had evaporated.

Despite such inconsistencies and omissions, *The Civil War in France* was printed three times in two months and was one of Marx's more successful publications from a sales perspective.[10] Its thoroughgoing optimism about the potential of the Paris Commune was partly genuine, in that the author really did believe that such forms of political organisation were the future, but it was also partly spun propaganda of the day. This duality is apparent from private correspondence, where Marx was more critical about the Commune and its members. He was particularly concerned about the apparent naivety of the leadership, for example in allowing time for their opponents to regroup and for a reluctance to provoke a full-blown civil war. In a letter to Ludwig Kugelman from April 1871, Marx judged about the Communards that: 'If they are defeated only their 'good nature' will be to blame. They should have marched at once on Versailles ... Second mistake: The Central Committee surrendered its power too soon, to make way for the Commune'.[11]

The first mistake being alleged meant that the Commune appeared reluctant to deal a final blow to its enemies, a fatal error in Marx's class-driven approach to political strategy. Given that the Commune was violently overturned, it might easily be concluded that he had been right on this matter, a hard-won tactical lesson that many of his later followers would take very much to heart. The second mistake was more ambiguous, since it appeared to suggest that the Commune was not the ultimate political form that Marx desired, or at least that it was not wanted quite yet. But if it was not required during proletarian control, then when was it wanted exactly?

The Civil War in France pamphlet also served to increase Marx's personal notoriety substantially, especially in Britain, as it had been written and published first in English, something uncommon for a Marx polemic. It was over 20 years since the revolutionary events of 1848 had occurred, and Marx had not been based in London at that time anyway. Consequently, association with the Paris Commune through authorship of *The Civil War in France* heightened his reputation as a subversive revolutionary after 1871, even though there had been no direct controlling link between Marx and the Parisian Communards. The publication of volume one of *Capital* in German had done little to raise his profile among the general public of his adopted homeland, but an association with the Paris Commune was something much more immediate and tangible. In consequence, the affairs of the International began to be covered in more detail in *The Times*, where in November 1872 it was reported by a disgruntled member of the International that the general council was 'at the complete devotion of Karl Marx'.[12] It is possible that Marx might have wished that this was the case, but ongoing conflicts within the International meant that it was not always so, as will be seen later in this chapter.

The experiences of the Paris Commune continued to influence Marx's political thinking even after the Commune had reached its bloody conclusion. For example, in a new preface written for the second German edition of the *Manifesto* in 1872, it was admitted that his views on the practical application of socialist principles outlined in 1848 had 'in some details become antiquated', due in part to the experiences gained by the proletariat during the Paris Commune.[13] However, the principles themselves were declared by Marx to be 'as correct today as ever'. Astute readers might immediately detect a contradiction between this idea of permanently valid socialist principles, apparently found in the *Manifesto*, and Marx's previously outlined suggestion from *The Civil War in France* that the proletariat had through the Commune 'no ideals to realise' that were in any way ready-made.

A more accurate formulation is even more problematic, in that a straightforward distinction between constant principles and variable strategy does not really hold much water. The Marxian variant of socialism was always an articulated combination of ultimate ends and immediate means, although the precise formula of the mix certainly changed as circumstances and individuals came and went. Perhaps, in suggesting that his own socialist principles were not the ready-made ideals that the Communards maintained, Marx was hoping at the time to prevent his French comrades from being too closely tarred with his own reputation. In truth the Paris Commune would have been ruthlessly suppressed whether Marx had been in any way associated with it or not.

LIFE IN THE EARLY 1870s

The destruction of the Paris Commune had a significant impact on Marx's life in a number of different ways. Various newspapers interviewed him as the supposed political inspiration of the French revolutionaries, and refugees fleeing from the massacre of the Communards soon found their way to London and to Marx's own door. Both Marx and Engels attempted to reinvigorate the International after the collapse of the Commune, but in reality after 1871 it fell into terminal decline. On a more personal note, Marx's daughter Laura and her husband were in Paris just prior to the momentous events, while his other two daughters (Jenny and Eleanor) were arrested on their attempt to return to London, after travelling to France in order to assist Laura in escaping from the aftermath. Laura and Paul Lafarge had conceived three children since their attachment, but all of them perished at a very young age in the early 1870s.[14]

In 1870 Engels had moved to Primrose Hill in London, occupying a grand address in Regent's Park Road, which was (and still is today) a very desirable location. This meant that he could visit Marx frequently and join with him in pacing up and down the well-used study in lively debate. In 1872 Marx's daughter Jenny became engaged and then married, characteristically to a French refugee and ex-member of the Paris Commune. Jenny and her husband Charles Longuest eventually produced six children, only one of whom died in infancy, and hence she was by far the most successful of Marx's children in reproductive terms.[15]

At around the same time Eleanor Marx had become romantically attached to Prosper-Olivier Lissagaray, who was again a Commune activist and author of the classic study *History of the Paris Commune* of 1876, which Eleanor subsequently translated into English from the original French. In the introduction Eleanor described Lissagaray resolutely as 'a soldier of the Commune'.[16] Marx, however, disapproved of the relationship, going as far as forbidding his daughter contact with the offending ex-Communard and causing a long-term estrangement between father and daughter. Although this opposition eventually subsided, when Lissagaray returned to Paris in 1880 Eleanor did not accompany him. Instead she later became seriously involved with Edward Aveling, a British socialist who helped to translate volume one of *Capital* into English after Marx's death.

In the summer of 1874 Marx took the bold (if not downright insolent) step of applying for British citizenship. On his application form he gave his profession as 'author', but refrained from providing any examples of his books. The Scotland Yard police report on this attempt at naturalisation was rather frank and not inaccurate: 'I beg to report that he is the notorious German agitator, the head of the International Society, and an advocate of Communistic principles. This man has not been loyal to his own King and Country.'[17]

Marx's request to become a British citizen was refused on the grounds that the Home Office report on his character was not satisfactory. This rejection was unlikely to have caused him any genuine distress, however, as the reason for the attempt at naturalisation was completely disingenuous. Marx had not suddenly been converted to a faith in the British bulldog; instead he anticipated trouble from the Bohemian police on a projected future visit to Carlsbad, and believed that British citizenship might have shielded him somewhat from this inconvenient fate.

Marx's health also began to worsen in this period. Liver problems and persistent headaches led him in 1873 to consult Engels' own doctor, who prescribed a regime of restricted work and long periods of rest and relaxation. Consequently Marx travelled to various health resorts, first in England and then later in Bohemia, the latter generating his faux attempt at becoming British. He adhered to the various (now quaintly antiquated) spa regimes quite strictly, and, probably due more to the absence of work than any accurate medical diagnoses, his health had improved to some extent by 1875. This facilitated a partial return to the usual work routine and hopes that the improvement would be permanent. One of the elements of the heavy workload that had led to this particular onset of illness was the preparation of various translations of volume one of *Capital*.

THE RUSSIAN TRANSLATION OF VOLUME ONE

The first edition of *Capital* had sold rather slowly in Germany and therefore a second edition was not required until 1872, five years after its first appearance. It was then re-issued in serial parts, rather than as a complete book, a form of publication that Marx believed would be more accessible to the working classes. This same year saw the publication of the first translation of volume one of *Capital* into a new language, which by no accident was Russian. Completed three years later, in 1875, *Capital* was translated into French, but (like the second German edition) in the form of a serial issue in sequential parts. Marx himself took great interest in these early re-issues and translations, and made various changes to the text of *Capital* especially for them that helped to indicate the evolving nature of his thought patterns. Marx also worked personally with some of the translators involved in order to get the various modifications correctly applied. The detailed content of these changes will be considered in more detail in the next chapter.

However, the Russian translation of 1872 came about not on Marx's own initiative but on the initiative of N. P. Danielson (who was known by the pen name 'Nikolai-on'), a Russian economist and social activist. Danielson was a *narodnik* (an agrarian Populist) in political terms, which meant that he opposed the implantation and development of Western capitalism in Russia, instead favouring the nurturing of indigenous Russian forms of economy such as the peasant commune. Russian Social-Democrats such as Lenin were strongly critical of the Populist approach, dismissing it as dangerously romantic and backward-looking. Danielson wrote to Marx in the autumn of 1868 with the idea of preparing a Russian translation of volume one, and Marx responded that he was in favour of the idea, if a little guardedly so. Russia as a country was of course Marx's pet hate, although he recognised the existence of socialist currents within it.

The proposed translator was G. A. Lopatin, and in July 1870 Lopatin visited Marx in London to discuss the translation in person. After first becoming acquainted with him, the author declared himself to be very happy with the translator's understanding of his work, and the process of translation began. However, after preparing four chapters Lopatin returned to Russia in order to aid a colleague and was imprisoned for his altruistic efforts, and so Danielson himself completed the remainder of the translation. 3,000 copies were printed in the spring of 1872, and sales were so good that by the summer a second Russian edition was being considered.

In one of the most infamously misjudged evaluations ever made by an official government censor, the book was declared not applicable to Russia and difficult to understand, and thus was passed for publication without much fuss. This was the equivalent of the British Board of Film Censors passing *Cannibal Holocaust* (1979) uncut with a 'U' (suitable for all) certificate.[18] Various genuine reviews of volume one appeared in Russian periodicals, i.e. reviews not planted pseudonymously by Engels, and the reception was generally more favourable than it had been in Western Europe. Irony of ironies, many people in the country that Marx had long hated the most apparently liked his work a great deal.

The Russian translation of volume one was only one component part of Marx's evolving interest in Russian affairs in this period. He had started to learn Russian in 1869 and thereby to study Russian history, and Danielson began sending Marx books by Russian authors. One significant example that was sent was N. Flerovsky's *Condition of the Working Class in Russia* of 1869, which by no accident was a Russian extrapolation of Engels' youthful work on the English working class. Marx described Flerovsky's book in a letter to Engels in 1870 as 'the first work to tell the truth about Russian economic conditions' and as 'the most important book which has appeared since your *Condition of the Working Class*'.[19] This was partly because (according to Marx) it showed that a social revolution was approaching in Russia, and exposed the basis of the 'schoolboy nihilism' that was fashionable among students.

Marx also received works by N. G. Chernyshevsky, a well-known radical most famous for his book *What is to be Done?*, and various different accounts of the Russian peasant commune. One estimate put the total number of Russian books in Marx's personal collection near the end of his life at 150.[20] Marx received these books eagerly and he studied them with the same level of seriousness that he was devoting to *Capital*. In fact, this newly constituted research on Russia *was itself* work on *Capital*, and should not be considered as a sideline to his more direct economic interests.

In this regard Marx continued to keep in touch with Danielson even after the Russian translation of volume one was published in 1872. In a letter to Danielson from March 1873, Marx requested information on the views of a specific author on the historical development of communal property in Russia. He asked rhetorically: 'How should it have come to happen that in Russia the same institution had been simply introduced as a formal measure, as a concomitant incident of serfdom, while everywhere else it was of spontaneous growth ...?'.[21]

The implication of this enquiry was that, in some instances, external forces (such as the state) might be necessary to create ownership structures, whereas in other instances such structures might develop spontaneously. The specific example under consideration in the letter to Danielson was communal ownership (i.e. the peasant commune), but the same question of 'forced' versus spontaneous creation applied to all the various modes of production. Marx had initially assumed that new modes of production were generated automatically from within the contradictions of the existing mode, but this Russian example could be interpreted as pointing to something else.

The question of the development of capitalism in hitherto non-capitalist countries, as outlined in the previous chapter, was central to Marx's own analysis of historical change within the various drafts of *Capital* that had been prepared by the early 1870s. In November 1877 Marx described the outcome of his Russian interest as follows:

> In order that I might be specially qualified to estimate the economic development in Russia, I learned Russian, and then for many years studied the official publications and others bearing on the subject. I have arrived at this conclusion: If Russia continues to pursue the path she has followed since 1861, she will lose the finest chance ever offered by history to a people and undergo all the fatal vicissitudes of the capitalist regime.[22]

By 'the finest chance ever offered' was meant the chance to bypass the capitalist stage of development and go straight to socialism, an alternative path that he obviously now believed might be possible to take. This seemingly innocuous change was in direct contravention to Marx's own previously articulated 'stages' account of historical progress, although it was presaged by his analysis of slavery in the USA. To paraphrase a much later work by Regis Debray, it could be seen as constituting a revolution in the Marxian conception of how social revolutions between modes of production occurred.

Of course Marx was not arguing that Russian society necessarily *would* bypass capitalism, only that under certain circumstances it could do so. But even this qualified position was a radical change, as in most previous accounts entire modes of production could not ever be 'skipped' or 'leaped over'. It was Marx's detailed study of Russia that had been a large part of engendering this change, and hence the Russian translation of volume one was significant not only for enabling access to his ideas for a Russian audience, but also in catalysing his own change of approach to economic progress. It is also unlikely to have been coincidental that this change was facilitated by personal contact with the Populist thinker Danielson, who not only believed that Russia could bypass capitalism but that it should make every effort to do so. Both Marx and Danielson agreed that the social consequences of the introduction of capitalism would be extremely negative for the vast majority of people in Russia, so the chance to avoid these dire consequences was not an unimportant one.

Marx also received various other eminent Russian visitors in London in the 1870s apart from Lopatin. Two such visitors were P. Lavrov (at the beginning of the 1870s) and M. M. Kovalevsky (at the end of the 1870s), both being authors of significant works on Russian history and society. Hence Marx's interest in Russia was fostered by a considerable amount of reading on the subject, together with personal contacts with some of the leading Russian intellectuals of the day. In the reverse direction, some of Marx's other more obviously political works, such as *The Manifesto of the Communist Party* and *The Civil War in France*, appeared in Russian translation, provoking further interest and debate about his ideas among Russian socialists. All things considered, Marx's *Capital*-based introduction in Russia in the early 1870s was certainly a qualified success, and therefore the October revolution in 1917 was not quite the complete surprise that some later commentators have made it out to be.

MARX AND BAKUNIN

One aspect of Marx's political, organisational and also personal life that is important to an understanding of his position within the general constellation of socialists in the second half of the nineteenth century has until this point in the book been ignored. This was Marx's relationship with M. A. Bakunin (1814–76), a leading Russian anarchist and (briefly) a fellow member of the International. The Soviet multi-volume edition of Marx's works described Bakunin as 'at that time, the principal opponent of Marxism', i.e. Bakunin was a leading left-orientated challenger to Marx as philosopher-king of the socialist movement.[23] Although they began on friendly terms, Marx came into conflict with Bakunin both on policy issues within the International and also in the realm of abstract ideas. Bakunin had a strong dislike of authoritarian state power and centralised political control, and he criticised Marx as a socialist advocate of precisely these negative features. Marx in turn criticised Bakunin and his supporters as a narrow sect and for a naive belief in the feasibility of an anarchistic variety of socialism. Given that precisely the issues that Bakunin highlighted were to haunt socialist governments throughout the twentieth century, the importance of his criticisms of Marx should not be underestimated.

The institutional aspect of the conflict developed as Bakunin had founded an organisation called the Alliance of Social Democracy at the end of the 1860s, and this organisation then applied to join the International. It was initially refused membership but was later offered affiliate status. Finally attempting to expel the Bakunin group as political dissidents, Marx feared the creation of an internal opposition within the International and an increase in the factionalism that he claimed publicly to detest. A less sympathetic analysis would also include the notion that Marx did not want another personality within the International whose stature was nearly as great as his own. Marx and Engels outlined their opposition to Bakunin's organisation in a private circular entitled 'Fictitious Splits in the International' from 1872. A basic theoretical difference presented in the circular was that Bakunin believed in the equalisation of classes, whereas Marx and Engels desired the abolition of classes. This might be considered to be a purely semantic distinction, but Marx and Engels made a great deal out of it. Interpreting Bakunin's class equalisation as meaning a desire for harmony between labour and capital, they summarily dismissed it as another variant of 'bourgeois' socialism.[24]

A more sympathetic interpretation would view Bakunin's equalisation of classes as being the more egalitarian position, as members of any ruling elite would be 'made equal' with workers, and Marx's abolition of classes as the more ominous process, as members of the ruling elites would (in some unspecified way) be made to disappear. As in many other instances, what would happen to individual members of those classes that had been 'abolished' was not precisely explained. Another point of conflict developed over the Paris Commune itself. Bakunin had travelled to Lyon just after the creation of the French republic in 1870, and he subsequently tried to organise a federated system of communes across France, including a very short-lived attempt at a Lyon Commune. This attempt quickly failed and Marx was quite scornful of such externally supported efforts, which was another reason why he had not discussed Communes outside of the Paris example in *The Civil War in France*.

On more abstract matters, Bakunin had written a book (in Russian) entitled *Statism and Anarchy* of 1873, in which his controversial opinions on the real consequences of authoritarian socialism were articulated. Marx wrote some revealing manuscript comments on Bakunin's book in 1874, in which parts of this book were copied out and then answered – comments that have survived for examination today. Marx described Bakunin's questioning stance in his usual unguarded manner as 'school-boy's asininity', 'democratic verbiage' and 'political drivel', and suggested that his opponent did not understand one thing about social revolution. One section of comments about the dictatorship of the proletariat, and the nature of the corresponding socialist state, is worth quoting in full:

> *Bakunin* [original text]: There are about 40 million Germans. Will ... all the forty million be members of the government? *Marx* [new comment] Certainly! For the thing begins with the self-government of the Commune. *Bakunin*: The whole people will govern and there will be no one to be governed. *Marx*: ... when a man rules himself, he does not rule himself ... *Bakunin*: Then there will be no government, no State ...[25]

This passage could be interpreted as Bakunin highlighting the contra-diction in Marx's position, which was that immediately after a socialist victory the state would need to be held in the form of the dictatorship of the proletariat. But if a separate state were to be maintained, then this would not be self-government in the style of the Commune. Hence Marx was apparently contradicting himself, although he could escape quite easily by pointing to the always-useful 'anomalies of the transition'.

Perhaps Bakunin's most resonant criticism of all was that Marx's pro-nouncements on the proletarian state were 'lies behind which lurks the despotism of a governing minority', which were even more dangerous in that this minority pretended to appear as an expression of the people's will. No more prescient prediction about the negative side of Marxist governments of the twentieth century was ever made by a socialist. Marx's reply was to send all of Bakunin's nightmares about authority 'to the devil' by citing the position of a manager in a cooperative; a rather feeble reply since, as far as is understood, Lucifer does not operate by committee. Needless to say, Marx frequently treated Bakunin as a political opponent with contempt. Ironically, it was Bakunin who was first offered the task of translating volume one of *Capital* into Russian. He initially agreed and was enthusiastic about Marx's economic efforts, but was quickly sidetracked by circumstances, and thus the task passed to Lopatin. This was regrettable, as a translation of volume one undertaken by an anarchist might have been a very interesting text.

Unlike many of his contemporaries, Bakunin was not in any way in awe of Marx, characterising him in *Statism and Anarchy* as a 'lifelong and incorrigible dreamer' and as either a madman or an abstract theoretician: there was a fine line between the two. Marx's programme would bring about only 'the (supposed) liberation of the proletariat' and his work lacked any practical instinct at all. Even more insulting, he was an 'alehouse politician' who really desired an impractical government of scholars. Bakunin's first description of Marx is worth quoting at length:

> Nervous, as some say, to the point of cowardice, he is extraordinarily ambitious and vain, quarrelsome, intolerant and absolute ... vindictive to the point of insanity ... he stops short at no intrigue, however 'infamous' ... These are his negative characteristics. But he has also a great many positive qualities. He is very 'clever' and extraordinarily versatile ...[26]

But perhaps the greatest insult that he dared to hurl at Marx was the subtlest one: he constantly referred to his opponent throughout the book as 'Mr Marx', i.e. forgetting to acknowledge that Marx had a doctorate, despite initially admitting that he had one.

This conflict with Bakunin was one of a number of factional contests that Marx had waged within the International since its first creation. In November 1871 Marx declared that the aim of the International had been to replace all the various socialist sects by a 'real organisation of the working class' designed to pursue the class struggle in a more disciplined fashion. He outlined three such factional battles that had been pursued, which were against the Parisian Proudhonists, the German Lassalle clique, and Bakunin's own Alliance.[27] When considering this issue it is difficult for an outside observer to refrain from suggesting that, if Marx had lost one of these internal battles, then the victors would have painted 'the London Marx clique' in exactly the same terms as Marx described his vanquished opponents. Moreover, the anarchist criticism of Marxist authoritarianism as being only a cover for Marx's personal elevation was itself thrown back on to Bakunin by Marx, who declared that Bakunin's own theory was 'merely a means to his personal self-assertion'.[28] Again, it is difficult for an objective observer to finally choose between sides in this conflict, as there was an element of truth in both claims, with such battles being characterised ultimately as 'my revolution is better than yours'.

All these various factional contests within the International, together with the experience of the Paris Commune, obviously weighed quite considerably on Marx and Engels as the supposed 'true' theoreticians of the vast majority of the working masses. These issues were so important that Engels decided to take on the accusation of authoritarianism directly in an article entitled 'On Authority', published in December 1873. The article was a model of clarity in the exposition of its arguments and in the conclusions to which it came. It was also the first truly Orwellian text written by a Marxist. Engels declared that:

> ... it is absurd to speak of the principle of authority as being absolutely evil, and the principle of autonomy as being absolutely good. Authority and autonomy are relative things whose spheres vary with the various phases of the development of society.[29]

Engels argued that the economic conditions of society determined the level of authoritarian control that was required, and hence that wanting to abolish authority within large-scale industry was tantamount to wanting to abolish such industry itself. The techniques of large-scale manufacture themselves, i.e. the needs of the physical machinery itself and the steam power on which it was based, set the framework for controlling the labour in the work involved. The notion that the authority managing this process could be abolished was utopian. Unsurprisingly, after presenting such a stark and uncompromising argument in favour of worker subordination to the manufacture process, Engels did not quote his much earlier work *The Condition of the Working Class in England*, which had carefully exposed the 'logic of capitalist machine production' to a withering humanitarian gaze.

The pro-authority arguments were developed still further. Engels cited the example of a political revolution, asking rhetorically whether the anti-authoritarians had ever witnessed an actual revolt. He continued:

> A revolution is certainly the most authoritarian thing there is; it is the act whereby one part of the population imposes its will upon the other part by means of rifles, bayonets and cannon – authoritarian means ... if the victorious party does not want to have fought in vain, it must maintain this rule by means of the terror which its arms inspire ...[30]

Echoing Marx's privately expressed views, Engels reproached the Paris Commune for not using its available armed power freely enough in protecting its existence. The article concluded by declaring that anyone who questioned the necessity of such authoritarian means was serving the reaction and hence betraying the proletariat: thus, they were 'enemies of the people'. Earlier on in the article, Engels had mocked the idea that authority in an anti-authoritarian sense meant 'a commission entrusted' as being irrelevant hair splitting. Apparently, those workers who had believed that a socialist revolution would result in the egalitarian redistribution of authority had misunderstood what Marx and Engels had meant. Property itself might be so redistributed, but the power to control this property might not be. This was an Orwellian distinction so far from hair splitting that it could be described as neck breaking.

It must also be highlighted that Engels' definition of a revolution as necessarily authoritarian and as inevitably being based on military might has today at least been conclusively broken. The peaceful 'velvet' revolution in Czechoslovakia in 1989 is one notable counter-example, although what Engels would have made of a successful civilised rebellion against East European communism cannot be known. The guerrilla revolutionaries of Latin America in the 1960s, basing their strategies on the writings of Che Guevara, did not really follow the European examples on which Engels based his account either, since the notion of a victorious guerrilla war against the state was considered highly unlikely. Even the

Bolshevik revolution in 1917, although closer to Engels' model than the previous two examples, utilised a conception of the communist party that would have been alien to him. It is more accurate to say that each new revolutionary wave in the twentieth century has developed some features unique to its own circumstances, and hence that Engels' authoritarian generalisations have long since become outmoded.

CONCLUSION

The tantalising model of Paris had allowed Marx briefly to smell the scent of socialist victory, although he knew in his heart of hearts that this particular example of the model Commune would not last. It had also brought to the surface various simmering issues relating to the politics of socialist government, and the proposed resolutions to these issues were not always comforting to those outside the inner circle of disciples. As Marx and Engels hardened through prolonged political struggle, their youthful humanism became transformed into something more angular. On a less ambiguous note, various new editions of volume one of *Capital* had appeared in the early 1870s, strengthening Marx's claim to be the most serious socialist thinker of the period. The content and significance of these translations are considered in more detail in the next chapter.

10

THE CIRCULATION OF

CAPITAL

In Chapter 8 some of the concepts and themes of volume one of *Capital* were outlined, together with an account of the various drafts that were produced along the road to publication. After 1867 Marx continued his research on those aspects of capitalist production that were not covered in volume one, while *Capital* as a book began to circulate. It would be pushing the analogy a little too far to suggest that it metamorphosed into its opposite during this circulation process, but certainly a number of variant interpretations of volume one were possible. In Chapter 9 the Russian translation of 1872 was discussed in some detail, although only the external aspects of its production were covered. What about the actual content of volume one of *Capital*? Did it change in any significant way in this overseas circulation process?

CIRCULATION IN EUROPE

In 1870 Marx had already expressed a desire to re-write parts of volume one, specifically the first theoretical part, although these revisions were not ready in time for inclusion in the 1872 Russian translation.[1] However, such revisions were made in the first French edition (of 1872–5, issued in serial parts) translated by Joseph Roy, and in the second German edition (also issued in parts, in 1872–3) prepared by Marx himself. The author explained in a preface to the French edition written in 1875 that:

> These revisions, made from day to day as the book was published in parts, were carried out with varying degrees of care ... Having once undertaken this work of revision, I was led to apply it also to the basis of the original text (the German edition) ... Hence whatever may be the literary shortcomings of this French edition, it possesses a scientific value independent of the original ...[2]

Marx meant that, although he was not fully satisfied with the literary qualities of his revisions for the French translation, he stood firmly behind them in intellectual terms, and had undertaken a similar revisions process for the second German edition. He commented in private correspondence that he had also added much that was new to these editions, and the French translation was a (relative) publishing success, despite being printed in double columns and on rather poor-quality paper.

A biographer very sympathetic to Marx as a socialist revolutionary described the process of preparing the French edition in intriguing terms, as follows:

> Roy, the translator, did his work well, but Marx had 'the deuce of an amount' to do all the same; not only had he to revise the translation, which was no light task in view of the condensed style of the original and the play made with Hegelian phraseology ... but he simplified passages here and expanded passages there ...[3]

As has been demonstrated throughout this book, Marx did far more than simply 'play' with Hegelian phraseology, as the dialectical method had formed the underlying structure of his economic analysis from the very beginning. But, as the previous quotation indirectly implied, the way that this Hegelian method was demonstrated within volume one of *Capital* was modified across the various translations, just as it had been across the various unpublished drafts of the text.

One structural change made by Marx for the French translation concerned the divisions into chapters and the sub-divisions within them. He mentioned these changes in 1878 when a second Russian edition was being considered, remarking that he desired that the chapter divisions for this new edition should be made according to the French translation, and therefore not according to the first German edition.[4] In the French version there were more sub-divisions within the early chapters, presumably to make the argument easier to follow. Another change that Marx made was to diminish the presence of philosophical terms by sometimes removing them and by taking away some of the highlighting of such special terms, thereby downplaying their significance.[5] He also removed the explicit reference to Hegel's *Science of Logic* (the central methodological inspiration) in the main text of the early part of the book.

Thus, ostensibly to improve the presentation of the topic being discussed – the nature of commodities and the theory of value – Marx consciously removed some of the philosophical underpinnings of his own approach for both the second German edition and the first French translation. This was done at least three or four years after the first edition of volume one had been published in 1867, and this additional lapse of time had allowed Marx more capacity to continue his research on various economics-related topics. Was this extra research at all connected to the decision to modify the presentation of the early parts of *Capital* in the French translation?

RESEARCH AFTER VOLUME ONE

What were some of the most important new elements of Marx's post-volume-one research effort? At the end of the 1860s Marx had discovered the 'exceptionally important' (his own description) books of G. L. Maurer (1790–1872). Maurer was a German historian of ancient tribal customs and archaic economic formations who had published various accounts of these topics in the 1850s and thereafter. Maurer's work received some dissemination in English through its use by Henry Sumner Maine, author of *Village Communities in the East and West* of 1871, but of course Marx could read it in its original format. Maurer argued that ancient German forms of village community had been important as the basis for more advanced structures of ownership and state control. This type of work was of interest to Marx as he was researching the initial expansion of capitalism into and within pre-capitalist economic formations, as part of the preparatory work for the later volumes of *Capital*.

Marx wrote to Engels in March 1868 in a revelatory tone regarding his own positive evaluation of Maurer's conception of historical development. It was now apparent to him that:

> Human history is like palaeontology ... even the best intelligences absolutely fail to see the things which lie in front of their noses ... They are therefore surprised to find what is newest in what is oldest ... right in *my own* neighbourhood, on the Hunsrucken, the old German system survived up till the *last few years* ... and primitive German villages still exist here and there in Denmark ...[6]

Marx was suggesting that, like fossils buried in different layers within the earth's crust, different social and economic structures could survive in layers embedded within and upon each other *inside* specific modes of production. Hence the form of the primitive German villages still existed in certain geographical areas, despite the fact that such forms had long since passed as the dominant type of social formation in the regions in question. The significance of this was fundamental, since it meant that within a given dominant mode of production subdominant formations from previous eras could survive, just like living fossils that had been perfectly preserved from various distant geological epochs.

The analogy being made by Marx between history and palaeontology was not merely accidental. As avid followers of new developments in the natural sciences, both Marx and Engels were well informed about the extraordinary discoveries being made in this period by the English dinosaur hunters. Gideon Mantell (discoverer of the *Iguanodon*) and William Buckland (discoverer of the *Megalosaurus*) were both mentioned explicitly by Engels in *Socialism: Utopian and Scientific* of 1880. Engels also related in the preface to volume two of *Capital* that Marx had studied geology after 1870. Hence this palaeontology-derived conception of historical layers accumulating over time was one that both Marx and Engels would have been quite familiar with from their varied scientific interests. Some years later, in 1881, Marx wrote again that 'our globe itself contains a series of layers from various ages, the one superimposed on the other', and then made the explicit analogy with social formations.[7]

There was of course a long section in volume one of *Capital* that had been devoted to the origins of capitalism in 'primitive accumulation', but this had focused mainly on the British example as exemplifying the most advanced case of the day. Here Marx had outlined how the usurpation of common land and its transformation into private property had created the preconditions for the development of capitalism, these being a landless proletariat and the accumulation of capitalistic control. He wrote that: 'The organisation of the capitalist process of production, once fully developed, breaks down all resistance'.[8] The idea that primitive economic forms could survive indefinitely alongside this development of capitalist relations had simply not been countenanced. Hence the acceptance of a 'geological layers' conception of historical change was a significant modification of the assumptions that had been tacitly accepted in volume one. The first chance that Marx might get to demonstrate this revised conception was in volume two. But did he actually take this opportunity?

THE PREPARATION OF VOLUME TWO OF *CAPITAL*

While working on the various translations and re-issues of volume one discussed above, Marx was simultaneously pursuing work on volumes two and three of *Capital*, at least to some (as yet) undefined extent. In the early 1870s various publishers began sending insistent letters enquiring about the state of play with regard to the continuing volumes of Marx's Herculean efforts, especially as volume one had done rather well in its French and Russian translations. In a triumph of revolutionary hope over practical experience, it was suggested in October 1876 that volume two would be 'tackled in a few days'.[9] Some considerable time later a submission date of the end of 1879 was being quoted. In fact Marx never completed volumes two and three before his death in 1883, the precise reason for this being contentious.

This did not mean, however, that the author had not conducted a great deal of research on the proposed contents of volume two, or had not composed draft versions of major parts of the book. As was frequently the case with Marx, he was in no way reluctant with regard to actually doing detailed and substantial research. Only (apparently) when it came to completing the research in published form was he characteristically reticent. Engels explained in his own preface to the first edition of volume two of *Capital* (eventually published in 1885) that:

> It was no easy task to prepare the second volume of *Capital* for the printer ...
> The great number of manuscripts, and their fragmentary character, added to
> the difficulties of this task. At best one single manuscript (no.4) had been
> revised throughout and made ready for the printer. And while it treated its
> subject matter fully, the greater part had become obsolete through subse-
> quent revision.[10]

What Engels meant was that Marx had prepared something close to a
near-complete draft of a substantial part of volume two, but had then
become dissatisfied with the manuscript as it stood. He then began to
prepare revised versions of sections of it, but never produced a finally
complete version of the entire work that he was satisfied with.

Engels explained in more detail that the first batch of manuscripts
devoted to volume two in their entirety were written by Marx between
1865 and 1870, and were presented in four parts. Marx had discussed
some specific points and issues relevant to volume two before this period,
but he had not begun focused work on preparing an entire draft until
1865, which was still two years before volume one was first published.
As already indicated, according to Engels manuscript no.4 of this first
batch of work on volume two was the most complete. However, after a
substantial gap in time, partly caused by poor health, Marx resumed
work on volume two in 1877, and then produced four additional manuscripts in 1877–80. These later manuscripts were not particularly long,
although they were (presumably) closer to Marx's final intentions in
what they did cover. Engels then explained that: 'About this time Marx
seems to have realised that he would never be able to complete the
second and third volume in a manner satisfactory to himself, unless a
complete revolution in his health took place.'[11]

Since such a positive health revolution never materialised, the implication was that the blame for not completing volumes two and three
should be placed squarely at the door of Marx's failing health.

Engels' account was partly true, in that Marx certainly did suffer
bouts of poor health that affected his ability to work to some considerable extent. However, it is revealing to explain what Marx actually did in
some of these periods of poor health that apparently prevented him from
working on the later volumes of *Capital*. One of his favourite diversions
from the difficulties of analysing economic theory from a socialist perspective was – wait for it – studying mathematics. Yes, this fact needs

to be repeated, Marx steeped himself in (for example) the history of higher algebra as a means of mental relaxation. Engels explained regarding the interrupted work schedule that: 'After 1870 came another pause caused mainly by the painful illnesses of Marx. By habit, he usually filled his time studying; agronomy, American and especially Russian land relationships ... geology and physiology, and particularly his own mathematical work ...'.[12]

The obvious point will nevertheless be made. If Marx had enough intellectual and physical energy to study mathematics (and the various other topics listed by Engels), then surely this was also enough strength to continue work on his own economics? The standard reason implied by many commentators was that the pure abstractions of mathematical thinking allowed Marx some relief from the 'stress' of working on the more immediate topic of economics, but whether this is a plausible explanation is debatable.

This relaxation technique is even more incongruous when it is considered that Engels himself (and some other commentators) have claimed that Marx's contributions to mathematics were original, and were of great significance to the subject itself. Thus, what was really being suggested was that Marx did not have the energy to complete an analysis of economics *that he had been working on for decades*, but he did have sufficient energy to make original contributions to some branches of mathematics, a subject with which he was far less conversant. Marx's mathematical efforts will be covered in some detail in Chapter 12, so readers can then decide for themselves if this type of work should be characterised as intellectually soothing. If Marx had been prevented from working on any subjects at all during and after all his various bouts of illness, then this explanation for the incompletion of *Capital* might be more believable.

In a long letter to Danielson from April 1879, Marx explained his real attitude to working on volume two. He first related that the existing government in Germany would not be sympathetic to allowing publication of this book, but then admitted that he was glad of this censoriousness, for the following three reasons. First, publication before the current industrial crisis in England had reached its climax was ruled out, as to study this crisis theoretically it must have finally worked itself through. Second, the receipt of a large amount of materials from Russia and from other countries such as the United States made it 'pleasant for me to have a "pretext" of continuing my studies, instead of winding them up finally for the public'.[13] And third, his medical adviser had warned him to shorten his working day.

The first reason is easily dismissed as irrelevant, as Marx had witnessed and analysed many trade cycles up until this date, and an empirical account of such cycles was not the essential feature of volume two anyway. The second reason was true, but the admission that he was using it as a 'pretext' suggested that Marx was looking for excuses not to finish. The third reason was again true, but it should be noted that this medical advice was only to shorten his working day, not to give up working completely. Thus if Marx had wanted to devote all his (shortened) working day to preparing volume two, he could have done so. Engels himself wrote the following comment in a letter from September 1879 concerning Marx's return from a recuperative stay in Jersey during August: 'Marx is back, apparently in the very best of health, so no doubt work on the 2nd volume of *Capital* can now go briskly ahead.'[14]

This hopeful statement seemed to contradict Engels' later claim, made in the preface to the first edition of volume two, that Marx had come to realise that he would never be able to complete the second volume in a satisfactory manner. At the time of the previously quoted letter in 1879, Engels obviously believed that he could and would finish it.

Moreover, even if publication of volume two in Germany was temporarily outlawed, which clearly it had not been for volume one, then other publishing options still existed. A German version could have been printed outside of Germany, or volume two could have been issued in another language. Admittedly, this last option would have required significant additional work, but since the fate of the entire socio-economic world was (allegedly) at stake this would not have been an impossible task to contemplate. It is therefore reasonable to conclude that the reasons for the lack of progress on volume two were more than simply health issues, without necessarily denigrating the real health problems that Marx had faced at this time.

THE CONTENT OF VOLUME TWO

But what of the content of volume two of *Capital* as Engels had finally presented it? This volume was certainly the driest and most technical of the three volumes, which meant that it was inevitably the hardest to engage with and probably the least read. The subtitle was 'The Circulation Process of Capital', and the book covered in great detail the various forms of the circuits of capital as they rotated through the production process, as expansions of the basic formula: $M - C - M'$. Perhaps the most well known part of it today was that it presented a set of equilibrium schemes for simple and expanded reproduction, or a series of equilibrium conditions that had to hold if disproportion between departments of production (and thus economic crises) were to be avoided. In this way Marx provided, firstly, a new method with which to explain disequilibrium within capitalist production, and secondly, a technique that might conceivably be of use in the process of economic planning.

One noticeable feature of volume two was that it contained far less historical and factual material than volume one, and far more analysis of the logical basis of circulation in an abstract form. The basic theoretical innovation was the division of all production within capitalism into two basic departments or sections: department I representing the production of means of production; department II representing the production of means of consumption. The equilibrium schemes for simple and expanded reproduction consequently posited a specific quantitative relation between the production of the means of production and the means of consumption that, when violated, generated economic convulsions. The implication was that sustainable growth could be maintained only if there was a certain balance between the production of consumption goods and the creation of new plant and machinery. There was also some historical discussion in volume two about previous economists' views on topics such as the distinction between fixed and circulating capital and various forms of reproduction.

At least as Engels edited together the draft manuscripts for the published version of volume two, the circulation formula $M - C...P...C' - M'$ occurred a mere four pages before Marx analysed the two departments of production (I and II) and simple reproduction, suggesting (accurately) to the reader that they were part of the same underlying approach to understanding capitalist expansion.[15] In creating the reproduction schemes Marx had in part been inspired by Francois Quesnay's *tableau economique*, but this creation itself was designed to illustrate the circular flow of economic life, and thus was ripe for young Hegelian reinterpretation. Textual evidence that there was some hidden

Hegelianism underlying the reproduction schemes is apparent from the following passage from volume two of *Capital*:

> The variable capital of [department] I passes through three metamorphoses ... 1) The first form is 1000 I_v in money, which is converted into labour-power of the same value ... its result is seen in the fact that working-class I confronts commodity seller II with 1000 in money ... 2) The second form ... functions as variable capital, where value-creating force appears in the place of given value exchanged for it ... 3) The third form, in which the variable capital has justified itself as such in the result of the process of production, is the annual value-product, which in the case of I is equal to 1000_v plus 1000_s or $2000\ I_{(c+v)}$ ...[16]

The posited triadic progression contained within this passage was thus: money-capital – productive-capital – commodity-value, which then returned to its point of origin in money. The metamorphosis of a concept through three distinct stages of itself was of course the underlying structure of Hegel's *Logic*.

In Marx's initial plan, volume two of *Capital* was supposed to deal with the circulation of capital in general as it created its own presuppositions by dissolving pre-capitalist economic formations.[17] The *Grundrisse* showed the Hegelian heritage of his work more clearly as products were transformed into commodities, commodities into money and money into capital by means of a historical pre-positing process, in which the simple forms of commodity production were initially presupposed, and then repeatedly pre-posited as the basis of the next presupposition for more developed capitalism, thus forming a self-reproducing spiral of capital across spatial and temporal bounds.[18] Volume two was designed to illustrate this process of expansion in more detail through use of the circuits of capital and the reproduction schemes.

One significant issue that was considered in relation to the expansion of capitalism both nationally and internationally was the time or period of circulation of capital, and how technological improvements affected this measure. Marx wrote that:

> ... the development of the means of transportation and communication by the progress of capitalist production reduced the time of circulation for a given quantity of commodities, the same progress, on the other hand, coupled to the growing possibility of reaching more distant markets ... leads to the

necessity of producing for ever more remote markets, in one word, for the world market.[19]

Thus the expansion of capitalism was being facilitated by improvements in technology, which enabled faster communication. But the fact that ever-more remote geographical areas were being brought within the capitalist orbit meant simultaneously a tendency towards the use of more protracted transport links. In volume two of *Capital* Marx considered this issue only in relation to the abstract circulation of capital, i.e. in terms of the effect of ever-longer periods of commodity travel on the time required for completing sales and hence realising monetary value. However, the same issue was also very important in terms of the effect of exporting capitalist relations to other countries – a crucial issue in relation to the ultimate fate of capitalism as a mode of production.

This issue was closely connected to the amount of research that Marx had undertaken on Russia after volume one of *Capital* was published in 1867. The geographical expansion of capitalism through the circulation of capital was something that could be modelled abstractly, as was supposed to have been done in volume two, but there was also a specific historical reality underlying this abstraction, i.e. the transplantation of capitalism to various unique nation states. Marx's ultimate aim was to connect these two areas together, and to model this process both theoretically and historically. However, here he had already come up against something of an anomaly. As previously detailed, Marx had come to realise that so-called antiquated forms of economy could still exist side by side with more modern forms, in a series of layers deposited through historical time. This did not necessarily completely invalidate his earlier conception of a sequence of 'pure' modes of production, but it certainly made analysing them much more complicated. It also made the abstract logic that they were portrayed as manifesting somewhat less realistic.

If volume two of *Capital* had attempted to deal with the historical reality of capitalist expansion in terms of the circuits based upon $M - C - M'$, then Marx would have needed to resolve this issue fully, otherwise his analysis would not have been convincing. As it stands today volume two does not really raise this issue, as, for some reason, Marx and/or Engels decided against covering it. A plausible hypothesis could be that, realising the monumental intellectual effort that would be required to achieve this unification of historical and theoretical materials, namely mastering the economic history of various non-capitalist and semi-capitalist countries in some detail, Marx was reluctant to attempt this task at this stage of his life. Remember that the three volumes of *Capital* were initially planned out at a time when this added complication was not an issue, since the already-outlined abstract logic was then accepted as being more accurate. Was part of the reason for the incompletion of *Capital* this added requirement for historical realism that Marx had understood fully only later in his life?

CONSTRUCTING VOLUME TWO

How volume two was finally constructed is worth considering in detail. Engels indicated in footnotes to the published text where sections of volume two had originated in relation to the various draft manuscripts that were prepared by Marx. He also provided a guide to the 'compilation of passages' that was used, which is shown here as Table 1.

Table 1: ENGELS' CONSTRUCTION OF VOLUME TWO OF *CAPITAL*

PAGE NUMBERS	MANUSCRIPT ORIGIN
1	2
2–13	7
13–17	6
17–93	5
94–97	(note from an extract)
97–105	4
105–107	8
110–117	2
130–140	4
140–340	2
341–349	2
350–383	8
383–385	2
386–389	2 (8)
389–392	2
393–418	8

PAGE NUMBERS	MANUSCRIPT ORIGIN
418–434	2
435–480	8
480–489	2
489–526	8

Source: Karl Marx, *Das Kapital: Buch II* (Hamburg: Meissner, 1885), p.xxiv.

Thus the first page or so of the text was from manuscript no.2, the next twelve pages or so were from manuscript no.7, the following four pages or so were from manuscript no.6, and the remainder of chapter one was from manuscript no.5. Thus the first chapter of around forty printed pages (divided into four subsections) was taken from four different draft manuscripts. Although a substantial part of the middle section of the book was from a single manuscript (no.2), this was not the manuscript that Engels had identified as being 'revised throughout and ready for the printer' (no.4). Moreover, manuscript no.1, the earliest and most philosophical of the draft manuscripts, was not used at all.[20] It should be explained that Marx left no detailed instructions for Engels to follow in assembling volume two, and hence that this manner of splicing the materials together was entirely due to Engels.

Perusing the first chapter today, it works perfectly well in introducing the topic ('the circulation of money-capital') to the reader, as does the book as a whole in conveying the content of the existing draft manuscripts. However, it cannot be claimed with any degree of certainty that Marx would have presented the materials in the same way that Engels did, simply because no one can know exactly how Marx would have finished volume two if he had found the energy to do so. He might have rewritten the entire book from the beginning, using the draft manuscripts only as notes. And he might even have added substantial new materials that were not found in any of the existing eight draft manuscripts, in order to explain more convincingly the real historical development of the capitalist mode of production in different countries. Simply because of the large number of edits and splices that were made in relation to the number of options available, the chance that Marx would have mirrored what Engels did exactly in the published version is close to zero.

It is also worth pointing out that the single reference to another author that was found in chapter one was to a Russian economist (A. I. Chuprov), who was a leading representative of the German historical school in Moscow – a school of economists who precisely recognised the historical specificity of economic structures that Marx had recently had reason to re-emphasise.[21] Thus, volume two of *Capital* as it stands today is a patchwork of draft chapters and sections, which do present many of the themes and ideas that Marx intended to cover in the book, but which do not articulate them in any finalised manner and do not connect them together (either externally in relation to volumes one and three or internally with all the chapters) as Marx would ultimately have desired. These failures are not necessarily due to any editorial flaws on the part of Engels but are simply the result of Marx's own incomplete legacy.

Even so, not everyone was entirely satisfied with how Engels had constructed volume two. Both the partial translator of volume one into Russia, Danielson, and the only person footnoted in the first chapter of volume two, Chuprov, expressed some concern that Marx's Russian studies were entirely absent from volume two.[22] The implication was that including this historical material would have added an important extra dimension to volume two, compared with the mainly abstract form that it was actually issued in. But, as has been argued, it is quite possible that this exclusion of Russian materials was deliberate, in that Marx had baulked at the task of integrating actual historical reality with his a priori-constructed theoretical scheme, and he consequently left this task to Engels. Engels in turn made no effort to accomplish such a grand unification, and instead simply edited together what Marx had already drafted in theoretical terms only. Or, as Engels himself explained, he confined his work on volume two to 'a mere selection of the various revised parts'.[23]

The only remnant of Marx's Russian efforts in volume two was a very short two-paragraph account of some of the problems that had been identified by Russian landowners. This suggested that the reason for a lack of available labourers for landowners to employ was that: '... the Russian farm labourer, owing to the communal property in land, has not been fully separated from his means of production, and hence is not yet a "free wage-worker"'.[24]

Marx admonished Russian landowners to have patience, as everything comes to those who wait. However, he then dropped something of a theoretical bombshell, outlining that the previously developed formula for the circuit of money-capital $(M - C...P...C' - M')$ was applicable 'only on the basis of already developed capitalist production'. If this was true, and Marx clearly believed that it was, then exactly how had capitalism first originated, and how could this genesis process be modelled using such circuit-based formulae? Answering this question would (presumably) have been aided significantly by the inclusion of the new research on non-capitalist and semi-capitalist economy, but of course it was entirely absent from Engels' published version of volume two. Marx repeatedly noted that agricultural producers had to become wage labourers if capitalism was to develop, but he never adequately explained exactly how this was supposed to occur by means of the natural circulation of capital, as the result of the motion of the capital accumulated in pre-capitalist systems.

If the hypothesis of deliberate (or enforced) exclusion of the additional materials is true, then it means that *Capital* as it stands in its three-volume form today is a long way from the completed system of economic analysis that its author had ultimately desired. And if it is a long way from Marx's real intentions, then it cannot be taken to finally prove anything one way or the other about the long-term historical fate of capitalism. Proto-capitalism was indeed (temporarily) supplanted in Russia after 1917, but this was the result of conscious human will and action; it was not the outcome of any historically inevitable processes that had been conclusively demonstrated in *Capital*. It was no coincidence that in volume one Marx had explained that the grounds for the genesis of capitalism in the UK had been laid by deliberate actions such as the Highland clearances in Scotland (the forced driving of the peasants from the land), not by any abstract laws of capital circulation.

In fact, nothing specific about the inevitable progression of economic systems had been finally proved in *Capital*, as the series of book was not completed, and Marx never actually confirmed that the additional historical examples that he was studying conformed to the abstract model that he had initially proposed. This abstract model was really only an internal theorisation of the motive mechanics of capital once capitalism had been created, deduced philosophically from the essence of the concepts on which this understanding of capitalism was constructed. The model explained little about the traumatic transitions between modes of production that were necessary for socialism to be born. Put bluntly, Marx's quasi-philosophical method had revealed its ultimate limit.

CONCLUSION

This might appear as shocking heresy to many devout Marxists, but what the three volumes of *Capital* actually consisted of was a series of preliminary 'studies towards' an understanding of capitalism. These territory-opening studies were undoubtedly brilliantly conceived, pioneering as economic history, and full of conceptual invention, but they were inconclusive nonetheless. In his heart of hearts Marx knew that this was true, and he left the manuscripts for Engels to make something of after his death. As an atheist, Marx believed that he would never have to account for how Engels managed to fulfil this remaining legacy. *Capital* was thus not a memento mori of capitalism; instead it was only a reminder of Marx's mortal limitations as a philosopher-economist.

This is being claimed not in order to denigrate the real contributions that Marx did make to an understanding of the evolution of economic systems, but only so that a more realistic benchmark of evaluation can be applied to his efforts as authentic research, rather than as messianic prophesy. Marx's stark prediction about the inevitability of capitalist collapse has not come true, but the fact that *Capital* was never finished can be interpreted as indicating that its author realised that such a prophecy had not been conclusively proved, if only on a subconscious level. Marx so desperately *wanted* capitalism to collapse that his emotional desires sometimes overruled what his (brilliant) intellect had actually demonstrated. This contradiction was the underlying contradiction of *Capital*. How it was manifested in volume three will be considered in what follows.

11

AND NOW RUSSIA!

Previous chapters have indicated the incomplete status of the later volumes of *Capital* in the early 1870s, but Marx apparently had many years in which to continue his research into economics and thus make up the intellectual deficit that remained. And, although French government forces had quickly crushed the political example of the Paris Commune, there were still various revolutionary prospects on the horizon in Europe and beyond. What would turn out to be the final years of Marx's life were thus potentially very active ones, both theoretically and in a practical sense, although whether they were fully successful remains to be seen.

DISPUTES OF THE PERIOD

As the 1870s progressed Marx began to turn his political energies back to Germany, where two separate proletarian parties had begun to achieve some significant degree of electoral success. It was decided as a result of this success to develop a united political programme, which came up for formal consideration by the parties involved in a town in Germany called Gotha in the spring of 1875. Marx was annoyed that his own input had not been explicitly requested in this process, and was also dissatisfied with the proposed programme itself. In consequence he wrote a work entitled 'Marginal Notes on the Programme of the German Workers' Party', in which his critical attitude was presented. This was later published as the *Critique of the Gotha Programme*, which is arguably Marx's most well-known political text from this later period of his life. It contained perhaps the largest amount of detail that he wrote in one document on the nature of future communist society, at least after the revolutionary events of 1848–9.

Certain key Marxian ideas were articulated in the *Critique of the Gotha Programme* in a forceful manner. The period between capitalism and communism required that the state should be 'nothing but the revolutionary dictatorship of the proletariat'.[1] In the first period of communist control each individual would receive back in labour certificates (a form of exchange voucher) exactly the same amount as they had contributed in working time, even through this was still a 'bourgeois' form of equality. Only much later, in a higher phase of communism, would the inspiring principle 'from each according to his ability, to each according to his needs' actually apply. The implication of this principle was that, given the material abundance that would eventually be produced in 'mature' communism, individuals could contribute and take back whatever they desired. There would be no 'bourgeois' accounting of profit and loss, or income and expenditure. In addition, the dictatorship of the proletarian state would eventually 'wither away' of its own accord, once its function of establishing proletarian control and facilitating the nationalisation of the means of production, distribution and exchange had been accomplished.

More subtly but still very significantly, Marx referred to the 'all-round development of the individual' and the end of the antithesis between mental and physical labour that would occur in the 'mature' stage of his future societal prediction. These two ideas pointed back to the philosophical origins of his conception of communism within the German idealism of his youth. Thus, echoes of the 'Economic and Philosophical Manuscripts' of 1844 could still be (faintly) detected in works from the 1870s, although exactly how the 'all-round individual' would be created was left unspecified. It should be pointed out that Marx's own life was the epitome of specialising in only mental labours, to the (apparently very unhealthy) exclusion of the physical. The *Critique of the Gotha Programme* also contained various criticisms of the German party programme that it was ostensibly directed against, such as that its specific proposals for a socialist redistributive policy, for an equal degree of elementary education and for the creation of a socialist 'free state' were flawed. Engels wrote a foreword to this *Critique* when it was finally published in 1891, characterising the 'ruthless severity' of Marx's dissection of the draft programme.

Another more focused conflict that broke out in this period was with Eugen Duhring, a German socialist philosopher who was based at Berlin University. As early as 1876 Engels had begun to assemble materials for an attack on Duhring's work, as his influence within socialist groups was seen to be rising, partly through followers categorised as Duhringians. A book-length study entitled *Herr Eugen Duhring's Revolution in Science*, the title of which was often shortened to *Anti-Duhring*, was eventually completed, written mainly by Engels, in which Marx contributed a chapter written in 1877 on Duhring's work on the history of political economy.

Duhring's crime was that he had criticised Marx for various deficiencies such as an over-reliance on Hegel and for a lack of foresight about exactly how a future communist society might operate. Unable to let this criticism stand without a reply, a lengthy counterblast was prepared by Engels between 1876 and 1878. It was originally written as a series of articles, but it was then published in book form under Engels' name. Parts of it went on to be used as a popular introductory text to the basic ideas of Marxism throughout the twentieth century, even though Engels had written the vast majority of it.

In May 1876 Engels wrote to Marx in a semi-humorous mood regarding his progress against Herr Duhring:

> You can lie in a warm bed – study Russian agrarian relations in particular and rent in general ... but I have to sit on a hard bench, drink cold wine, and all of a sudden drop everything else and break a lance with the tedious Duhring.[2]

Engels then outlined how one of Duhring's major political crimes – writing a whole chapter in one of his books depicting how a future communist society would operate, including syllabi for primary and secondary schools – would be dealt with. Taking a leaf from Marx's sophisticated vocabulary of put-downs, Engels later described Duhring as a 'conceited ignoramus'.[3] The book itself was repeatedly described in correspondence as 'the Duhring', suggesting a superior length of detachment and a degree of annoyance that such a petty individual might have the gall to criticise the great Marx himself. It is worth pointing out that Duhring is mainly known today as the target of Engels' book. If Engels had not written it, then Duhring would probably be long forgotten by most commentators.

ENGELS POPULARISES MARX

After recovering somewhat from another bout of illnesses, throughout 1880 Marx continued to work periodically on volumes two and three of *Capital*, as well as on studying related topics such as ground rent and finance. Early in 1881 he continued his research on the historical development of the Russian economy by reading various Russian authors. However, he was unable to finish or finalise anything on the later volumes of *Capital* in this period, the usual reason that is offered in the existing literature being that of continued poor health.

By the beginning of the 1880s, some works by other authors had appeared that included an account of Marx's own theories: both sympathetic outlines and also more critical analyses. Moreover, in the first three months of 1880 Engels prepared one of his most well-known and frequently read works, *Socialism: Utopian and Scientific*. In fact this work was simply a revised version of three chapters taken straight out of *Anti-Duhring*, and it has subsequently served as a general introduction to the Marxian variant of socialism within socialist circles for many decades. How accurate an introduction to Marx's own ideas it actually was is debatable.

In *Socialism: Utopian and Scientific* Engels gave a chronological account of the development of socialist ideas from their initial philosophical roots, and also provided an introduction to the materialist conception of history. This work did not contain a discussion of Marx's economic theory in any detail, and it did not present the formulae used to represent the circulation of capital or to calculate the rate of surplus value. Marx wrote an introduction to the French edition of Engels' popularisation, but was not involved in any way in its composition. Thus it represented Engels' interpretation of some of Marx's ideas on the philosophy of historical development. One example of its content is particularly indicative, this being Engels' presentation of the idea of 'dialectics'.

It would be incorrect to state that Engels' presentation is 'wrong', only that it fails to fully convey the 'spirit' or 'impetus' of dialectics. Another way of putting it is that Engels' had described the content of dialectics without fully conveying an appreciation of its form, or even that he was guilty of presenting a non-dialectical account of dialectics. As a result he translated the philosophical language of German idealism into the (for him more familiar) positivistic language of the natural sciences of the day. For example, he referred to a 'fundamental law of dialectical reasoning' as if it were a mathematical formula describing the motion of inanimate bodies.[4]

This led Engels to declare the existence of three 'basic laws' of dialectics, such as 'the law of the transformation of quantity into quality', which were not really found (as this type of strict formal law) within Hegel's philosophical method. Hegel had certainly described the notion of such a transformation, but not really as a basic law of dialectics. For Hegel dialectics was a method of analysis, not a series of set laws. Thus Engels transformed a philosophical method of comprehending the movement of conceptual understanding into a prescribed system of basic laws that were applicable to the physical world. Later, in the USSR, this detached translation would be continued even further to produce the notion of 'dialectical materialism' as the underlying philosophical foundations of Marxism-Leninism, but this was a term that Marx himself never ever employed. Hence, in his attempt to popularise Marx, Engels had to some extent unconsciously distorted his friend's true intentions, or at least diffracted them through his own intellectual prism.

RUSSIA LOOKS TO MARX

By the beginning of the 1880s Marx's influence in Russia (unlike in many other European countries) was growing. The most famous and perhaps the most contentious passages on Russia that Marx ever wrote were contained in preparatory work for a letter to Vera Zasulich, who was a Russian exile living in Geneva. Zasulich had written to Marx in early 1881 asking if the views being attributed to him about the inevitable disintegration of the Russian peasant commune were accurate. The commune was a form of agrarian cultivation based on common ownership of arable land and collective managerial control. Given that this topic was very close to what Marx had been studying as part of his research for the later volumes of *Capital*, it might be assumed that this enquiry would be seen as a gift of a question allowing a detailed reply of many pages, if not an entire essay. In fact the letter that Marx sent in reply was a mere 34 lines of text (as later printed). What had been the problem?

In fact Marx had initially composed three lengthy draft letters on this question before drafting the actual short reply, but he chose not to send them. These drafts went into much more detail than the letter that was finally sent, and provided a clear account of Marx's attitude on the question that had been raised. But why had he decided against sending one of the longer versions? Perhaps the differences between the drafts and the actual letter might provide a clue. One obvious difference was that Marx was much more enthusiastic about the peasant commune as a social formation in the drafts. For example, in the first draft he wrote that research on the topic had established the fact that:

> (1) the vitality of primitive communities was incomparably greater than that of Semitic, Greek, Roman, etc. societies, and, *a fortiori*, that of modern capitalist societies; (2) the causes of their decline stem from economic facts ... not at all analogous with the historical surroundings of the Russian commune of today.[5]

A more glowing endorsement of the commune's nature and potential would be hard to conceive. Yet, in the actual letter that was sent, all that Marx could muster on this point was that the analysis already given in *Capital* 'assigns no reasons for or against the vitality of the rural community'.[6] Technically he was right – the analysis given in volume one of his proposed trilogy was neutral on the issue – but of course he had actually planned to cover the topic in the later volumes of *Capital*, not in the first. In general, although Marx outlined in the drafts that there were various interests in Russia working against the perpetuation of the commune, he believed that its dissolution was not inevitable, and that it could conceivably (in revived form) provide a springboard to create a socialist society directly, if certain other conditions were met. These conditions related to a simultaneous successful revolution in Western Europe.

In the drafts Marx also mentioned an organisation called the *artel*, a Russian form of workers' collective, which according to him had facilitated the transition from parcel labour to cooperative labour, i.e. had assisted in enabling the move from individual to social forms of farming. Yet in the actual letter the *artel* was not mentioned at all. One point of similarity was that Marx had emphasised that his theory of the historical inevitability of the genesis of capitalism was limited to the countries of Western Europe alone. This meant that the circulation of capital would indeed transform all pre-capitalist relations into capitalist ones, but only within the geographical bounds of Western Europe. In presenting this explicit limit to the validity of his proposed sequence of modes of production, Marx was tacitly accepting that the circulation of capital to countries outside of Western Europe would not inevitably create capitalism beyond the areas that were indicated. Thus the prevalent modes of production in (say) India and China were sufficiently resilient to prevent the inevitable rule of capital. This was a conclusion that Marx had reached only after his detailed study of non-capitalist countries such as Russia across the 1870s.

Perhaps in toning down his support for primitive economic formations such as the peasant commune in the letter of reply compared with the drafts, Marx had experienced a modicum of trepidation about the consequences of his explicit support for such an antiquated form of social economy. Socialism was (conventionally) supposed to be about creating a bright new future, not reinventing archaic forms from the past. Perhaps Marx had baulked at the consequences of being seen to explicitly advocate the preservation of the traditional culture of old Russia, which after all was the basic definition of being conservative. Had Marx mellowed a little politically as he grew to middle age (and studied more about the Middle Ages), and was he reluctant to admit it publicly? It is true that he viewed the commune's potential as enabling a return to previously existing collective forms of control, but this was still 'back to the future' rather than 'ever onwards and upwards'. Apparently the latent political conservatism buried within Hegel's philosophical method was difficult to completely annul, even if the rational kernel was removed from the mystical shell.

The letter to Zasulich was not Marx's last word on the issue of Russia. In a new preface composed for the Russian edition of *The Manifesto of the Communist Party* published in 1882, written mainly by Engels but corrected and co-authored by Marx,[7] the following passage gleefully admitting the political volte face that had occurred in respect to projecting Russia's historical destiny was found: 'And now Russia! During the Revolution of 1848–9 ... [the] tsar was proclaimed the chief of European reaction. Today ... Russia forms the vanguard of revolutionary action in Europe.'[8]

The change that this represented in Marx and Engels' scheme of national political understanding cannot be overestimated. It was the equivalent of Margaret Thatcher's hypothetical conversion to state socialism after hell had frozen over. For decades 'Team Marx' had rallied against the 'reserve army of European reaction', but now Russia was seen as being at the leading edge of socialist potential. Part of the explanation for this dramatic reversal must be seen in the detailed study of Russia that Marx had undertaken in the 1870s, and part in the actual political changes that had taken place in Russia after the emancipation of the serfs in 1861.

One major circumstantial catalyst for the changes that Marx was referring to had been the Russian–Turkish war of 1877–8. Ever the neutral objective observer on current events that he was not, in 1877 Marx immediately took the side of Turkey in this conflict. His reasons were twofold: that the Turkish peasantry were seen as brave and 'morally upright' peasant representatives, and because a Russian defeat would accelerate the social transformations that he desired.[9] Note that the rights or wrongs of this war from a diplomatic or international relations perspective were not even considered. The defeats suffered by Russia in the early stages of the war Marx hailed as hastening the coming social revolution. For example, Marx wrote to Engels in July 1877: 'I trust that the Russians' impudent goings-on beyond the Balkans will stir up the Turks against their old regime ... the Russian defeats in European Turkey are leading straight to revolution in Russia ...'.[10]

However, when the war was concluded in a diplomatic congress after Turkey had failed to capitalise on early military advances, the hopes for an immediate Russian revolution receded. Marx blamed the Turkish defeat partly on British treachery and support from Bismarck, and partly on indecisive action by the Turks. By September 1878 he was reporting that Russian military ploys were of 'little interest to me now', probably because the predicted social revolution had been studiously avoided.[11]

War, whatever the outcome, is frequently the catalyst for social change, even in the sense of generating growing frustration at hindering the changes that are desired, and so the revolutionary forces within

Russia sharpened their anger a little as a consequence of the Turkish war. Although the political forces for radical change in Russia were only a minuscule drop in a vast peasant ocean, these forces believed very strongly that their day would eventually come.

It is in the context of Marx's Russian studies of the 1870s that one of his most famous (and misunderstood) utterances – 'All I know is that I am not a Marxist' – can be comprehended. Engels reported this statement in a letter from August 1890, explaining that Marx was commenting on French 'Marxists' of the late 1870s when he made this particular remark. What he meant by the apparent disavowal of his own movement was that the beliefs being attributed to him by some who called themselves Marxists were inaccurate. The same reasoning can be applied to some of Marx's Russian followers, who claimed that Marx believed in the inevitable disintegration of the peasant commune. Hence, if the label 'Marxist' was given to those who believed in this particular inevitability, then Marx himself was certainly not one. Taken out of these specific contexts the disavowal makes no sense at all, since Marx never recanted on his basic critique of capitalism and his concomitant support for socialism as a political movement. He did, however, on various occasions have reason to dispute that some of those who acted in his name were actually correctly representing his own views on various contentious topics.

'TO THE DEVIL WITH THE BRITISH'

Although after the Paris Commune of 1871 Marx had begun to receive some attention from British commentators, he was still only infamous in the UK rather than famous, and his work was not taken very seriously by most British intellectuals. In return Marx was scathing about 'the British philistines' who ignored his ideas, and relations between Marx and representatives of British socialism were intermittently rocky to say the least. A good example was Marx's friendship with H. M. Hyndman, an English well-to-do socialist and the author of various books expressing reformist ideas. In 1880 Hyndman had been so impressed with volume one of *Capital* that he arranged to meet Marx in person. After being introduced the two socialists became acquaintances and (for a while) they met periodically to discuss prospects for political change.

For example, Marx wrote to Hyndman in December 1880 evaluating the 'revolution versus evolution' question for the UK: 'If you say that you do not share the views of my party for England I can only reply that the party considers an English revolution not necessary, but – according to historical precedents – possible'.[12]

The implication was that socialism might be achieved in the UK by ongoing gradual change, rather than by instantaneous forceful convulsion. As this passage implied, Hyndman was a strong advocate of this type of peaceful revolution introduced from above, not of violent revolution forced from below, and in 1881 he published a book in which such an approach was outlined. In this book Marx's economic ideas were employed to some considerable extent, but Hyndman acknowledged the source of this aspect of the book only indirectly, not by name.

In response to this silent usage Marx was furious, both that his name was omitted from the references and that his ideas had apparently been hijacked by a reformist. A short spat followed and the friendship was over.[13] The most obvious question to ask is, in their long hours of previous conversation, had not Marx realised that Hyndman was fully a reformist? And might it not have been wiser for Marx to request calmly that in any future editions of Hyndman's book his own name was either explicitly acknowledged, or, if the offence taken was so great, that the particular ideas and their source should be removed entirely? But perhaps this would have been a peaceful 'reformist' response, not a violent revolutionary one.

Hyndman evidently forgave Marx for the argument, as in the preface to his 1896 book *The Economics of Socialism* both Marx and Engels are explicitly listed as the founders of a 'scientific school of political economy' to which Hyndman wanted to introduce his readers.[14] Moreover, in the frontispiece picture of the book's author, Hyndman was shown sporting a beard uncannily like that worn by Marx. Hyndman's description of Marx as a political orator is worth quoting:

> Whilst speaking with fierce indignation ... the old warrior's small deep-sunk eyes lighted up, his heavy brows wrinkled, the broad, strong nose and face were obviously moved by passion, and he poured out a stream of vigorous denunciation ... The contrast between his manner and utterances when thus deeply stirred by anger and his attitude when giving his views on the economic events of the period was very marked.[15]

Marx's impassioned heart for politics and cool head for analysing 'the whole economic muck' were clearly displayed.

The episode with Hyndman indicated very well Marx's fractious relationship to the British intellectual scene. British empiricism and a penchant for practical compromise did not sit easy with Marx's German idealist roots and his love of struggle and ongoing conflict. Yet it was Great Britain that had allowed the infamous firebrand to settle within its capital city, when both France and Germany had ingloriously rejected him. It was the initial development of capitalism in Great Britain that had allowed its political opposite (socialism) to be first conceived in theory by (great) British thinkers such as William Godwin and Robert Owen. And it was the (great) British Museum that had provided Marx with a large proportion of the materials that he had used to write *Capital*. He paid back this large debt to his adopted homeland with a final recorded epitaph: 'To the devil with the British'.[16] As Marx was a lifelong atheist, this dismissive insult did not really make any intellectual sense.

A TURN FOR THE WORSE

In the last period of Marx's life, between 1881 and 1883, the fluctuating health problems that had repeatedly dogged him and his family for many years finally turned very serious indeed. In the mid-1870s Marx had been used to travelling to continental Europe to take various spa-based cures, but in 1878 the passing of anti-socialist legislation in Germany prevented him from doing so. His wife Jenny suffered various bouts of illness in this period, but then she developed a very serious illness which turned out to be cancer of the liver, and was consequently unable to leave the house for significant periods of time. In the summer of 1881 it became apparent that Jenny was terminally sick, and, to add to the family difficulties, in the autumn Marx contracted a serious bout of bronchitis.

Although he eventually recovered from the worst of this chest infection, Jenny did not recover from liver cancer, and she finally passed away in December. Marx was still too ill to attend the funeral, so instead Engels spoke at Jenny's graveside. Marx was deeply grief-stricken by the loss of his wife, and Engels judged in the heat of the tragic moment that his friend's heart for serious work had been broken. Although this was not quite true, Marx's capacity for work was dramatically curtailed, and this meant that the chances of *Capital* being completed in the form that had initially been outlined were remote. It was only at this point that it is accurate to judge that ill health and its associated consequences finally rang the death knell for the remaining volumes of *Capital*. Up until this time, Engels had hoped that the periodic fluctuations in Marx's health would still permit some serious work to continue.

Early in 1882 Marx travelled to Algiers on medical advice, where he stayed for around ten weeks, but the winter weather was still cold and wet so his poor health did not really improve. It is perhaps a little surprising to realise that this was the first time that Marx had ventured outside of Western Europe. Although since the publication of volume one of *Capital* in 1867 Marx had devoted a great deal of energy to studying non-European history, he had never visited any of the countries he had consequently studied, i.e. countries such as India, China and Russia. Certainly he had supporters in (for example) Russia who would have been delighted to receive him in person, although whether the Russian authorities would have allowed such a trip cannot be known. But Marx had not attempted to visit and then been denied access. The issue of conducting fieldwork for his research in person never really arose, perhaps partly because in methodological terms this first-hand approach to economic investigation was still uncommon.

After the stay in Algiers Marx travelled on to Monaco, where he described the casinos of Monte Carlo as 'childish' in comparison with the gambling that occurred on the London stock exchange. Further travel took him to Argenteuil to stay with his daughter Jenny in the summer of 1882, and then to Lausanne and Geneva in the autumn, all in search of relaxation to recover both from his various illnesses and from his grief. He had become a sort of detached nomad searching for some type of inner peace, which apparently was very difficult to find. The health problems that he has been identified as suffering in this period include bronchial catarrh, blisters and pleurisy, with the associated symptoms of spitting blood, painful skin and weight loss.[17] After returning to London for a brief respite he continued travelling, while his daughter Jenny began to suffer serious health problems of her own. She eventually died in January 1883, and on hearing this terrible news Marx returned to London. By this time it is impossible to deny that Marx had experienced the full range of personal losses, and it is difficult to see him other than as a melancholic figure wandering across Europe, perhaps in search of valediction for his entire life.

Although the popularity of his ideas in certain limited quarters was growing, he had not witnessed the great cataclysmic successful revolution across Europe that he had frequently predicted. His magnum opus in economic theory was still incomplete, although volume one of it had obtained a favourable reception among a few outlying political factions. And what part of it was published had certainly not accomplished anything like an intellectual revolution in prevalent conceptions of the subject. Marx's main contribution to proletarian political organisation, the First International, was by now long deceased, and it had left a legacy of continued factional splits within revolutionary leftist groups. It is thus impossible to describe Marx's success as a revolutionary socialist by the early 1880s as anything other than mixed. And he would certainly have realised the only partially successful nature of his legacy, at least privately when being honest with himself.

DEATH OF A PROPHET

Marx's demise was as far away from the heat of political battle as it was possible to conceive. Back in London following his daughter Jenny's death in January 1883, Marx had another relapse of bronchitis, and in February his lung problems flared up again. Difficulties with swallowing food compounded his general poor health, liquid nourishments such as milk becoming a major component of his diet, and he consequently weakened as the days passed by. In March his body finally gave up the struggle it had been pursuing valiantly for many years, and after a haemorrhage he passed away quietly while sitting in a chair. The great socialist prophet was dead, aged only 64. Although this is not particularly old by today's standards, it was a fair innings at the crease by the standards of the day.

Engels was comforted a little by the thought that Marx had been spared months or even years of vegetative existence and thus the possibility of 'dragging out his death to the glory of medical technique'. He was also glad that Marx was not forced to survive any longer for intellectual reasons: '... having in front of him so much unfinished work, burning like Tantalus with the desire to complete it, and being unable to do so ...'.[18]

Although it is easy to forgive Engels expounding this simplification of the issue just after his best friend had died, as has been demonstrated Marx's various illnesses were only part of the explanation of his inability to finish *Capital*. In the next chapter Engels' own attempt at completing volume three will be considered in detail.

Marx's funeral was a small-scale affair. In attendance were political associates such as Liebknecht, Lafargue and Longuet, and members of his close family. He was buried in Highgate Cemetery where his grave remains today, a large imposing bust being placed in his honour at a later date. At the graveside Engels gave a speech on Marx's scientific legacy and his numerous political struggles. Complaining of a 'bourgeois campaign of vilification' directed against him, Engels claimed that Marx had nobly brushed it all aside like cobwebs, answering only when compelled to do so. He proudly declared that:

> Marx was above all else a revolutionist. His real mission in life was to contribute, in one way or another, to the overthrow of capitalist society and of the state institutions which it had brought into being ... Fighting was his element.[19]

Prophesying that Marx's name and work would live across the centuries, Engels said his final fond farewell to his lifelong friend, with much affection called the Moor. However, although his death affected those around him very profoundly, the wider intellectual community had hardly noticed Marx's demise in any significant manner. He had, after all, continuously predicted social revolutions that had only rarely actually materialised, and was probably seen by some as a socialist 'cry wolf'. It thus seemed to many outside observers in the early 1880s that Marx's reputation would only decline further after his mortal remains had been laid to rest.

CONCLUSION

The reader of this book knows of course that this was not the end of the story; that in the early part of the twentieth century a society came into being which professed strict adherence to Marx's ideas, i.e. the Union of Soviet Socialist Republics (USSR). If these same readers think that this demonstrated that Marx's desire (as outlined in Engels' graveside speech) to 'overthrow capitalist society' had finally been realised, then perhaps they should think again. Russia was in 1917 a semi-feudal state, meaning that the transition to capitalism had certainly been interrupted by the Bolshevik assumption of power, but capitalism had not really been overthrown there. It had not fully developed by the time of the outbreak of World War One, so by definition it could not have been overthrown immediately thereafter.

Moreover, Marx's political analysis from the later 1870s that envisaged a revolution in Russia occurring alongside a successful socialist revolution in Western Europe was certainly not realised, despite some brief failed attempts along this path in the 1920s, for example in Germany. Consequently the Bolsheviks were forced to 'go it alone' in an economically backward country that for most of his adult life Marx had regarded as the bulwark of anti-socialist reaction. If Marx is regarded as only a revolutionary prophet of future societal transformations, then his record is really quite poor. But of course Marx was not only a socialist agitator – he was also a theorist of social economy, and in this area his contributions have proved much more durable.

12

VERY LATE MARX

Marx's death in 1883 was not of course the final chapter in his intellectual life. Engels went on to publish his own version of volume two of *Capital* in 1885, but even then the concluding volume in the series still remained to be issued. Thus, although Marx's actual brain was no longer alive encased in flesh and bone he continued to communicate to his band of followers through the intermittent publication of his unfinished legacy. He had missed his own final deadline (literally) for completing *Capital* by a long way, but luckily for him he had a very dedicated friend who was prepared to sacrifice a great deal of his own time to continue publication in the revolutionary cause.

THE CONSTRUCTION OF VOLUME THREE OF *CAPITAL*

Chapter 10 described exactly how Engels constructed volume two of *Capital* from the manuscripts that Marx had left after his death. The state of the prepared manuscripts for volume three was less developed than for volume two, and hence it took Engels an even longer period of time to publish the final volume of Marx's trilogy. Nine years passed between the first publication of volume two in 1885 and the printing of volume three in 1894. Engels provided an account of his protracted efforts in the preface, and this needs to be considered in detail if the real nature of volume three as it stands today is to be comprehended.

First of all, Engels admitted that within the discussion of the topic of ground rent, which occupies around 200 pages of analysis in part VI of volume three as it now stands, Marx had intended to use the materials on Russia that he had been studying for many years. As Engels correctly noted, the Russian example was to have played 'the same role in the part on ground rent that England did in volume 1 in the case of industrial wage-labour'.[1] But – hold on a minute – Marx employed the example of England as the essential empirical example throughout volume one. If Russia was to have occupied anything like this function in volume three, even if only in one major part of the book, then its use would have been crucial. Surely, then, Engels attempted to replicate, as best he could, how Marx would have used the Russian materials, at least in some way or another. Except that he did no such thing, protesting simply that Marx was prevented from carrying out his plan, and providing no explanation for why he himself did not even attempt in any way to follow Marx's scheme in this area.

Second, certain parts of the text were entirely written by Engels. For example, he explained regarding the state of the draft materials left by Marx that: 'Nothing was available for chapter IV but the title. But as the point of issue, the effect of the turnover on the rate of profit, is of vital importance, I have elaborated it myself.'[2]

Hence Engels attempted in certain instances to bridge the gaps left by Marx. This might seem perfectly reasonable, but the important point to understand is that he did this only in some cases and not in others. He did not attempt to elaborate by himself on including the use of the Russian materials. Engels was thus bringing his own preconceptions and normative judgements to the preparation of volume three, regarding which of Marx's stated intentions could be carried out and which could not, even more so than he had done with volume two. If volume two can be described as a 'cut and paste' job, then volume three was a selective 'fill in the blanks' effort. Another example of this was Marx's intention to include a critical account of the confused ideas of the nature of money and capital as revealed on the money market, i.e. in the attitudes of businessmen and writers. Engels decided that such a chapter could not be composed, so he simply abandoned the idea.

Third, Engels admitted that the whole of part V of the book, over 300 pages on interest and credit that included a chapter on pre-capitalist conditions, was not finally presented as Marx would have wanted. This was because Engels had attempted three times to elaborate and complete the basic first draft that Marx had left, but had found the task impossible, as the amount of new research that would have been required would have made this part Engels' work rather than Marx's. So, instead of completing the task, Engels 'cut the matter short' and confined himself to only arranging what was available. The consequences of this incompletion for the conceptual integrity of Marx's system of economic understanding were not discussed. Finally, it is necessary to recognise that Marx might very well have added additional new components to volume three, i.e. elements that were not indicated to Engels in any way on his death, if he had had the opportunity of completing it.

The overall result of these various problems that were either ignored or sidestepped by Engels was that volume three of *Capital* in its issued form was, like volume two, not the book that Marx had intended to publish. Its inconclusive status is aptly symbolised by the concluding passage of the book. The denouement of Marx's entire life's work on a groundbreaking trilogy of economic theory written from a socialist perspective, for which he had sacrificed a big part of his health and happiness, was the following emphatic flourish: 'For instance, the landlords are divided into owners of vineyards, farms, forests, mines, fisheries. [Here the manuscript ends.]'[3]

A complete damp squib of an ending, if ever there was one. No rousing call for proletarian solidarity, no prediction of the coming collapse of the 'bourgeois' order, no drum roll for the sunny socialist new order: only a bland statement on the various categories of landlords. Surely, no one would honestly suggest that this was how Marx himself would have rounded off his entire 'Critique of Political Economy' – or at least the theoretical part, as the historical sections discussing the development of 'bourgeois' political economy were planned to be prepared after volume three, and to be issued as a supplementary fourth volume.

This latter task proved too much even for Engels, who died before it could be completed. But it should now be clear that, for whatever reason is taken as the real cause, Marx's projected 'Critique of Political Economy' was never completed in the manner that the author had intended it to be. *Capital* is not a complete work in the sense that Adam Smith's *Wealth of Nations* is. It is debatable precisely what percentage of what purports to be the latter two volumes of *Capital* as they stand today are as Marx would have intended, but the fact that this is substantially less than 100 per cent is indisputable. But, and here is the crucial qualifier, most (if not all) of Marx's followers have treated *Capital* as a completed text, and have claimed that in it he solved all the problems associated with a revolutionary socialist perspective on economic theory. How could he have, when two-thirds of the work was without question incomplete?

THE CONTENT OF VOLUME THREE OF *CAPITAL*

There is not the space available here to cover every aspect of the content of volume three, but in some ways it was the most interesting of the three volumes, being subtitled 'Capitalist Production as a Whole'. A substantial part of the book was concerned with the various types of capital, such as merchant and commodity capital, and the various forms of interest and rent. One part of volume three proved especially controversial even within the extended Marxian family, and this was a section called 'the law of the tendency of the rate of profit to fall'.

At this point in the analysis it is necessary to introduce Marx's notion of the organic composition of capital, which he defined as: constant capital divided by constant and variable capital ($c/c + v$). This ratio was a measure of how much accumulated or dead labour was used in manufacture compared with living labour, or how much was spent by capitalists on plant and machinery compared with wages. Marx posited that within capitalism this ratio was constantly increasing, as the labour-saving bias of technical change led to workers being continually replaced by machines. The consequence of this for capitalists was that the amount (in percentage terms) of variable capital that they could use in extracting surplus value was constantly declining, leading to problems in obtaining sufficient profits. Marx developed this idea into a 'law of the tendency of the rate of profit to fall', which was one of the underlying factors that he claimed demonstrated that capitalism could not continue to exist indefinitely.

Instead it would inevitably collapse through its own internal logic, Marx having discovered the underlying economic law of motion proving this to be the case.

Readers will be aware that capitalism is still flourishing today, so they might naturally enquire what went wrong with Marx's new discovery. The clue was in the rather awkward-sounding name of the law, the 'law of the tendency of the rate of profit to fall'. The 'falling profits' part of the law was in fact only a tendency, which was offset by various counteracting causes that also operated in capitalism. Examples of these offsetting causes were increasing the intensity of exploitation and cheapening the elements of constant capital. Hence, in order to save appearances (a still-flourishing capitalist system), what is often claimed by diehard Marxists is that the counteracting causes have matched the basic tendency in the period since Marx's death. Only in the future will the basic tendency finally assert itself.

The 'law' that Marx had discovered obviously operated over a very long timescale indeed, the lonely hour of the last instance having still not yet been reached. Capitalism is currently very late indeed for its very important date with historical destiny. Or, more likely, Marx had indeed discovered various contrapuntal economic tendencies with capitalism, but the idea that one was a 'basic tendency' and the others only secondary phenomena was political wishful thinking. As always with Marx, his insightful analysis of economic development was tainted by his desperate political desire to prove that capitalism would and should collapse.

MARX AS A MATHEMATICIAN

As was noted in Chapter 10, Marx's broad range of research interests and wide reading across many different fields of intellectual pursuit even went as far as the detailed study of mathematics. There were a number of reasons for Marx's interest in this subject, one of the most important being that he wanted to use mathematical analysis (in particular, algebraic formulae) in his analysis of the 'laws of motion' of capitalist production. As previously described, Marx sometimes turned away from economic study and towards reading in other subject areas when his illnesses apparently hindered him in his writing efforts, and his interest in mathematics can also be partially understood in this light. But how original were his efforts in this field?

One sub-discipline within mathematics that Marx wrote about in detail in various manuscripts that he sent to Engels was differential calculus. Calculus had been a controversial topic within the canon of mathematical analysis in that it was based upon the contentious idea of 'infinitely small quantities' that were sometimes taken to equal zero (or to vanish), and sometimes were not (i.e. were seen as being greater than zero). One philosopher had famously referred to this phenomenon as comprising 'the ghost of departed quantities'. Calculating instantaneous measures (such as the instantaneous speed of an object at a given point in time) was a corollary of this method of taking limits infinitely close to zero. Marx had documented some of the disputes that occurred within the historical development of calculus in a separate manuscript.

In characteristic style, Marx added his own twist to this set of mathematical ideas by applying Hegel's form of reasoning to the calculus method, in order to elucidate the operations being applied. He first emphasised that the idea of a 'variable' quantity in mathematics necessarily implied the concept of change. Marx then declared that the derivative of the function $f(x)$ – or dy/dx in mathematical notation – should be conceived as the motion (or movement in Hegelian terms) of the function $f(x)$. He wrote that:

> First making the differentiation and then removing it therefore leads literally to *nothing*. The whole difficulty in understanding the differential operation (as in the *negation of the negation* generally) lies precisely in seeing *how* it differs from such a simple procedure and therefore leads to real results.[4]

What Marx meant here was that in Hegelian logic, the idea that the unity of opposites led both back to the initial point of origin and also to a new point of synthesis was an intrinsic part of the method. In calculus a given quantity x was first made different from itself (transformed into x_1), and was then made the same again (transformed back to x), in order to produce the required mathematical result. This movement of double negation yielded a real result, according to Marx, because the dialectical method was in operation. The final x was indeed exactly the same as the initial x, but it was also different from the initial x. What many mathematicians had experienced difficultly in grasping was that reality itself was composed at the most fundamental level from motion. Marx was implying that calculus was an appropriate mathematical method because it reflected this dialectical motion in its structure of calculative operation.

The vast majority of Marx's mathematical writings date from the 1870s, but the quotation given above was from a manuscript written in 1881, i.e. two years before his death. It is thus clear that he was still actively employing Hegel's method to illuminate a range of problems well into the final decade of his life. Indeed, Hegel himself had included mathematical concepts within his *Science of Logic*. For example, the latter two terms of the triadic progression 'Quality – Quantity – Measure' had included within them other triadic progressions such as 'Pure Quantity – Continuous and Discrete Magnitude – Limitation of Quantity', indicating Hegel's direct interest in mathematical concepts. In analysing this topic, Marx was thus just following in the footsteps of his philosophical master.

Marx's study of mathematics was also pertinent to understanding the nature of gaps in his prolonged study of 'bourgeois' political economy. The decade of the 1870s had witnessed the 'marginal revolution' in British economics, in which the mathematical idea of a limit (also employed in calculus) was applied to the theory of value to formulate a neoclassical approach to economic analysis. The basic idea of marginal economics was that it was the final or marginal degree of utility (rather than total utility) that declined as the individual consumption of any good increased, and in consequence it was marginal quantities that should be used by the economist to explain observations about exchange value. The limit that the marginal utility of any good approached as its consumption increased could be expressed by means of mathematical analysis.

However, Marx had simply ignored this new marginal approach to economic analysis in his studies from the 1870s and 1880s, and he never attempted to criticise this new way of understanding economics in any direct manner. This meant that in some ways he was employing what many saw as an outdated 'classical' approach to the subject in the final years of his life. The labour theory of value, the cornerstone of Marx's conception of surplus value and hence exploitation, had in the 1870s been sidestepped by the use of a marginalist theory of exchange, yet he did not ever attempt to counter this challenge in any immediate way. Some socialists had derided the marginalist idea on its initial appearance as 'bourgeois subjectivism', implying that it was too unimportant to devote much effort to, but this turned out to be a strategic error of great magnitude, as marginalism eventually swept to victory (at least among many academic economists in the West).

THE ENGLISH TRANSLATION OF VOLUME ONE

Finally, aspects of the story of the progress of *Capital* into the English language can fruitfully be considered. The first complete English edition of volume one of *Capital* did not appear until 1887, i.e. four years after Marx's death and twenty years after its first publication. The first English translation of the 1859 *Contribution to the Critique of Political Economy*, the principal account of Marx's economics that was available in German before *Capital*, was not published until 1904.

These facts of delayed translation might be seen as rather odd, as volume one of *Capital* took the British economy as the paradigm example of capitalism, and was packed to the brim with discussion of British factory conditions and references to the writings of British economists. It might be thought that English readers would have been more interested than most in reading Marx's analysis of capitalist production. Moreover, since in one version of the Marxian framework it was the advanced proletariat of Britain that were fated to be the vanguard carriers of historical progress towards socialism as the first revolutionary class, it might be thought that Marx would have been very keen to allow them access to *Capital* through an English translation. Engels remarked in 1886 that the 'damned English edition has cost me almost a year', although he followed this by stating that it was absolutely necessary.[5] In fact Marx had discussed the idea of an English translation of volume one as early as 1867, but his own notoriety in England had worked against this idea coming to early fruition.

The English-language edition was of wider relevance than many other translations since it was also accessible to American readers, who alone made up a larger market area than many European countries taken together. The first English edition of volume one of *Capital* was actually a translation of the third German edition of this book, which had been prepared by Engels in the year of Marx's death. In his preface to the third edition Engels revealed that the earlier parts of the book, i.e. the theoretical analysis of the categories of capitalist production to which Marx had attached great significance, had previously undergone a 'thorough elaboration' in comparison with the original version, meaning that it had been comprehensively revised.[6] Hence English-language readers have not easily been able to access the exact manner in which Marx had analysed the categories of capitalism in the true first edition of *Capital* as it was published in his own lifetime.

To give readers a flavour of the original text in the true first edition, the following passage was the closing paragraph of the first chapter on commodities:

> The commodity is [the] *immediate unity of use-value and exchange-value*, thus of two opposed entities. This is an immediate *contradiction*. This contradiction must enter upon a development just as soon as it is no longer considered as hitherto in an analytic manner ... but is really related to other commodities as a totality. This *real* relating of commodities to one another, however, is their *process of exchange*.[7]

In the English translation, this passage was entirely absent from this part of the text.

The fourth German edition of *Capital* was issued in 1890, and a guide to the alterations and additions that were made by Engels in preparing this fourth edition alone occupied 22 printed pages. Later English-language editions included changes made in the fourth German edition as well. Moreover, the English-language edition of the *Contribution to the Critique of Political Economy* that was issued in 1904 was a translation of the second German edition that had also been revised.

As has already been suggested, one of the most important regularities underlying the changes that were made by Marx to the various drafts and then editions of the first volume of *Capital* was that he made a conscious decision to reduce or remove the Hegelian form of reasoning that he had used to indicate the logical basis of capitalist development. It is sometimes stated that in this process Marx was merely removing residual Hegelian language from the text, in order to present a less philosophical mode of expression that would be more easily understood by non-specialists. In fact, as has been argued throughout this book, Marx's use of Hegel was not just a mode of expression but went to the root of the structure of his entire system of analysis. Marx's 'Critique of Political Economy' was (at least in its earlier formulations) based upon Hegelian logic in the most direct manner. One element of the story behind the removal of the dialectical structure was that he had come to realise that the concrete reality of capitalist expansion did not always conform to his pre-established philosophical scheme.

But in wading through 'the whole economic muck', Marx had claimed to be revealing the 'laws of motion' of capitalist production. Consequently it was second nature for Marx initially to use Hegelian logic in order to understand this particular type of economic motion. Given his national background and personal history, nothing could have been more natural than for Marx to attempt to apply Hegelian reasoning to political economy. However, nothing could have been more alien to the existing tradition of political economy than Hegelian logic. From this collision of approaches a great deal of confusion has arisen.

For example, the leading historian of economics Mark Blaug has written that: 'most of the *Grundrisse* is unintelligible, being written in a sort of Hegelian shorthand'.[8] For someone well versed in the history of mainstream economics, Marx's use of Hegelian logic might appear very strange indeed. But to Marx himself, the existing methodology of political economy was itself very curious, and consequently much of his criticism of economics was methodological in nature. Underlying all of this was a massive clash of cultures: German idealist philosophy against British analytical political economy. Marx relished this type of dialectical collision, but others have found it difficult to appreciate. It is hoped that readers of this book are now in a better position to understand it for themselves.

CONCLUSION

Returning to where it all began, to Marx's hometown in the Mosel, a recently published touring guide of the surrounding region declared the following about how the current inhabitants of Trier viewed their own internationally renowned wines:

> The fascination of Trier comes from its long and many-faceted history, in which wine plays a central role. However, contemporary Trier rarely takes Mosel wine anything like as seriously as its international success and fame would lead one to expect. One wonders what Trier's most famous son, Karl Marx, would have to say about this, as some of his earliest writings were about the plight of the Mosel vintners during the mid-19th century. The house where he was born is now one of Trier's museums.[1]

Something similar about taking the subject-matter seriously might be claimed about Marx himself, as his undoubted international success and fame have not always been recognised within specific nation states such as (West) Germany itself, or the UK and the USA. The contradiction between the geographical regions of Marx's actual political triumphs and the regions where he *believed* his ideas were most likely to take root has been a theme explored throughout this book. It is perhaps only a (poetic) coincidence that the famous *Trockenbeerenauslese* (TBA) wines of Germany are known for their amazing interpenetration of sweetness and acidity, an apparently impossible combination of opposite flavours held harmoniously together by expert viticulture. Of all the major grape varieties found across the world, only the Riesling grape grown in some parts of Germany can produce such directly contrasting complexity.

EVALUATING MARX AFTER COMMUNISM

How is it best to evaluate Marx's long-term legacy in the various areas of his influence? One especially relevant way is to introduce a distinction made by the subject of this book himself in order to evaluate the progenitors of grand philosophical systems of thought, including those of Kant and Hegel (and by extension that of Karl Marx). In a letter to M. M. Kovalevsky from April 1879, Marx wrote that:

> ... a writer should distinguish between what an author really gives and what he gives only in his imagination. This is true even of philosophical systems; thus, what Spinoza considered the cornerstone of his system and what actually constitutes that cornerstone are two entirely different things.[2]

What Marx considered the cornerstones of his system of economic thought – the theory of surplus value and the law-like proof of capitalist collapse – might thus be viewed not actually as the foundations of the system but rather as only two pieces of encouragement used to foster belief in it. His own system of thought operated more as a teleological account of the stages of human development, a prophecy of future liberation for those deemed in most need of it, based upon a historical account of the development of the interactions between the material forces of production, and the relations between different socio-economic groups. It was also based upon a utopian projection of human potential that is not always easy to identify with recent socio-political reality, amid the various bloody world wars and sporadic mass genocides of the twentieth century.

The fact that Marx's legacy is still so contentious even today is an indication that 'what Marx really meant' as the basis of his system of thought will remain in some ways permanently open for debate. This book has emphasised the Hegelian structure of reasoning that Marx often deployed in understanding the various topics that he investigated, but some French Marxists such as Louis Althusser, who were influenced by 1960s structuralism, would probably disagree. Althusser posited the idea of an epistemological break in Marx's thinking around 1848, after which Young Hegelian reasoning was decisively rejected and a 'scientific' Marx was born. The evidence presented in this book should go a long way to dispelling Althusser's erroneous claim, especially the discussion of the *Grundrisse* and the various early drafts of *Capital*, but the ghosts of departed radicals often remain in circulation long after their intellectual reason for existence has faded from view.

Thus, different schools of followers have taken different aspects of Marx's theories as their points of origin, constructing revised and more developed systems of their own that were really only partial accounts of all his ideas taken as a whole. One element favouring these tendentious developments was the fact that not all of Marx's writings have been available in print across the twentieth century; another was the incomplete intellectual legacy that he had left on his death. A third was the diverse and dramatically changing contexts in which Marx's ideas were utilised across the twentieth century. The most well-known such context was that of the USSR after the Bolshevik assumption of power. Since this was the very first attempt to implement Marx's ideas in practice, some judgement about its success is now required.

THE SOVIET EXPERIMENT

Marx's most obvious political legacy was the socialist experiment that was begun in Russia in 1917, and which was then imported into various East European countries after 1945. The mechanism of much of this importation, the positioning of the Red Army at the end of World War Two, was not one that was explicitly considered by Marx, although he had continually emphasised the revolutionary potential of war. Without question the progress made in terms of economic development in Russia after 1929 was very significant. From being a semi-feudal country up until World War One, Russia became the leading country in a superpower bloc after World War Two, that went on to rival the USA in exploratory grand gestures such as sending men to the moon. This was certainly an impressive achievement, but it must be recognised that it had only a very tangential relationship with what Marx had actually predicted for socialism or prescribed for a socialist state.

The basic idea of developing a new type of planned economy was due to Marx, but that was where the connection to the experience of the USSR really ended. The idea of using this planned economy to foster industrialisation was due entirely to the Soviet context, where it was thought necessary quickly to rival the West in terms of economic might, or risk being destroyed in an anti-socialist war. Marx had in no way envisaged that economic planning would be directed primarily towards industrialisation, since he believed that it would be advanced capitalist countries that first made the transition to socialism.

Later in his life he came to accept that less-developed countries such as Russia *might* be able to make the switch directly to socialism, but only on the condition that advanced capitalist countries made the change alongside them. The idea that a single less-developed country on its own could proceed directly to socialism was entirely excluded from consideration as being patently absurd. And the particular organisational form that planning assumed in the USSR in the 1930s, for example the five-year period of plan operation and party political control of plan targets, was also not due to Marx, as no specific details had been provided by him on these issues. This latter fact can easily be interpreted as a major deficiency on his part.

Regarding the internal dynamics of the planned economies that were created in Marx's name, it is clear from today's perspective that the progenitor of the idea of planning had failed sufficiently to consider how this system would initially be born, and how it might develop in any detail at all. The vague phrases that he did supply, such as 'dictatorship of the proletariat' and 'from each according to his ability, to each according to his need', were quickly exposed as inadequate to fill the managerial chasm that opened up. Consequently, the actually existing socialisms that were built in the twentieth century had various significant inbuilt flaws that rivalled those of the capitalist economies that Marx's system was designed to replace. For example, exploitation of proletarian labour by capital within the free market system was replaced by exploitation of comrade workers by party bureaucrats in the central planning system. As was soon discovered by the animals that took control of Manor Farm, with numerous voices shouting in anger and all sounding alike, was it possible to say which was which?

Whether 'socialist exploitation' was any better than its capitalist forebear is a debatable point, but Marx never considered this possibility in any serious way at all. He just assumed (erroneously) that if property relations were formally equalised then so would all the other sets of social relations. But the experience of the USSR proved that the forces determining the structural forms of social relations could not simply be reduced to those surrounding private property. Proceeding only to change property relations, as Marx had advocated in his political writings, was not nearly enough to guarantee that exploitation would disappear. New forms of property relations simply generated new forms of exploitation, as necessity was the mother of invention.

It could be argued that on this topic Marx the political advocate was not taking enough notice of Marx the theorist of economic structures. As was outlined regarding the *Grundrisse*, Marx had glimpsed a more fundamental conception of social relations that was not limited only to forms of property ownership, but he was not able to overcome the dead weight of his own political certainties in order to translate this conception into practical policies. To do this would of course have taken Marx outside the boundaries of what is conventionally described as Marxism, but intellectual revolutions were what he accomplished best.

WHAT CAN BE SALVAGED FROM MARX?

According to David McLellan, Marx was a nineteenth-century Victorian rationalist who greatly overestimated the ability of the conscious human mind to solve social and economic problems that were really of super-complex (and even of spiritual) constitution. Mirroring F. A. Hayek's notion of the dangers of extreme rationalism, Marx's fatal error was intellectual hubris. According to James White, Marx's most significant error was is positing capitalism as a *deus ex machina*, a near-perpetual motion machine that drove itself to destruction through its own internal logic. Marx discovered too late that the conscious action of the state was required in order to lay the ground for capitalist expansion, and this was one of the reasons why his system of thought remained incomplete on his death. Both McLellan and White situate themselves broadly on the left, as critical sympathisers to Marx's basic aims. The author of this book claimed in the Introduction to be both sympathetic and hostile to Marx's goals in equal measure. How should such a political sceptic view Marx's achievements?

One important conclusion is that Marx today is most appropriately seen as a 'revolutionary explorer of social economy' rather than as a political deity whose ideas should be worshipped as eternal truths. Accepting that Marx was an intellectual explorer, it is easier to see how his various intriguing theories (such as the materialist conception of history and the importance of the all-round development of the individual) should not be taken as the final word on these subjects but were meant merely as the starting points for further avenues of exploration. Marx's ideas were taken by many of his immediate followers (and even sometimes by Engels) as the ultimate declarations of socialist truth, but in fact they were only pioneering visions that had begun the search for future enlightenment, rather than being designed to close the door to further innovation. It was this 'casting into stone' of Marx's legacy at the end of the nineteenth century that was so dangerous, and that caused so much political strife across the twentieth century. If the critical (Young Hegelian) approach to understanding is to be followed in its true spirit, Marx's most faithful follower would be the one that subjected his own historically limited conclusions to the most rigorous and insightful refutation, within the new and ever-evolving contexts of the time.

The absurdity of the 'setting into iron and steel' of a patently incomplete work such as *Capital* has been explored in some detail within the pages of this book. But many of Marx's other now-famous works have a similarly problematic status. For example, the 'Economic and Philosophical Manuscripts' of 1844 were never finished and were not prepared by Marx for final publication, yet today they are sometimes treated (and quoted) as a completed text. The fact that Marx's works were so often incomplete should tell the reader something important: his system of thought itself was also not complete. But basing an entirely new type of human society on an unfinished legacy might be considered a rather hazardous project, perhaps even a foolhardy one.

Thus, at the expense of sounding trite, it is important to understanding that Marx's single greatest legacy was the exploratory intellectual journey that he took across his life, not any single specific idea or conclusion that he came to along the way. We must today relive Marx's overall journey, not his specific end points. Most of the tragedies and suffering that have come about as a consequence of attempting to implement his ideas have resulted because these intellectual end points were ossified into rigid dogma by some of his most fanatical disciples. But Marx did not want to be treated as a religious thinker, as (by his own maxim) religion, even of the political variety, was the opiate of the people.

His favourite motto was *De omnibus dubitandum*, or 'you must have doubts about everything', and this is a much more accurate statement of his underlying philosophical attitude – something that people who call themselves Marxists today would do well to remember. The moment that a thought appears to be definitely true (even a 'Marxist' one), all the foundations and consequences of this idea must immediately be questioned in the most rigorous and unflinching manner. Never allow thoughts to become set into tablets of stone, as this is the most dangerous intellectual path of all. Having first discovered what are deemed to be ultimate truths, people tend to act on them, but invariably with an overly simplistic conception of the consequences of their actions. Dialectical results inevitably ensue.

Marx's own intellectual journey had begun with the Young Hegelian philosophy of his youth, but then it traversed the path through French socialism and British political economy before finally being beached on the historical specificity of the development of capitalism in various individual nation states. Starting from the universal abstractions of the dialectical method, Marx's efforts were subsequently devoted towards understanding the particularity of various political and economic structures, until he realised it was in fact the individuality of unique geographically specific countries that required comprehension: Universality–Particularity–Individuality. As noted in the Introduction, this trajectory can be characterised as moving from idealist philosophy, through European politics and classical economics, finally coming to rest somewhere close to the methodology of the German historical school. Marx never explicitly admitted this final development, but how else can the emphasis towards the end of his life on Russian history be explained? If the development of modes of production was the same everywhere, then why study any country other than the UK, which Marx had initially taken as the paradigm case of capitalism?

And why did the paradigm case never make the transition to fullblown socialism that Marx had continuously predicted? A major part of the answer was that the methodological foundations from which he had deduced this prediction were mistaken, as Marx himself came to realise at least to some extent while working on the later volumes of *Capital*. Thus his magnum opus, despite being a great classic of economic literature, was already half-scuttled before it was anywhere near finished.

It was partly (in its specific economics content) the last gasp of the 'one size fits all' approach of the classical school, being published in 1867, or just before the beginnings of the marginal revolution in economic theory after 1870. But the classical elements, such as the labour theory of value and the law of the tendency of the rate of profit to fall, which Marx had attempted to tweak with a socialist spin, were the less original and least substantiated parts. It was also partly (in its general dialectical structure) an attempt to widen the scope of economic analysis through the import of historical context and a philosophical heritage. But for mainstream economists this meant that *Capital* was already out of date in methodological terms three years after its first publication.

And, just like the plays of Shakespeare, everyone today should read it – but few would maintain that the attitude to human relationships on show in (say) *Hamlet* accurately reflects all of contemporary social mores. Both *Hamlet* and *Capital* are still relevant to an understanding of today's world, but they are not to be taken as literal or complete portrayals of it. To obtain a more rounded view of economics, the knowledge contained in *Capital* has to be added to that in Adam Smith's *Wealth of Nations*, J. M. Keynes's *General Theory of Employment*, Thorstein Veblen's *Theory of the Leisure Class* and so on. The danger arises when any one of these pioneering texts is taken as gospel truth. This is a religious attitude, not a scientific or a scholarly one, and in some parts of the world in the twentieth century, dogmatic Marxism became the opiate of the people.

WIDER INFLUENCES FROM MARX

Undoubtedly, the total number of national governments created in the twentieth century that claimed adherence to Marx's system of thought was large. They included the USSR, China, Cuba; East European states such as Hungary, Poland and East Germany; African states such as Mozambique and Angola; Indian states such as West Bengal; and Central American states such as Nicaragua. However, in geopolitical terms only the USSR and China could claim membership of the most powerful group of nations alongside the USA and Western Europe, and no advanced Western countries were ever declared by their governments to be Marxist states. Euro-communism had some political influence in continental countries such as Italy and France, but never really threatened to assume ultimate control. And, as a further irony, Marx was a dedicated internationalist, which meant that the direct association between revolutionary socialism and nationalism that prospered in the twentieth century was certainly not one that he had intended to promote.

At the beginning of the twenty-first century, it is apparent that the high tide of Marxist government has long since ebbed away as an international force. It is of course logically possible to conceive of a new wave of Marxist governments coming to power across the globe some time in the future, but the experiences of the USSR and Eastern Europe under communist control makes this (at the moment) seem very unlikely to most mainstream commentators. Consequently, in direct policy terms, Marx appears to have experienced his political zenith, and – as our subject famously proclaimed – historical events rarely repeat themselves, except perhaps as tragedy and farce.

The number of theoretical offshoots that have emanated from Marx's writings – such as Leninism, Trotskyism, Maoism and Che Guevara-style guerrilla warfare in terms of political organisation; and the New Left, analytical Marxism, the Frankfurt school, Bernstein-type reformism, and even existentialist Marxism as intellectual currents – has also been very large. These intellectual influences are likely to survive for far longer than the various Marxist governments ever did. What Marx himself would think of these various groupings as developments of aspects of his own ideas is impossible to know, but, certainly, factionalism within the Marxist family has been facilitated by the latent ambiguities within his own theories. Marxist movements have been characterised by a state of constant splitting (or permanent revolution?) as personalities clashed and contexts developed: a classic example being the ruthless communist government suppression of protest movements in Poland in 1956 and then Czechoslovakia in 1968. These were defining events of the day that served to split diehard Stalinists from those who could no longer stomach communist-style repression.

Moreover, being true to the dialectical nature of Marx's own thought processes, many of the experiences of twentieth-century Marxist states exhibited contradictory tendencies, both within their own countries and in the wider world. A classic example was that of the Cuban revolution after 1959. The founder of communist Cuba, Fidel Castro, was originally a Latin American nationalist who was pushed into the Soviet orbit largely by an insensitive US foreign policy. Cuba's subsequent record under Castro was ambiguous, with improved health and education systems sitting alongside political repression and growing economic dependence on the USSR. Despite the CIA's failed attempts to assassinate Castro, for example by means of an exploding cigar, and despite an association with the pre-revolutionary culture of decadence that socialists saw as redolent of 'Yankee imperialism', the production of fine Havana cigars continued to flourish in revolutionary Cuba.

For example, at a gala dinner held at the plush Dorchester Hotel in London in 1995, boxes of 90 Cohibas made with a solid gold lid and personally signed by Castro commanded over $100,000 each, yet the commercial importation of Cuban cigars into the USA was still officially prohibited. Surely it should be the USA's role to encourage such market-focused commercial activities, and Castro's role to encourage its replacement with more lofty socialist aspirations to personal self-improvement? Somewhere along the way the political wires have evidently been crossed into their opposites. Marx himself would doubtless be doubly frustrated by this development, as his own prolonged poverty forced him to smoke very cheap and rough-tasting cigars that were an ongoing bane to his family, as well as to those who were invited to visit his perennially smoke-infested study.

In China too, in the early twenty-first century, the apparently contradictory features of communist political control allied to market-driven economic development is producing a level of material growth that Mao could only have dreamed about, but which is starting to generate ecological and energy-supply nightmares for the Western world. In this seemingly unlikely combination, some echoes of Engels' policy from the draft 'Principles of Communism' of 1847 might be found, where communist forces were initially directed to employ private ownership in order to develop the productive forces.

More generally, the (backwards) transition from communism to capitalism in Russia and Eastern Europe in the 1990s was obviously a systems transition too far for Marx's own mature system of thought, constituting a complete reversal of the path of historical development that he believed his own theories had proved was occurring. And the post-communist ethnic conflicts that have erupted in countries such as the former Yugoslavia constituted a return of the repressed nationalist forces that Marx claimed would die out in socialism but were in fact simply lying dormant, waiting for an opportunity to arise in an ever-more virulent form. Thus, many of Marx's concrete political certainties crumbled to dust in the most direct and immediate way at the end of the twentieth century. In a much earlier period of similarly fluctuating circumstances, the young Marx wrote to his father in November 1837 declaring that:

> There are moments of one's life that represent the limit of a period and at the same time point clearly in a new direction. In such a period of transition we feel ourselves compelled to consider the past and present with the eagle eye of thought in order to come to a realization of our actual position ... every change is partly a swansong, partly an overture, to a new epic that is trying to find a form in brilliant colours ...[3]

Perhaps what remains for sure in the 'actual position' of Marxist theory today is only the form of a constantly surprising dialectical progression. For the true Hegelian this process is certainly not the end of history, but only another twist in its ever-spiralling continuous form of motion.

MARX IS (NOT) DEAD

So in conclusion it can now be seen that Marx was a great intellectual pioneer across the fields of history, political analysis and even economics, without whom scholarly analysis would today be noticeably poorer, and who set a new benchmark for investigation into the economic sociology of nation states. He also was an active campaigner for the rights of workers and the dispossessed, a process that has yielded many improvements in living conditions for millions of people across the globe ever since he first became a communist. This is Marx's positive 'Being'.

However, plausible interpretations of his ideas have also cost millions of lives in horrific mass genocides across the twentieth century, and Marx's own political propaganda, employing stark and simplistic caricatures of class structure, has often hindered greater understanding between different people rather than fostered its improvement. The class hatred that his writings often encouraged is only another form of discrimination, alongside racial prejudice, and murdering someone simply because of their class origins is a hate crime. This is Marx's negative 'Nothing'.

The reader might now be able to predict the logical outline of the next sentence. What exactly will constitute the synthesis of these two poles of Marx's legacy, or how these two opposites will be unified into a future 'Becoming', is up to each and every individual person alive today, if they so desire it. Although certainly not always in circumstances of their own making, people still make (the best and the worst of) human history, sometimes at the very same time.

NOTES

INTRODUCTION

1 T. Bottomore and M. Rubel (eds), *Karl Marx, Selected Writings in Sociology and Social Philosophy* (Harmondsworth: Penguin, 1963), p.84.

2 F. A. Hayek, *The Counter-Revolution of Science* (Illinois: Free Press, 1952), p.206.

3 Michael Inwood, *A Hegel Dictionary* (Oxford: Blackwell, 1992), pp.44–6, pp.199–202 and pp.268–71.

1 RULED BY A DEMON

1 Karl Marx and Frederick Engels, *Collected Works* (London: Lawrence & Wishart, 1975), vol.1, p.8.

2 Eugene Kamenka (ed.), *The Portable Karl Marx* (Harmondsworth: Penguin, 1983), p.8.

3 Marx and Engels, *Collected Works*, vol.1, p.522.

4 Ibid, p.545.

5 Kamenka (ed.), *The Portable Karl Marx*, p.10.

6 David McLellan, *Marx before Marxism* (London: Macmillan, 1980), p.53.

7 See M. A. Rose, *Marx's Lost Aesthetic* (Cambridge: CUP, 1984).

8 Marx and Engels, *Collected Works*, vol.1, p.389.

9 Karl Marx and Frederick Engels, *Collected Works* (London: Lawrence & Wishart, 1975), vol.4, p.19.

10 Karl Marx and Frederick Engels, *Collected Works* (London: Lawrence & Wishart, 1975), vol.2, p.336.

11 Kamenka (ed.), *The Portable Karl Marx*, p.42.

12 Friedrich Engels, *The Condition of the Working Class in England* (London: Penguin, 1987), p.30.

13 Marx and Engels, *Collected Works*, vol.4, p.280.

14   F. J. Raddatz (ed.), *The Marx-Engels Correspondence* (London: Weidenfeld and Nicolson, 1981), pp.14–15.

2   EARLY WRITINGS

1   Karl Marx and Frederick Engels, *Collected Works* (London: Lawrence and Wishart, 1975), vol.1, p.577.

2   Ibid, p.707.

3   Ibid, p.45.

4   Karl Marx, *Early Writings* (London: Penguin, 1975), p.67.

5   Marx and Engels, *Collected Works*, vol.1, p.204.

6   Ibid, p.221.

7   Karl Marx and Frederick Engels, *Collected Works* (London: Lawrence and Wishart, 1975), vol.3, pp.171–2.

8   Ibid, p.187.

9   Ibid, pp.440–43.

10   Ibid, pp.375–6.

11   Karl Marx, *Early Writings*, pp.264–5.

12   Ibid, p.384.

13   Ibid, p.386.

14   Ibid, p.348.

15   Ibid, pp.353–5.

16   Ludwig Feuerbach, *The Essence of Christianity* (New York: Harper, 1957), p.281.

17   Karl Marx, *Early Writings*, p.393.

18   Karl Marx and Frederick Engels, *Collected Works* (London: Lawrence and Wishart, 1975), vol.5, pp.53–4.

3   THE SPECTRE OF COMMUNISM

1   Karl Marx and Frederick Engels, *Collected Works* (London: Lawrence and Wishart, 1976), vol.6, pp.556–7.

2   Karl Marx and Frederick Engels, *Collected Works* (London: Lawrence and Wishart, 1977), vol.7, p.33.

3   Ibid, p.538.

4   Ibid, p.147.

5   Ibid, p.431.

6   Hal Draper, *Karl Marx's Theory of Revolution* (New York: Monthly Review, 1978), vol.2, p.232.

7   Karl Marx and Frederick Engels, *Collected Works* (London: Lawrence and Wishart, 1977), vol.8, p.162.

8   Ibid, p.317.

9   Karl Marx and Frederick Engels, *Collected Works* (London: Lawrence and Wishart, 1977), vol.9, p.487.

10   Franz Mehring, *Karl Marx: The Story of his Life* (London, Allen and Unwin, 1936), p.203.

11   David McLellen, *Karl Marx: His Life and Thought* (London: Macmillan, 1973), p.454.

12   Mehring, *Karl Marx: The Story of his Life*, p.217.

4   POLITICAL WRITINGS, 1848–1852

1   Gareth Stedman Jones, 'The Reception of the Manifesto', in Karl Marx and Friedrich Engels, *The Communist Manifesto* (London: Penguin, 2002), p.19, fn.10.

2   Karl Marx and Frederick Engels, *Collected Works* (London: Lawrence and Wishart, 1976), vol.6, p. 350.

3   Ibid, p.352.

4   Karl Marx and Frederick Engels, *Collected Works* (London: Lawrence and Wishart, 1976), vol.5, p.75.

5   Karl Marx, *Surveys from Exile* (London: Allen Lane, 1973), p.35.

6   Karl Marx and Frederick Engels, *Collected Works* (London: Lawrence and Wishart, 1977), vol.8, p.158.

7   Ibid, pp.40–1.

8   Ibid, p.58.

9   Karl Marx and Frederick Engels, *Selected Works* (London: Lawrence and Wishart, 1968), pp.165–6.

10   Connection inspired by the works of James D. White.

11   Marx and Engels, *Selected Works*, p.96.

12   Marx and Engels, *Collected Works*, vol.8, p. 213.

13   Marx and Engels, *Selected Works*, pp.114–15.

14   Ibid, p.137.

15   Ibid, pp.177–8.

16   Karl Marx, *Selected Essays* (London: Parsons, 1926), pp.202–5.

17   David McLellan, *Karl Marx: Selected Writings* (Oxford: OUP, 1977), p.341.

18   Marx and Engels, *Selected Works*, p.170.

19   McLellan, *Karl Marx: Selected Writings*, p.506.

5   THE WHOLE ECONOMIC MUCK

1   David McLellan, *Karl Marx: His Life and Thought* (London: Macmillan, 1973), p.286.

2   Karl Marx, *The Eastern Question* (London: Sonnenschein, 1897), pp.3–7.

3   Ibid, p.19.

4   Ibid, p.81.

5   Frederick Engels, 'The European War', in Karl Marx and Frederick Engels, *Collected Works* (London: Lawrence & Wishart, 1979), vol.12, p.557.

6   Karl Marx, 'Russian Finances during the War', in Marx and Engels, *Collected Works*, vol.12, pp.603–4.

7   Karl Marx, *Secret Diplomatic History of the Eighteenth Century and The Story of the Life of Lord Palmerston* (London: Lawrence and Wishart, 1969), p.108.

8   Karl Marx and Frederick Engels, *Collected Works* (London: Lawrence & Wishart, 1983), vol.40, pp.8–10.

9   Karl Marx, *Secret Diplomatic History of the Eighteenth Century*, p.174.

10   Ibid, p.212.

11   Ibid, p.88.

12   Robert Payne, *The Unknown Karl Marx* (New York: New York University Press, 1971), p.144 and p.227.

13   David McLellan, *Karl Marx: His Life and Thought*, p.288.

14   Marx and Engels, *Collected Works*, vol.12, p.xxix.

15   David McLellan, *Karl Marx: His Life and Thought*, p.265.

16   Franz Mehring, *Karl Marx: The Story of his Life* (London: Allen and Unwin, 1936), p.240.

17   Frederick Engels, 'The Russians in Turkey', in Marx and Engels, *Collected Works*, vol.12, p.339.

18   S. Shuster, 'The Nature and Consequence of Karl Marx's Skin Disease', *British Journal of Dermatology*, vol.158 2008, p.2.

19   Frederick Engels, letter dated 29 July 1857, in Marx and Engels, *Collected Works*, vol.40, p.150.

20   Karl Marx, 'The Monetary Crisis in Europe', in Karl Marx and Frederick Engels, *Collected Works* (London: Lawrence & Wishart, 1986), vol.15, pp.113–14.

21 Karl Marx, 'The Trade Crisis in England', in Marx and Engels, *Collected Works*, vol.15, p.400.

22 Karl Marx, 'The Causes of the Monetary Crisis in Europe', in Marx and Engels, *Collected Works*, vol.15, p.117.

23 Ibid, pp.255–7.

24 Karl Marx, *A Contribution to the Critique of Political Economy* (New York: International, 1904), p.24.

25 Karl Marx, 'The Emancipation Question', in Karl Marx and Frederick Engels, *Collected Works* (London: Lawrence & Wishart, 1980), vol.16, pp.145–6.

26 Ibid, p.147.

27 Karl Marx, 'British Incomes in India', in Marx and Engels, *Collected Works*, vol.15, pp.349–52.

28 Karl Marx, 'Great Trouble in Indian Finances', in Marx and Engels, *Collected Works*, vol.16, pp.284–5.

29 Karl Marx, *Herr Vogt*, in Karl Marx and Frederick Engels, *Collected Works* (London: Lawrence & Wishart, 1981), vol.17, p.153.

6 'OUTLINES OF A CRITIQUE OF POLITICAL ECONOMY'

1 Karl Marx and Frederick Engels, *Selected Works* (Moscow: Progress, 1968), p.183.

2 Karl Marx and Frederick Engels, *Collected Works* (London: Lawrence & Wishart, 1986), vol.28, p.28.

3 Ibid, p.30.

4 Ibid, p.36.

5 Ibid, p.132.

6 Karl Marx, *Grundrisse* (Harmondsworth: Penguin, 1973), pp.332–3.

7 Karl Marx, *Selected Writings on Sociology and Social Philosophy* (Harmondsworth: Penguin, 1961), p.110.

8 Marx and Engels, *Collected Works*, vol.28, p.46.

9 Marx, *Grundrisse*, p.495.

10 Marx and Engels, *Collected Works*, vol.28, pp.246–7.

11 Marx and Engels, *Selected Works*, p.181.

12 Ibid, pp.181–2.

13 Marx, *Grundrisse*, pp.477–9.

7 AN IMMENSE ACCUMULATION OF RESEARCH

1   Quoted in David McLellan, *Karl Marx: His Life and Thought* (London: Macmillan, 1973), p.354.

2   Karl Marx and Frederick Engels, *Collected Works* (London: Lawrence & Wishart, 1987), vol.42, p.322

3   Quoted in Anitra Nelson, 'Marx and Medicine', *Journal of Medical Biography*, vol.7 1999, p.54.

4   Marx and Engels, *Collected Works*, vol.42, p.22.

5   Ibid, p.281.

6   Quoted in Nelson, 'Marx and Medicine', p.100.

7   Karl Marx, *Surveys from Exile* (London: Penguin, 1973), p.351.

8   Ibid, p.341.

9   Ibid, p.345.

10 Eugene Kamenka (ed.), *The Portable Karl Marx* (Harmondsworth: Penguin, 1983), p.366.

11 David McLellan (ed.), *Karl Marx: Selected Writings* (Oxford: OUP, 1977), p.538.

12 Franz Mehring, *Karl Marx: The Story of his Life* (London: Allen & Unwin, 1936), p.384.

13 McLellan (ed.), *Karl Marx: Selected Writings*, p.525.

14 Ibid, p.526.

15 Marx and Engels, *Collected Works*, vol.42, p.464.

16 Karl Marx and Friedrich Engels, *Correspondence, 1846-1895* (London: Lawrence & Wishart, 1934), p.219.

17 Ibid, p.220.

18 McLellan, *Karl Marx: His Life and Thought*, p.358.

19 Marx and Engels, *Collected Works*, vol.42, p.309.

20 Ibid, p.334.

21 Ibid, p.63.

22 McLellan, *Karl Marx: His Life and Thought*, p.356.

8 VOLUME ONE OF *CAPITAL*

1   Karl Marx and Frederick Engels, *Collected Works* (London: Lawrence & Wishart, 1987), vol.42, p.173.

2   Karl Marx and Friedrich Engels, *Correspondence, 1846–1895* (London: Lawrence & Wishart, 1934), p.205.

3   Karl Marx and Frederick Engels, *Collected Works* (London: Lawrence & Wishart, 1988), vol.30, p.172.

4   Karl Marx, *Theories of Surplus Value* (Moscow: Lawrence & Wishart, 1963), part I, pp.45–52.

5   Ibid, p.106.

6   Karl Marx, *Theories of Surplus Value* (London: Lawrence and Wishart, 1971), part III, p.101.

7   Karl Marx, *Theories of Surplus Value* (Moscow: Progress, 1968), part II, pp.500–1.

8   Karl Marx, *Capital* (London: Penguin, 1976), vol.1, pp.949–50.

9   Ibid, p.1022.

10   Karl Marx and Frederick Engels, *Selected Works* (Moscow: Lawrence & Wishart, 1968), p.38.

11   Marx, *Capital*, vol.1, p.1062.

12   Karl Marx, *Capital* (London: Penguin, 1992), vol.2, p.184.

13   James D. White, *Karl Marx and the Intellectual Origins of Dialectical Materialism* (London: Macmillan, 1996), p.166.

14   Karl Marx, *Capital* (Moscow: Lawrence and Wishart, 1954), vol.1, p.292.

15   Karl Marx, *Capital* (Chicago: Kerr, 1906), vol.1, p.13.

16   Ibid, pp.506–7.

9   THE TANTALISING MODEL OF PARIS

1   Karl Marx, 'The Civil War in France', in Karl Marx and Frederick Engels, *Selected Works* (Moscow: Lawrence & Wishart, 1968), p.269.

2   *The Times*, 9 June 1871, p.8.

3   David McLellan, *Karl Marx: His Life and Thought* (London: Macmillan, 1973), p.393.

4   Karl Marx and Friedrich Engels, *Correspondence, 1846-95* (London: Lawrence & Wishart, 1934), p.314.

5   Ibid, p.312.

6   Marx, 'The Civil War in France', in *Selected Works*, p.287.

7   Ibid, p.290.

8   Ibid, p.291.

9   Lissagaray, *History of the Paris Commune* (London: New Park, 1976), p.108.

10   McLellan, *Karl Marx: His Life and Thought*, p.400.

11   Karl Marx, *Selected Works* (London: Lawrence & Wishart, 1942), vol.2, p.530.

12   *The Times*, 12 November 1872, p.4.

13   David McLellan, *Karl Marx: Selected Writings* (Oxford: OUP, 1977), p.559.

14   McLellan, *Karl Marx: His Life and Thought*, pp.402–3.

15   Ibid, pp.414.

16   Lissagaray, *History of the Paris Commune*, p.1.

17   National Archives, 45/9366/36228.

18   In fact it was completely banned.

19   Marx and Engels, *Correspondence, 1846-95*, p.283 and p.284.

20   James D. White, *Karl Marx and the Intellectual Origins of Dialectical Materialism* (London: Macmillan, 1996), p.244.

21   British Library, Ms 38,075, p.16.

22   Karl Marx and Friedrich Engels, *Basic Writings on Politics and Sociology* (New York: Fontana, 1959), p.477.

23   Karl Marx and Frederick Engels, *Collected Works* (London: Lawrence & Wishart, 1989), vol.24, p.658.

24   Karl Marx and Frederick Engels, *Collected Works* (London: Lawrence & Wishart, 1988), vol.23, p.88.

25   McLellan, *Karl Marx: Selected Writings*, p.562.

26   Marx and Engels, *Collected Works*, vol.24, p.513.

27   Marx, *Selected Works*, vol.2, p.616.

28   Ibid, p.617.

29   Marx and Engels, *Collected Works*, vol.23, p.424.

30   Ibid, p.425.

10   THE CIRCULATION OF *CAPITAL*

1   James D. White, *Karl Marx and the Intellectual Origins of Dialectical Materialism* (London: Macmillan, 1996), p.228.

2   Karl Marx, *Capital* (London: Allen and Unwin, 1938), p.842.

3   B. Nicolaievsky, *Karl Marx: Man and Fighter* (Harmonsworth: Penguin, 1973), p.394.

4   British Library, Ms 38,075, p.18.

5   White, *Karl Marx and the Intellectual Origins of Dialectical Materialism*, p.208.

6   Karl Marx and Friedrich Engels, *Correspondence, 1846-95* (London: Lawrence & Wishart, 1934), pp.235–6.

7   Teodor Shanin (ed.), *Late Marx and the Russian Road* (London: Routledge, 1984), p.103.

8   Karl Marx, *Capital* (Chicago: Kerr, 1907), vol.2, p.809.

9   David McLellan, *Karl Marx: His Life and Thought* (London: Macmillan, 1973), p.421.

10   Marx, *Capital*, vol.2, p.7.

11   Ibid, p.10.

12   Karl Marx, *Mathematical Manuscripts* (London: New Park, 1983), p.ix.

13   Karl Marx and Frederick Engels, *Collected Works* (London: Lawrence & Wishart, 1991), vol.45, p.355.

14   Ibid, p.415.

15   Karl Marx, *Capital* (London: Lawrence & Wishart, 1956), vol.2, pp.396–401.

16   Ibid, pp.450–1.

17   White, *Karl Marx and the Intellectual Origins of Dialectical Materialism*, p.194.

18   Hiroshi Uchida, *Marx's Grundrisse and Hegel's Logic* (London: Routledge, 1988), Chapter 2.

19   Marx, *Capital* (Chicago: Kerr, 1907), vol.2, p.287.

20   White, *Karl Marx and the Intellectual Origins of Dialectical Materialism*, p.194.

21   Vincent Barnett, 'Historical Political Economy in Russia, 1870–1913', *European Journal of the History of Economic Thought*, vol.11, summer 2004, pp.239–43.

22   White, *Karl Marx and the Intellectual Origins of Dialectical Materialism*, p.281.

23   Marx, *Capital*, vol.2, p.11.

24   Ibid, p.41.

11   AND NOW RUSSIA!

1   David McLellen, *Karl Marx: Selected Writings* (Oxford: OUP, 1977), p.565.

2   Karl Marx and Frederick Engels, *Collected Works* (London: Lawrence & Wishart, 1991), vol.45, p.122.

3   Ibid, p.310.

4   Karl Marx and Frederick Engels, *Selected Works* (Moscow: Lawrence & Wishart, 1968), p.409.

5   Karl Marx and Frederick Engels, *Collected Works* (London: Lawrence & Wishart, 1989), vol.24, pp.358–9.

6   McLellen, *Karl Marx: Selected Writings*, p.576.

7   Karl Marx and Friedrich Engels, *The Communist Manifesto* (London: Penguin, 2002), p.259.

8   McLellen, *Karl Marx: Selected Writings*, p.583.

9   Franz Mehring, *Karl Marx: The Story of his Life* (London: Allen and Unwin, 1936), p.517.

10　Marx, *Collected Works*, vol.45, p.242.

11　Ibid, p.332.

12　McLellen, *Karl Marx: Selected Writings*, p.594.

13　David McLellan, *Karl Marx: His Life and Thought* (London: Macmillan, 1973), p.446.

14　H. M. Hyndman, *The Economics of Socialism* (London: 20ᵗʰ Century Press, 1896), p.i.

15　Quoted in Mehring, *Karl Marx: The Story of his Life*, p.505.

16　McLellan, *Karl Marx: His Life and Thought*, p.447.

17　Anitra Nelson, 'Marx and Medicine', *Journal of Medical Biography*, vol.7 1999, p.107.

18　Quoted in Maximilien Rubel, *Marx* (New York: Facts on File, 1980), p.124.

19　Marx and Engels, *Selected Works*, p.430.

12　VERY LATE MARX

1　Marx, *Capital* (Chicago: Kerr, 1909), vol.3, p.16.

2　Ibid, p.13.

3　Ibid, p.1032.

4　Karl Marx, *Mathematical Manuscripts* (London: New Park, 1983), p.3.

5　Karl Marx, *Capital* (London: Allen and Unwin, 1938), vol.1, p.843.

6　Ibid, p.875.

7　Karl Marx, *Capital First Edition* (New York: Labor, 1972), p.38.

8　Mark Blaug, *Economic Theory in Retrospect* (Cambridge: CUP, 1985), p.288.

CONCLUSION

1　Stuart Pigott, *Touring the Wine Country: The Mosel and Rheingau* (London: Beazley, 1997), pp.26–7.

2　Karl Marx and Frederick Engels, *Collected Works* (London: Lawrence & Wishart), vol.45, p.452.

3　David McLellan, *Karl Marx: Selected Writings* (Oxford: OUP, p.1977), p.5.

FURTHER READING

As a biography, David McLellan's *Karl Marx: His Life and Thought* of 1973 is excellent on detail and atmosphere and on chronicling the ongoing events of Marx's life, and this book has been reissued in various updated forms. All of McLellan's books on Marx (and Marxists) are of significant scholarly value and are certainly still worth consulting today, for their balanced and informative presentation of the topic. However, McLellan is primarily a political scientist and hence was less attuned to the economic aspects of Marx's contribution, especially with respect to documenting the dynamic development of his critical project. Another highly recommended book, one of the most important works published on Marx since 1945, is G. A. Cohen's *Karl Marx's Theory of History: A Defence* of 1978, which, though not a biographical account, tries convincingly to get under Marx's philosophical skin.

Francis Wheen's more recent biography, *Karl Marx: A Life* of 1999, although celebrated in some quarters, cannot really be recommended as a balanced account of his life and work. The basic problem is that Wheen makes little effort to understand Marx's ideas or goals in their own terms. Instead he strings together various less-than-flattering episodes in Marx's life, with the aim of de-mythologizing the stereotype of 'Marx the revolutionary'. Wheen's interpretation of *Capital* as Victorian literature is certainly interesting, but it cannot replace a detailed understanding of the concepts that Marx was trying to develop through his 'Critique of Political Economy'. Criticising Marx's ideas head-on is to be lauded, but not even attempting to understand them is scholastic indolence.

In contrast to Wheen's semi-populist effort, James White's *Karl Marx and the Intellectual Origins of Dialectical Materialism* of 1996 is, despite having a misleadingly obscure title, the most ferociously original book on Marx published since the collapse of the USSR. It really requires an understanding of Marx's ideas in order to get the most out of it, but even the interested novice will find its scholarship impressive and its arguments difficult to ignore. This was the first book to attempt a historical reconstruction of the relationship between Marx and Hegel's ideas as live philosophical concepts, rather than as discarded excess baggage.

Boris Nicolaievsky's *Karl Marx: Man and Fighter*, first published in English in 1936, is written from a Marxist perspective, and it focuses much more on the everyday political battles that Marx was periodically engaged in, rather than on his more scientific endeavours. Franz Mehring's *Karl Marx: The Story of his Life* of 1936 is also overly sympathetic to Marx, although both books are still worth consulting as examples of a Marxian flavour.

Unquestionably the best source for studying Marx's theoretical legacy is his own writings, which have now been issued in an excellent multi-volume English-language edition by Lawrence and Wishart. Anyone who is serious about understanding Marx at a level beyond what can be obtained from any single biography is encouraged to consult the *Collected Works*. Marx was rarely a dull or a boring writer (with the notable exception of volume two of *Capital*), especially so in his journalism, although he could certainly be tendentious and juvenile as well as brilliant and powerful. The *Collected Works* also contain numerous volumes of letters, and these allow a first-hand insight into Marx's personal life.

Penguin has issued a series of Marx's most famous works in paperback editions, and the introductions to these books are often well worth consulting as further context. Also published by Penguin is a single volume called *Karl Marx: Selected Writings in Sociology and Social Philosophy*, edited by T. Bottomore and M. Rubel, which is an excellent thematic introduction to a range of Marx's ideas in the areas specified.

For a beginner selecting which of Marx's works to read first, the best choice is probably as follows. To discover Marx the philosopher, read the 'Economic and Philosophical Manuscripts' of 1844. To discover Marx the political theorist, read *The Manifesto of the Communist Party* of 1848 and the *Critique of the Gotha Programme* of 1875. And to discover Marx as an economist, read the first volume of *Capital* of 1867. Interested readers are strongly advised against reading any of Engels' own individually authored works as a guide to Marx's ideas. In particular, do *not* read Engels' *Socialism: Utopian and Scientific* expecting to gain an understanding of Marx, as all of Engels' works indicate only how he interpreted his best friend's ideas.

Finally, to understand the philosophical method that Marx employed throughout his life, read Hegel's *Science of Logic*. Hegel's other works do not present this method in itself, and hence are not recommended for this particular purpose. There are two basic versions of Hegel's *Logic*. The two-volume 'greater' version is superior to the single-volume 'lesser' presentation, but each conveys the unique 'feel' of dialectical thinking very well.

NAME INDEX

SUBJECT INDEX